MELVYN BRAGG

Melvyn Bragg is the author of fourteen novels, including the bestselling CRYSTAL ROOMS, THE MAID OF BUTTERMERE and A TIME TO DANCE. He also wrote the screenplay for the BBC television dramatisation of A TIME TO DANCE and has written several works of non-fiction including RICH: THE LIFE OF RICHARD BURTON and film screenplays. He is editor and presenter of *The South Bank Show*, and Chairman of Border Television. Born in Wigton, Cumbria, Melvyn Bragg now lives in London and Cumbria.

D1103065

Melvyn Bragg

AUTUMN MANOEUVRES

sceptre

Copyright © Melvyn Bragg 1978

First published in Great Britain in 1978 by Martin Secker and Warburg Ltd

Coronet edition 1979
Sceptre edition 1993

Sceptre is an imprint of Hodder and Stoughton Paperbacks, a division of Hodder and Stoughton Ltd

British Library C.I.P.

A CIP catalogue record for this title is available from the British Library

ISBN 0-340-51856-1

Printed and bound in Great Britain for Hodder and Stoughton Paperbacks, a division of Hodder and Stoughton Ltd, Mill Road, Dunton Green, Sevenoaks, Kent TN13 2YA. (Editorial Office: 47 Bedford Square, London WC1B 3DP) by Cox and Wyman Ltd, Reading.

For two good friends
David Jones and Phillip Whitehead

'*A human life, I think, should be well rooted in some spot of a native land, where it may get the love of tender kinship for the face of the earth, for the labours men go forth to, for the sounds and accents that haunt it, for whatever will give that early home a familiar unmistakable difference amidst the future widening of knowledge . . .*'

George Eliot (from *Daniel Deronda*)

I. THE LIVING-ROOM

Chapter One

(i)

The surging sound of the wind in the trees had been so wild through the night that it had brought back childhood fears. She had slept badly and abandoned her bedroom at dawn to seek the tranquillity brought by the first light. She had soon strayed from the garden and on to the fellside and there she now stood, her eyes closed against the early morning sun, swaying voluptuously in the stillness.

Her slippers were sodden, her dressing-gown was inadequate, her guilt and anxieties lurked ready to pounce – but, for a few moments, nothing could break the spell she had cast on herself. A woman of fifty, yet youthful, slender, in some way unused, her eager pale face yearning for whatever warmth would come even from the thin autumn rays. She was at peace with herself. That was rare. She held on to the moment as if for dear life.

The storm had blown itself out. A great shower of yellow, golden-brown and russet leaves had newly fallen. They lay on her path through the garth. They had made her way soft but she had been conscious, as she trod, that she was pressing them to decay. She did not like the autumn. Year after year on this same spot she had watched the flowers die, the trees stripped by the wind, the hedges become skeletons of themselves, and after the last of the fruit, only the firs and evergreens with colour. And they were so dull, she thought. Except for the holly – and then only when it was enriched with berries. There was the famous copper beech, of course, down in the garden, but it was too heavy, too dark. No, she preferred to escape on to the bare hillside where the orange fern and last patches of purple in the heather gave evidence of life: the slow death into winter depressed her. But the hills were a comfort. On the fells, she thought, you found grandeur, not prettiness, endurance, not annual birth and death. On the fells she felt more free.

On such a morning the fells were at their best. They were in the north of the Lake District – on the peak of England – bare thin grass and large pools of bracken on the sweep and fall of the oldest rock in Europe. From where Elaine stood she saw range enfolded behind range, snow-tipped, some mist – empty land, soothingly empty to her as she tried to force out of her mind the frightening image of her husband embracing another woman. The previous afternoon. She had not been spying but she felt unclean. He had done it so tenderly – tenderness which she had long learnt to live without. He treated her as a child now – gently, not as an equal. He had simply embraced the young woman and yet the picture flared up in Elaine's mind violently, as if he had been brutal. The memory smacked against her eyes.

She turned from the hills, from the sun, as if she had been hit in the face. She was determined to use this dawn, to draw strength from it. Before her now was the sea, the Solway, the long sliver of rapid tides and treacherous sands which had had the final say in so many Border battles. As a girl she had watched it for hours, waiting for a ship, picking out the white houses on the dark Scottish hills, dreaming about the salt water on her skin, the hard dry sand coarse and hot on her body. The land dropped away so quickly to the shore; farms, fields, cattle, sheep, a few small copses, the plain, and then the glitter of water. She had often imagined herself striding down there in a few minutes in the seven-league boots of the fairy tale. When she looked at the sea she had felt like someone in a fairy tale. As if, up on the mountain, she was waiting to be rescued or released. She had made up stories of her Hero coming ashore and taking her away down the firth and into the ocean. She had been careful enough to keep such fantasies – which had lasted well into her adolescence – strictly to herself. Yet another secret to hug, perhaps to fester.

But again she turned away. Such small peace as might have been possible had come and gone. The panic and the terror were tormenting her again. She took a few steps up the hill towards the screes but discovered that she was soon out of breath. The years of pills, she thought hopelessly, they even stop you walking. Once she could all but dance up the hillside. Their poison had to be purged. She turned downhill to face the long strip of woodland, the tiny, isolated hamlet with its four hill farms, three cottages, the ruined and robbed Great House and the old vicarage, her home, massive and ugly on the sloping land, like a great galleon beached. She was afraid to express this opinion to anyone, but – she hated it.

(ii)

Jimmie, though in the next bedroom, had not heard his wife go out. He got up promptly as the ancient alarm clock began to gather pace. He quenched it almost immediately, concerned that it should not disturb Elaine. She was heading into another of her bad times by the look of things and she needed all the rest she could get. By now he had a reliable routine: he could, generally, gauge and pace her breakdowns to the week. They were a settled part of his life.

His bedroom was cold, big and uncomfortable like all the bedrooms in the house. There were fires but they were only used when someone was bedridden and more than averagely ill. The antiquated central heating system operated downstairs only, and even there unevenly. He dressed quickly and neatly as he had done since a boy in this same room. Then it had been to stave off the cold; now it was a habit of efficiency.

13

He had cleared away his childish mementoes when Elaine had moved in with him after their marriage. But his mother's death had released the adjacent bedroom and Elaine's first serious onslaught of nervous depresssion had made it seem sensible that she should have a room to herself. She had not wanted his mother's room but, as he had explained, it was next to his and he could be available whenever she wished. And so it had stayed – separate rooms. His room was anonymous. It was without the model aeroplanes, the maps and school photographs, the toys and illustrated books of boyhood; nor had it any trace of conjugality. It was like a bedroom in one of those large Victorian hotels which still exist, unmodernised, bleak, splendid dinosaurs among the fawning mammals of the contemporary motel–hotel world. Jimmie had come to like it. He thought that it enabled him to get on with more work more quickly.

There was a study downstairs but his father's old desk had been brought up to his bedroom. He was at work within a few minutes of getting out of bed. Although he would never admit it to anyone, he had been greatly influenced, as a youth, by a small volume of Arnold Bennett's which had explained to the reader how to get full value out of twenty-four hours in a day. To Jimmie, idling but seeking a higher purpose at his middling public school, this text had appeared as the foundation on which he could build his life. He had been forced to practise in the holidays. It was not done to be 'keen' at that school, which was heavily weighted in favour of the sons of clergymen. Jimmie had conformed but he had not lost touch with his text.

During Elaine's first illnesses, he had re-discovered work as an anaesthetic: now it was the only way he could be at ease with life. In Parliament and in his constituency he was noted for his hard work and for his capacity to keep many and various activities going simultaneously. Yet his political career had been undistinguished.

The problem facing him for the next hour was the matter

of his campaign literature. The election was exactly three weeks away. The polls were not strikingly favourable but the Prime Minister had little room for manoeuvre. This autumn gamble had surprised the commentators, who had prophesied that he would hang on until the spring. Instantly they declared themselves unsurprised and both left and right proved that the Prime Minister had, after all, no real alternative. The explanation which the Prime Minister had given to his parliamentary colleagues was precisely that which he had given the press and the public. The parliamentary majority was too small, government by hairsbreadth voting was tiring and belittling –a clear mandate was necessary. Once upon a time Jimmie would have believed every word of this and gone to the hustings (as he could still call them) ready to defend this statement in the teeth of all contrary evidence. Now, a sadder and, as he said, a more ignorant man, he suspected that the Unions, the IMF or the CBI had threatened to cut up rough in the winter and an autumn election was the best way to spike their guns. The polls, too, though not good, were at least better than they had been for months.

Swiftly and expertly, Jimmie drew up the main points for his pamphlet. His agent would have some good ideas. Helen had produced some useful facts and figures. The hortatory missives from Transport House supplied much bulk, rather like those chunks of bread that fill out a lean meal. But he had always taken pride in speaking directly to his constituents in his own way and out of his own truest convictions. He had to temper and trim in Parliament, but not before the electors. That was his credo. To those who voted for him, he told the truth of his convictions.

Yet he knew that he was forcing himself. He had less heart for the job than ever before. What *were* his convictions? He knew that if he laid down his pen to think them over, he would meander into an endless and melancholy labyrinth of doubt.

When he had first become a Labour Member of Parliament, as a young gallant ex-captain, everything had been clean and clear. He had admired 'the ordinary men', 'the working chaps' in his regiment. He thought they needed a much better deal and deserved a bigger slice of the cake. He met the trade unionists like Ernie Bevin, and was deeply impressed by their authority, their sense of rightness and the utter confidence they had that they spoke for the majority of their countrymen. He admired Major Attlee and was overawed by the likes of Cripps and Dalton. When, eventually, he came to be acquainted with Nye Bevan, then he knew that he had made the right choice without question. 'Bevan brought poetry into Labour politics' – that was how James (Jimmie) Johnston, MC, put it unblushingly. The achievements of the 1945-51 Government made him 'proud to belong to the Labour Party' *and* 'proud to be British'.

He had been fortunate enough to get a seat just a few miles from his father's house. The house, in fact, overlooked much of the constituency, which mostly lay on the industrial fringe of the Solway Plain in Cumbria. He held the seat in 1951 and there was well-supported talk that, had Labour been returned, he would have been offered a junior job. He was a man to watch, they said.

In the fifties, euphoria had gradually slithered into desolation. The split in the Labour Party dismayed him. It seemed such an act of self-indulgence and such a waste of energy when there were so many things which only a Labour Government could achieve. Although he supported the Labour Party over Suez, he found the reasoning of some of his closest friends to be glib. He was enthusiastic about the Ban-The-Bomb Campaign and marched, once, from Aldermaston at Easter – only to find himself mocked and, later, even spurned by those whose cause he had taken to heart. He was bewildered by the fight over Clause Four and came into Gaitskell's camp too lamely and too late. In the Tory-triumphant Macmillan election, he lost his seat and felt that he had let down his ideals, his colleagues and above all those who had worked and voted for him in the constituency. He was ashamed of himself and wanted to run away and start again. But when he reviewed his actions, he could not see that he might have acted otherwise except by seizing an opportunistic line which would have been a greater betrayal, he thought, than his confused blundering.

He was persuaded to stand again in 1966 by the constituency party, with whom, on principle, he had never lost touch. They had tried to find another man but failed to agree. The attempt had been half-hearted. It was Jimmie they wanted. He came back rejuvenated. A large majority, an avowedly socialist policy, he wanted it to be 1945-51 all over again. He wanted to see big changes, a more just and tolerant society, the poor raised up, the rich curbed – he had never lost his naïve, even innocent do-gooding socialism. He discovered, to his astonishment, that he was regarded with great affection by many of his old colleagues; he was seen as one of those who had endured – a fine old-fashioned middle-class Labour man. Even his Christianity was considered to be proof of his integrity. Once again he was widely tipped for a ministerial post.

It never came. He held his seat through the next three elections and still it did not come. The time had passed him by. His growing dislike of Harold Wilson could not be concealed – but other men were given jobs without having to swear affection for the man. Jimmie was tactless. He always pushed forward his own and, as he saw it, the Party's principles and yet he stood for the notion that you must put country before party. He was able, amiable, eloquent, persuasive and rejected.

In a perceptive but dismissive little profile in the *New Statesman*, the writer half-playfully suggested that Jimmie's fatal flaw might be his good looks. Even now, in his fifties, Jimmie was an extremely handsome and graceful man in a passé, matinée-idol manner. Thick grey hair, strong features, bold grey eyes, tall, squarely built, polished – the sort of man, the *New Statesman* proposed, who was guaranteed to raise the hackles of Harold ('I can understand the man in the street *and* beat the intellectuals at their own game better than anybody') Wilson. Jimmie was neither clever enough nor was he sufficiently plebeian, he was not young enough nor was he dependent enough – and besides that he had lately taken to asserting his belief in the stand taken by Gaitskell, the dead leader whom Wilson had replaced and seemed to wish to efface. The writer tactfully omitted to say that perhaps Jimmie simply was not tough enough, but he did suggest that Jimmie's Christian and clerical background had somehow left him 'forever just that bit out of touch with contemporary reality'.

As he covered the broad-lined pages of the blue exercise book with his appeal to the voters, Jimmie found that it was as if he were driving in neutral. The active part of his mind was not engaged. He considered turning to something else, but there was no time. His agent needed the first draft today and besides, would thought make it different? He wrote on: about the Welfare State, North Sea Oil, Nationalisation, Comprehensive Schools, Race, Inflation, Unemployment and the special problems of the area he knew so well and had represented so faithfully. Yet he felt he had let the people down. They deserved a minister. In this cut-off and historically neglected area they needed someone with pull, someone who could begin to have a positive effect on their apparently intransigent problems. Not him. Jimmie was a shy, solitary man whose heartiness and hail-fellow attitude was no more than a smokescreen to protect himself and enable him to appear to be making the ordinary contacts he found so difficult. Yet they would have no one else.

This loyalty touched him very deeply. It was because of this loyalty that he was preparing to work sixteen hours a day for the next three weeks. Because of this loyalty that he put his mind to the eternally recurring difficulties of his sick wife. Because of this loyalty that he feared to break out of the conventional life which had slowly suffocated him and grab the chance of a new life which seemed to be before him. And because of this loyalty that he dreaded the arrival of his friend Harold Ruthwaite with news which could make him a public scandal within the next week.

Chapter Two

Elaine's son, Gareth, had driven down from London the previous night and arrived in the early hours of the morning. In his nervous, almost alarmed gestures he clearly resembled his mother, although in looks he was so different that, as a boy, strangers had remarked on a likeness to Jimmie. This was embarrassing. Jimmie was his step-father, although that fact had not been admitted within or without the family for many years, not, in fact, until Gareth was in his mid-twenties.

Marianne had heard the car, got out of bed and come down to meet and be persuaded to stay to sleep with him.

Gareth reached out and touched her bare back. There was a very slight spread of hairs. He rubbed them with his thumb. He let his hand trail down the spinal cord emphatically but gently, playing his fingers on the discs. At the buttocks he paused and touched all about them as if sizing them. Then his hand went up once again to the waist, girl-slim again and as trim as it had been five years before. He knew that she was not asleep. He hesitated, to lull her, and then, quite suddenly, drove his hand down between the thighs.

She twisted violently on the makeshift bed and pulled away from him, taking most of the rough blankets with her. Gareth grinned to himself, as if he had scored an important point. He swung his legs over the edge of the chaise-longue which they had pushed against the large sofa in the early hours of the morning to make a double bed. The curtains were badly drawn. Sunlight came through the gaps. The drawing-room looked even larger than usual, heavy with inherited furniture, hungover with its ecclesiastical past in the pictures and the Gothic Window motif on the walls. There was even a lectern, brass eagle's wings outspread, at the ready for the next lesson. Jimmie used it as a writing desk when he wanted to stand and ease the monotony of sedentary work.

Gareth glanced at her and then looked elaborately about the room, like a stage villain. He knew that he had used her and he should have felt ashamed. But he did not and took refuge in mock-theatricality. He had his back to Marianne, who again pretended to be asleep. If Gareth had an audience for the monologue which followed, then it would appear to have been his genitals. The fact that Marianne did not watch did not matter. All that he wanted was to find some way to get out of the exasperating feeling of responsibility she always put on him.

'Arise, *Cerne Abbas*, and go into thy kingdom.' He waved his hands before him like a pantomime conjuror. 'Abracadabra – we are alone, deep in the bowels of the manse – arise.' He glanced over his shoulder at Marianne, 'Game's up, love' – the melodramatic delivery became Cockney camp – 'don't put on airs, dearie. Ladies want it just as much as gentlemen. Come along now, my darling, the old pecker's peckish.' He did not desire her, nor did it matter to him whether or not they made love again, but there was a game of domination he had always played with her and the habit had stuck. 'Come on, gal.' The American deep-bass-virile-cigarette-advertising tone. 'Sometimes, a man's gotta do what a man's gotta do. Time we hit the trail. Remember.' He recited very slowly as a dirge. 'Remember, gal,

Rip Van Winkle slept a long long time
When he woke he was old and grey.

'So!' he reverted suddenly and wildly, leaping up like a marionette, to stage queer – a wacky faggoty voice full of innuendo:

'Wakey – Wakey! Give a shakey!
It's gonna be a glorious, I say glorious, yes a glorious Da – a – a – ay.
GETTING UP TIME, CAMPERS! I *mean.* Mother's waiting!'

He finished, half-turned to her, one hand on hip, the other patting the back of his hair, knees primly together in what Quentin Crisp had described as the classic transvestite pose. In that instant, but only for that instant, when imitating some fantasy figure, Gareth felt a rare burst of contentment.

Marianne was not looking.

'Cock-a-doodle-do!'

'What time is it?' Her voice faked sleepiness. She had, once upon a time, enjoyed his mimicking and strutting. Now it wearied her.

'I understand. Cock a doodle *don't* if I'm not a good boy then.' He clambered across to his trousers and pulled out a large pocket watch. 'On the third stroke it will be – resist the temptation – 7.24 a.m. precisely. I wonder if God knows that. Do You?' He looked up at the ceiling, which was the floor of his mother's bedroom. '7.24 precisely. We have our own fix on the universe now – so watch it, sun.'

'Time I was out of here,' Marianne said. She was apprehensive and Gareth, in some callous part of him, enjoyed that.

'First the little matter of the morning call.' He stood up, naked, lean, dark, and ran a few steps on the spot – high knee raising. He stopped abruptly. 'Knock knock, who's there?'

'Not again.' Marianne pulled the blankets up to her neck and looked at him gravely. She had no influence on his

22

moods these days. There was no way she could control him.

'It's a crime against the appetites! Don't you realise your responsibilities as a liberated female? Lie back and take your medicine like a man.'

Marianne sat up, took a half-smoked cigarette from the ashtray, lit up, and coughed. 'I'm sore,' she said, fanning the smoke away from her watering eyes. 'You're too rough. I'm not used to it.' Her excuses were lame but he did not see through them.

'Let me rub your bum.'

Gareth darted forward – she loved his quick, greedy movements – lifted the blankets, levered her on to her side and then delicately patted her bottom. Then he let her sit up, replaced the blankets and once more stood before her, bristling with the desire that she join in his play.

'What a generous thought on the part of the Great Inventor, that bum of yours – that beautiful double mould' – his hands shaped them in the air – 'that shapely beasty-breasty bum, all laid on to decorate nothing grander than the glum little terminus of your intestinal organs. A Henry Moore original! Genius.'

'They'll be up soon. I'd better get dressed.' It was over. He had not changed. She had been weak to give in.

'Whereas,' he continued, watching her carefully, almost threateningly now, 'compare and contrast the lack of craftmanship that went into the old pecker. With twice the responsibility – like a withered bit of old rhubarb – why so old? Why were you born so old? Do you hang your head in shame? Or are you exhausted by the millions of half lives which have passed through you? Or is it guilt? Alas poor prick! Hampton, Tool,' the names came popping out, like balloons being burst by an unruly child, 'Ding-a-ling, Member – of what? Couldn't you inspire us a little more than that? Take *penis* – well, you can't take it anywhere. Snake? No fun. *And tventieth-scenchury men demends*

23

fun! "John Thomas." "Willie." "Dick." Never Fred. "Little Man." O Mother.'

Marianne stubbed out the cigarette and shivered. She was afraid of him when he got carried away in one of his moods. She saw him wilfully damaging himself, contradicting all that once had been so gentle and decent in his nature. However funny he started out to be the result was just the same as when he was nasty – once she had never known him to be nasty, but now, half stranger, she never knew how he would turn. He ignored her restlessness and went on, still addressing his groin.

'St. Augustine said that you had a will of your own. Do you know that? Do you forget nothing and learn nothing? *Cock*'s the only decent word. But why does it mean rubbish at the same time? Tell me.'

It was true that in the last two or three years he had become a stranger to her, Marianne thought; although she had known him for so much of her life, all the quick strength she loved became petrified now in an argument he was having only with himself. She felt detached and saw him isolated, odd, straining – for what? She had lost him. She did not know. Now he stood, naked, holding himself, glaring at his crotch, even comical: yet she dared not laugh.

'I want to know,' he said, apparently in all seriousness, 'why? – and believe me, the answer could bring peace to the world – why? – this could unify the dualities of good and evil – why? – it could release the central absurd agony of man or, better still, anaesthetise it – why? – it could staunch the wound which the ridiculous makes in the poetic, it could be the sensual splitting of the atom – it is, in short, the riddle Oedipus should have proposed to the Sphinx. Why, O little cock, must we pee out of you as well?' He glared at her.

She put her hand to her mouth so as not to make a sound. She had experienced his anger – blown up suddenly and meaninglessly, just as seemed about to happen now. He smiled at her yet she felt alarm swoop up into her throat like nausea.

'I'm getting up,' she said, dry-throated, bewildered by the strength of her fear for this man she had known and loved for so long.

'Not really.'

'Yep.' She pulled on her jeans hurriedly, hauled the sweater towards her, that would do – underclothes, shoes, tights could wait.

'Not really.' Still he smiled and waited for her to stop running away.

'I'd hate to play gooseberry to you and your – thingummy there.' She was in a panic to have the protection of her clothes.

'You were listening! She was listening, Cerne Abbas. Monologues are for us monos, my girl.'

She was dressed. She took some deep breaths, carefully so that he would not notice. She needed to do something. She reached out to fold a blanket. Now that she was clothed, her confidence returned.

'Still bloody anti-life.' No play in his tone now. But she was dressed – and the bed was between them.

'Pass my shoes. Please.'

He ignored her request and slowly began to draw on his tight jeans.

'I've said I'll marry you,' he said calmly, his usual self now; cool. 'I've said it ever since Alan was born.'

'The way you say it makes it impossible for me to accept it – doesn't it?' She punched the cushions back into shape and tugged at the chaise-longue to disengage the temporary coupling of furniture. Why was he always so serious when she was least prepared for it? He made no effort to reply. Surely he ought to reply when it was so important. 'Don't you? Say it that way? It's just saying it for the sake of saying it. But do you love me?'

'No,' he said. 'I don't. It's unfortunate.'

She was never prepared for his honesty. It hurt and shocked her. She turned to check the tingling in her eyes. Gareth was well aware of the effect his words had on her but he calmly continued to dress, carefully pulling his denim shirt on, fastening the cuffs as if he were securing fine cuff-links, breathing in deeply to tuck the faded blue shirt into his trousers. He was back in himself and played her like a hooked fish.

'I could say "I'm sorry, Marianne", but that would be hypocritical.'

She nodded, her back still towards him. She was well trained. By him. No one else. If only they could talk it all over nicely, quietly, in a relaxed way, she thought, instead of barging into the most important issue in their life – her life anyway – like some obstacle in the dark. She had told herself to fight back a hundred times when he had been far away from her. Recently, as he had noticed, she had begun to assert herself strongly. He merely increased his pressure and watched. She had to find courage now, she thought, and she braced herself.

'You look like a schoolgirl from the back,' he said. 'Having your hair cut short did it. And that grey pullover I suppose, one of Holy Jimmie's, is it? How old are you?' he paused. 'Twenty-two; twenty-three just after Christmas.'

'Why did you just make love to me then?' she asked, facing him, trying to be fierce.

'I like it. You know that.'

'You've always thought you could – whenever you wanted. And ever since I had Alan you've treated me like a doormat.'

'That's a poor analogy,' he said. 'You can do better than that.'

She ignored his attempt to check her anger. 'I don't need you. He'll be at school soon and I'll get a job. I won't need your money either.'

'You'll get it.' He spoke tiredly, not out of affectation –

26

although that tint was never quite absent from the character or characters he played with when teasing her – but because the subject of their child exhausted, he would say bored, him. 'You always have. On the dot.' This was the worst part of coming home: the child, the talk of the child, the final proof of his lack of all true feeling, for he sinned against all that was right by feeling so little for his child.

'On principle,' Marianne retorted. 'Not because you want to give it to me. And certainly not because you want to give it to Alan. But because you want to be able to *say* that you've given it to us.'

'Say to whom?' She was right, he knew that, and he appreciated her acuteness.

'Yourself, of course!' She tugged the heavy furniture over the room, knocked her shin against the leg of the piano and felt giddy. She straightened up to clear her head. 'You say everything to yourself, don't you? Who else would listen? You're the most self-centred man in the word. *Your* articles, *your* radio programmes, *your* ideas about everything under the sun. I'm surprised you even find time to talk to that thingummy of yours. Mind, you make a lovely couple!'

He laughed. Bullseye for another cliché, he thought. Beautiful women *did* become more interesting when they grew angry. Another truism rises from the dust. She was black-haired, jet, shiny: the face a small oval which would have been too pretty but for the uneven gash of mouth and the biting blue eyes. He liked to laugh at her when she was angry. It made him feel rich to control her so absolutely. It was the nearest, these days, he came to real emotion.

'*You* wanted the child, Marianne,' he said, slipping in the thrust. '*You* missed the pill.'

'I forgot it.'

'You forgot it?' He replied with flat disbelief. 'You still maintain that, do you?'

'I loved you. You don't understand that any more, do you?' She rapped out the sentimental phrases urgently.

27

Marianne was someone who always believed there was one last chance. 'You were wonderful then. You said you loved me. And I believed it. I'd been brought up to believe in love.' He looked the same. More tired, thinner, more tense, but he was the same man, she thought. How could he not be touched by what she said? How could he not remember? She wanted to scream at his coolness – WE MADE LOVE! WE HAVE A CHILD!

'What are you trying to tell me, Marianne?' His battery razor worked almost silently: the buzzing cushions of mini-blades grazed safely over his jaw.

'I want a life of my own. I want to get away from you.'

'So why did you do it last night?'

'When I phoned you yesterday to tell you that Elaine had had a bad turn, you were up here in no time.' She strove to keep the envy out of her voice.

'So I went to the top of the class. "The boy loves his mother: can't be all bad." '

'You twist everything.'

'Everything's twisted.'

'You do love *her*, don't you?'

Gareth winced as if he had cut himself and did not answer. Marianne had said what she wanted to say but felt no better for it. Two forces struggled inside her: one which knew it was hopeless and degrading to beg for his love and saw strength and sanity only in breaking free: the other which feared to leave what had once been strong and still hoped desperately for a happy ending. But that was out, she could see: the ending was behind her.

'I'm going to have to do it all by myself, aren't I?' she said quietly – suddenly aware of this. 'You'll give me no help at all. You'll come, you'll want me to go to bed with you, then you'll go away for weeks and months on end and our only communication will be the monthly cheque at the bank. I'm on my own, aren't I?' The force of this final realisation made her want to sit down, to have time to absorb it, to reassure herself that she could face up to it. She had not owned up to it in front of him before now.

'You always were,' he said thinly, even, she sensed, kindly. 'That was clear from the start. Those were the terms.'

'You can't have terms when people fall in love.'

He shrugged.

'Nobody's free of other people,' she said. 'Are they?'

Again he gave no answer and she made herself fold up one of the blankets, feeling that she had done something important, unsure exactly what it implied, wanting to stay until the instinct was confirmed. 'Do you know what *you* want, Gareth?' she asked him finally. He was only seven years older than she was, but his education, his position as the son of this big house, his strange ways of talking had always made him appear to her as much a teacher, even a guru, as a lover.

'I know exactly what I want, Marianne,' he said. He had finished shaving. He rubbed the nectarine smoothness of his skin with an approving thumb and forefinger. And indeed, when he was with Marianne he *was* confident of his role. Had he followed this through, he would have been surprised to discover how much he looked forward to their meetings for this very reason – the relaxation of knowing where he was. With her, he *did* know exactly what he wanted.

'I thought I did,' she replied sadly.

'You do. You want to be free from me. Remember?'

'Yes.' Not even her sorrow could reach him now. She was chilled by how completely he had cut her out of his feelings: for her self-respect, she fought to disguise it.

'That's a start.' He smiled at her. She could have been his secretary, he thought, or a young student a bit down-in-the-mouth – in need of that little bit of extra personal encouragement. 'We are all free. That's the message. That's all the message.'

'You keep saying that.' Her response was weary. She had

to take on the burden of living without hoping for anything from him and this first intimation tired her.

'Thank you for last night,' he said, enjoying the switch to this tone of genuine gratitude, enjoying her puzzled expression. 'You're very good in bed. Muchas gracias.'

She shook her head and further folded the already folded blanket.

'Stop behaving as if we're due for kit inspection,' Gareth said gently. He leaned across and twitched the blanket away from her. She let it fall on to the carpet. 'If you want to pretend that I slept here alone – for reasons of propriety which must be as curious as can be imagined all things considered – then, please leave the bed scruffy as I would. A little social realism. Never let it be said the fifties lived in vain. Nice and untidy.' He threw a cushion to join the blanket. 'There.'

'You'd make a good criminal.'

'I've often thought that.'

'I'm going.' She began to walk to the door which led to the back stairs. It was clear that she wanted to be called to stop. He waited until the very last second.

'Marianne.'

'Yes?'

'Stay loose. Take care. Good morning.'

He nodded and she had no reason to stay.

Gareth took out a crumpled Disque Bleu from his breast pocket and wandered around the large room. He remembered how in Jane Austen's novels people had 'taken a turn' around the drawing-room. It was not such a bad idea. He looked at the books, well bound, complete sets, leather and gilt; the three bronze statuettes Jimmie had bought just after the war from a sculptor friend who since had become famous, thus making these writhing headless almost shapeless hermaphrodite bodies quite valuable – each little piece worth about six months' average wage, he calculated: madness. There were just two jardinières which Gareth liked for their absurdity and a nineteenth-century miniature tapestry on the theme of the Crucifixion which always mesmerised him by its bloodless implausibility and bad taste. 'Elaine's piano', always so called although it had been there, she said, before her arrival, formerly subject to a weekly pounding from Canon Johnston as he had ground through the Friday-night friends-and-family sing-song ritual with the same joyless relentlessness as appeared to have characterised his attitude towards all other rituals, sacred, secular and sexual. Canon Johnston had existed in the district much as the old parson-squire of eighteenth-century novels. Now he seemed further away than the Tudors. A valuable vase, often caused to wobble, never yet to crash, stood on a massive mahogany side-table. Heavy, comfortable, now very chic and expensive, Victorian furniture. A Georgian bookcase, two Adam mirrors slung high on the walls to avoid all but the tallest human eye. A civilised, settled place, crammed with some of the achievements of an imperial past: to Gareth's eye it looked like so much debris.

Several times in his recent past Gareth had felt like smashing this room to pieces with a poker. Now he regarded it with calm contempt.

He whistled a ragtime tune and stubbed his cigarette on a Wedgwood dish. He had no desire to look out of the window. He put the light on, took out a pad and made some notes for his next article. He sipped gently from the hip flask of malt whisky.

Lionel popped his bald brown and crinkled old head around the door. With its flying wisps of grey hair skewered out above the ears, it looked like some puppet's face swivelling about half-way up the door.

'I go, I come back?'

'Come in.'

The head withdrew, the door was pushed open, and Lionel hobbled in, legs bowed as if from riding (though it was from mining), black waistcoat and trousers, white collarless shirt, sleeves rolled up above his elbows revealing tight biceps which made a mockery of his seventy-four years, at the end of one arm a bucket of coal, in the other hand a bucket of newspaper and twigs.

'Phew!' He paused dramatically. 'O dear me.'

'Good morning.'

'Good night by the smell of it.' He put down the coal bucket, licked his finger and held it up. 'Fresh, very. O yes.'

Gareth was irritated by the old man's intimacy and homeliness. Once upon a time he had made a great fuss over Lionel. Now he was glad to be out of his company although he took great care that no one should notice, least of all Lionel himself. 'Keep the home fires burning.' Gareth was vexed that he should descend to such a fatuous mandarin-matey remark. He could do better than that. 'I need some air,' he said. Not much better.

'I bet. Did it end up on t'floor then? A fight to the finish?' The old man grinned and stubbed his toe on the hectic pile of blankets.

Again Gareth felt the kick of irritation.

'You are the occupying power, clearly. I'll be gone.'

He jumped up, scarcely able to control the fierce surge of anger he felt for this amiable cheerful old man whom he had once idealised as an 'unsung working-class hero' – the best friend of his mother's legendary (in her eyes) father – someone who had helped to raise him. Yet Gareth could not bear to be in the same room as him. He made for the door.

'Hey! Just a minute. I want to take you up on something you said on that daft programme of yours last Thursday – no, Friday – no, wait a minute – Thursday – Thursday.' Gareth was forced to stop: Lionel was making a point of it.

'Later. Please, Lionel. We can have a talk later.'

'I turned it off anyway. I can't listen to all those squawkin' records you put between the interviews and the political stuff. Why do you mix it all up? Irritatin' everybody.' Still the old man's insistence held him. Then he wrenched himself free.

'Life, Lionel! Life! Good morning. Draw the curtains. Reveal the french windows. Set the stage for the usual Victorian farce.'

He was gone.

Lionel nodded. Recently he had pestered Gareth deliberately in order to test his conclusion about him. There was no doubt. Gareth had lost himself, he thought.

The old man drew the curtains very slowly, afraid to disturb the rather rickety curtain rail which he had meant to attend to for months.

There were two sets of stairs in the house and it was the servants' stairs Gareth chose to use to take him to the attics. That way, he was less likely to meet anyone and he wanted some time alone before he met Elaine and took on Jimmie.

He chose the attic in which Lionel had laid out the apples. They covered the floor, wall to wall, safely stored, already filling the room with a rich cidery fug. Gareth pushed them aside gently, his feet wading through them so that they scattered and bunched untidily, breaking the neat pattern which Lionel's careful work had given them. He sat on the floor, his back against the wall. The effect of the journey, the false alarm about Elaine (Marianne had been apologetic when he arrived: she had thought Elaine was about to enter one of her *very* bad times whereas it now appeared that she was still within the limits of her own 'normal' behaviour), the lovemaking with Marianne ... he could make up lists of reasons for his feeling of utter emptiness ... lists that would reach back into childhood.

It was odd that in the room below was his son, being brought up in the same house as he had known as a child. Elaine and Jimmie had urged Marianne to come and live with them. The advantages for Alan and the temptation to be in contact with Gareth had easily persuaded her to accept their offer. Her mother, down in the town a few miles away, saw it as yet another betrayal. Gareth avoided thinking about the troubles Marianne must have faced in that small community: pregnant, unmarried, whisked out to the house of the widely known and respected Member of Parliament, and all because of that Gareth Johnston who had done so well for himself in the papers and on the radio. He could not burn for her.

Since he had found out the truth about his father he had been so self-consumed that he could scarcely reach out to anyone. Sometimes he thought that it was simply a question of energy: the amount of thought, of re-consideration, anger, self-pity, reorganisation, misery, regret and confusion thrown up by the over-late discovery that he was not the son of his apparent father – of Jimmie, whom he had called 'father' innocently for years – this had given him so much preoccupation that there was nothing *left* for anyone else.

But it was too straightforward and too infantile to blame it on that. For years before then, since his adolescence, Gareth had felt a split in himself, a division which he could heal only by play-acting at being someone he was expected to be, or, alternatively, someone he was not expected to be. For, since his adolescence, he had experienced an acute sense of bleakness and an insoluble sense of loss. He would wake up to the crushing thought that yet another day had to be got through. He would see the prospect of years before him as an appallingly, unnecessarily vast acreage of time which yawned emptily, greedy for things to fill it – but what had he to offer? In those moments of stillness, when you sink to the root of yourself like a diver going down to the bottom of the ocean in a bell-jar, he felt only nothingness, meaninglessness, a despair which he could not describe or understand but which was there, however much he might mock or blame himself for it, it was there, like a black hole in the heart of his life relentlessly sucking into itself all that he constructed. To escape this he ran: he ran to work, to women, to drink, to different jobs, different places, different creeds; he took risks, he was reckless rather than bold, and he found that, as if some inevitable process were at work, one thing after another lost its savour until now he was at the most extreme point possible from where he had started.

As a schoolboy and undergraduate and at first with Marianne, with his friends in London, he had been able to appear warm-hearted, interested in everything about him, even a little naïve. Now he saw himself as a cynical man, bitter, without decent feelings, prepared to be cruel as he had been with Marianne that morning, not even prepared to be polite to old and faithful friends such as Lionel. 'Saw himself' was the correct expression of his state, for to escape the bleak, draining despair within himself he had begun to act more than one part. That was the division, between the centre of him which did not change but drew him in endless circles around some grave of faith, and the face he put on to the world which was so animated and various that people would say he was 'full of life'. And so to blame his sudden access to the knowledge of his past for what he was feeling now was unfair. But he felt like being unfair. He had come back to be unfair. That was his present rôle.

He felt sleepy and took up one of the smaller green apples. It was pocked and misshapen and hard but he bit into it and relished the sourness, 'His present rôle': it was uncanny now how he 'saw' himself as if his body existed apart from some central and guiding spirit. He laughed: perhaps there *was* a soul after all! That would be a joke, he thought, and wonderfully ironic and absurd if he should discover such a thing here, in an ex-Anglican vicarage of all places! An unlikely place for religion: his contempt for Jimmie's quiet Christianity was intense.

But if it was not a good place for souls, it was certainly a fine place for acting out a part. Long ago, Gareth had noticed how the vicarage was organised about that main room as about a stage. The basic reason for this was that as it was the only reliably warm room in the entire vicarage, it was naturally the spot where everyone came together for warmth: this primitive huddle was still part of the life-style of a house geared to austere Edwardian notions of domestic fortitude. There was always a fire on in the living-room and the ancient radiators were allowed to function.

More had been added to that. Elaine's illnesses had meant that she was often convalescing, and for quite long periods of time. It was much more companionable for her to be allowed down into the big room – a bed made up for her rather in the way Gareth had made up the bed for himself and Marianne – and there she could at least seem to be part of the life of the house. Jimmie had got into the habit of doing the less taxing work – many of the letters, some of the reading – there in the big room in order to spend some time with his wife: otherwise he could have moved from Westminster to the train, to his local committee-rooms, to the various functions and to his study-bedroom without seeing her for weeks on end. Elaine's mother had always liked the room and she, too, like Jimmie, saw that it was the only focus they had. Gareth could extend the similarity to a stage much further. For as they tended to arrive from such different worlds – Jimmie from Parliament, Elaine from the private concentration of her illness and loneliness, himself from the loose and corrupting metropolitan mixture of extremist politics and jaded hedonism – they tended to make announcements to each other, statements from their worlds which were so different it seemed to Gareth a wonder they met at all. Add to that the long-rooted home-binding local certainty of Elaine's mother, who acted as unacknowledged housekeeper (a rôle she had held officially for Jimmie's father), and the straightforward, as he saw them, difficulties of Marianne, and the room became a little theatre for them all. All the better, he thought viciously, for him to play his final part before he pulled down the curtain on Jimmie.

Gareth bit again into the sour green apple. The acid spurted stingingly inside his mouth and began its trickle down his throat, bitterly. Tears came to his eyes. He felt invigorated.

Chapter Three

(i)

The walk usually cheered Jimmie up. It was the same walk.
Every morning that he was in the vicarage he would set off
right after the eight o'clock news and pound the two-and-a-
half miles around the lanes which linked the hamlet with
other small farming outcrops in that sparsely populated
region. He kept off the fell. It was too strenuous and too
spectacular for the purpose he required. He liked these un-
dulating lanes. He passed by farmyards and nodded to
neighbours he had known all his life, he would meet the mail
van, the Milk Marketing lorry overtook him on the way
back, he felt part of the place and that mattered increasingly
to him.

The wind was getting up again. The clouds were on the
move, scudding across the tops, pouchy with rain. It was
cold. Jimmie liked all weathers. He used to say that those
who lived under perfect blue skies and clear hot sun did not
know what they missed. He would be bored stiff, he declared, just gazing at a bare blazing disc of flame all day
long. He enjoyed rain in all its varieties, snow, hail, sleet,
mist – above all, the wind, the stronger the better. To fight to
keep his foothold made him feel firm in his sense of being
alive.

There was so little time left. A few years and then senility.
He walked briskly, as if to beat back the grim reaper.

Though his head turned this way and that looking at familiar landmarks and features, Jimmie was no countryman.

He knew only the most common flowers, birds and trees by name. What he liked, he would say, was the feeling of it all, the sweep and space, the drama of the landscape, not the minutiae of a garden. And yet he admired Lionel's skill and knowledge in the garden and envied him his erudition on these matters. Close learning of nature had been neglected in his education; just as he had never learned how to be practical – brought up, indeed, to despise the man who worked with his hands or was mechanical as someone inferior to those, like himself, who would think. He regretted the snobbery and stupidity which had brought that about, but it was too late to change now. So many things he did not know. The workings of his own body, for example, were as unknown to him as the latest laws of physics. The best in his own literature remained but scantily read, and yet he gutted three or four newspapers a day and as many magazines a week. Whatever he thought of he thought of with regret. However quickly he walked he could not shake that off. So much was coming to a head.

Hill farms, small lowland acreage and spans of fell for the sheep. Hard-living, constant work. Farms tucked into every advantage of the land. Well-kept, these days, with the money to spend on them. Clean beasts in the green fields. A few ponies. Still hens, ducks, geese, guinea-fowl in the farmyard. The lean black-and-white sheep-dogs, long-haired, keen-faced. Plain small hamlets and villages set in the hillsides. Names that went back for centuries, like his own. Three generations of clergymen before him and before that, gentlemen farmers and before that 'statesmen'. Like the famous huntsman John Peel, who must have trekked over these same lanes many a morning – lived only a mile away. The hunting still went on, the shooting, the fishing, the old pubs, the showing of animals, the market and auction at Thurston, the hound trails, the competing with vegetables and flowers and baked bread and cakes at the agricultural shows, the fêtes. It was all there to be part of and he wanted

39

to be knitted into it, he wanted to draw from it the strength of endurance.

Yet his finer instincts told him that he had no real place here any more. The gentry had not disappeared, but its function as leader, provider and exemplar was obsolete. Affluence, increased independence and the change of mood had altered the relationship which his father had found so fruitful and easy. Jimmie's good nature and open-heartedness made him generally well liked, but among his immediate neighbours there was not much more than amiable politeness. He felt it a mark of weakness that he should want more, but he did. When he walked about the quiet high-hedged lanes he felt sure of himself: when he spoke to a farmer or a labourer or a factory worker or a teacher, he was conscious, within seconds, that he was slithering about, fighting for a grip. The social ladder had been pulled away and yet its marks remained; however loud the protests, the system persisted and it embarrassed him.

He had friends, scattered about the country. One or two from his old school, one or two from the army, a few family friends – some of them thirty or forty miles away up in the Borders where feudal play could still be taken half-seriously. His political inclination had not put them off – they rather enjoyed the company of a 'Red'; some of them welcomed him to berate him with their complaints about death duties, income tax, corporation tax and the unions. Living this far from London, at an extremity of England, was not unlike living in one of those tax havens – Malta, the south of Portugal, Barbados – where Anglo-Saxon cash-exiles cluster together and attempt to make a common life out of the common cause of their monetary grievances. He did not despise them, though, and would defend them when his colleagues at Westminster became virulent about 'privilege'.

Yet Jimmie was losing touch with these friends through neglect. His time was taken up in London or in the main town within his constituency – a coal and steel town now in trouble, trying desperately to attract light industries, be-devilled by the inconvenience of its position, stuck way off the main trade roads with no populous hinterland. Although he clung to this vicarage and sought refuge and support in it, he felt most himself in that prosaic industrial constituency so apparently alien to his past and his nature. He had work to do there and the work gave him a validity he could no longer lay claim to among these fells which he had roamed on foot, by bicycle, on his first pony and, in the fifties, on horseback with the hunt – 'The Sporting Pink or the Socialist Squire' one popular paper had, unfortunately, called him at the time, and a large photograph had appeared. He had never been careful enough about cutting himself off publicly from his past. His version of a Labour Party did not impose penalties on you for whatever you had been born, rich or poor. Individual freedom was a keystone of the Party. Yet in time he *had* dropped away from his county set. He had come to feel that he did not truly 'belong'.

It was a longing which had always been with him. It seemed insatiable. And, over the past week with Helen, he had felt a rare potential for just that sort of intense companionship. He could not burden her by telling her of it. That would be unfair to her, he thought. He had gone too far in that one impulsive embrace he had given her, although, he reasoned, ruefully, his explanation of it as the over-effusive act of a tired old man had seemed to satisfy her completely. She had shown up his emotional life for the barren rump it was, a compact of cowardice, despair and hopelessness, he thought: he was hard on himself, and he needed to be, for with Helen, he dreamed, there could be a new life – and that was not permissible even as a thought. There was Elaine. There had always been Elaine.

He decided to go into the church. It was not on impulse. He had known that he would go into it from the moment he had left the vicarage. He always went in when he needed peace. He used it as religiously and as superstitiously as

41

Mediterranean women use the foot of the statue of a favourite saint or the Virgin, touching it for more than luck.

The church had been shut down for over thirty years but it was still well looked after. It stood in the middle of a field. There had been a path to it but the farmer had let it grass over. You could just see the outline, though, and Jimmie followed it conscientiously. The graveyard was kept trim by the church-wardens from the nearby village whose church had absorbed the parishioners once faithful to the small whitewashed twelfth-century foundation now standing bright in the morning sun. The door was always unlocked.

There was an altar, a cross and no other furniture. The floor was flagged; tombstones had been used for patching and where the chancel had been there were more tombstones deliberately laid to mark the graves of the family which had held the living. Jimmie's father had held services here: his mother had declared it to be her favourite spot on earth and she was buried beside his father in the ground outside the East Window. Nowadays it was Mrs Burns, Elaine's mother, who trudged across the field to see the flowers were fresh and sweep the place out. Her brush and shovel were behind the door. Lionel sometimes came with her, bringing a ladder to climb up and clean the windows. There were only four: the East Window, and three on the North side. Plain glass. Jimmie could feel at peace here.

He could no longer pray and he was ashamed of that but he could not clasp his hands together and address God. He knew he believed, not in the First Cause of a Clockwork Universe, nor in the Jealous Jehovah of the Israelities – though more in Him than in the uncommitted and abstracted entity of modern churchmen. He believed in God although he did not know who or what God was. He knew he had a soul but was utterly crushed by the knowledge. On this holy spot the best he could do was be still and attend.

Elaine needed him. The rest was wrong. She needed his help as she always had done and his duty to her was clear.

Helen must not be loved: he had already done her a disservice by showing overmuch affection.

In among the flowers Mrs Burns had put one or two twigs from the copper beech tree.

Once, in Jerusalem, he had spent an evening with Professor Sholem, a scholar whose life's work had been devoted to the mystics and the cabbala. 'I can understand agnostics,' Sholem had said, after an evening where he had disputed every 'proof' of God, 'but atheists I cannot understand. It is up to *them* to prove there is no one, nothing. Already I know that there could be. They never prove there is not.' In his worst moments, Jimmie rested on that. Yes: atheists he could not understand. Elaine needed him. He nodded at the cross, paused and went out.

The weather had changed again and a cascade of hailstones met him at the door. He stepped out, enjoying the sharp pricks they made as the pellets struck his hands and face. On the road before him they bounced in their thousands, as if someone had taken a giant scoop of hard wedding rice and poured it all over the land.

Chapter Four

Lionel led Elaine into the room with elaborate care, holding her arm tightly as if helping her pass through a hostile crown. He sat her down in the chaise-longue, put a blanket about her shoulders and went to the drinks cabinet, where he poured out a brandy. She held on to the large copper-beech twigs tightly.

'Drink this.'

She took a sip, shook with a spasm of cold, and then forced another mouthful down, clearly grateful.

'I don't know. What a lass! You need a cup of something hot. You're shaking like a leaf. I'll get you some tea.'

'Don't worry.' Elaine sat bolt upright to make her point and the blanket slid down her shoulders. Lionel carefully repositioned it. 'I'm afraid Mother saw me. She'll be bringing tea.' She held out the half-empty glass to Lionel and noticed the twigs in her other hand. 'These were lying on the ground. I didn't pull them off.' She spoke intently: it was important to her that Lionel should know that she had not pulled off the twigs.

'You wouldn't have the strength. And you wouldn't do it anyway.' Lionel took the glass back to the cabinet, emptying it down his throat on the way. He felt a surge of sentiment for this daughter of the man who had been the best friend of his youth. There was something orphaned about her, he thought, and he turned, feeling the brandy sting his stomach, to say, 'You're too good for this life. That's your whole trouble. I'll make up a fire.'

To be of service to her, he all but scurried across the big room and knelt before the grate, working rapidly. Elaine stood up, drew the blanket about her like a cloak, and walked around. She let her slippers fall off and rubbed her feet dry in the old blankets piled on the floor. Then she stopped and looked across at Lionel, who could have been at worship on his knees before the fireplace. 'And who's been sleeping in *my* bed?' she asked, curious about the blankets. Lionel did not answer. She picked a blanket and began to fold it. 'Father used to sleep downstairs when he was on the morning shift. "You needn't all suffer," he used to say.'

'Your father was like you,' Lionel said, eager to divert and indulge her. 'Too soft.' Afraid he might have given offence, he added, 'Best mate I ever had.' The old man loved talking with her: she was so light and eager, so full of relish for the moment even though what she spoke about was so often the past and so often in a seeming dream.

'It's so curious how you remember people.' She had folded one of the blankets and picked up another, her face flushed from the spirits. 'I was only seven when he died. We still lived down in the town then. Shops in the street, a picture house.'

'Two,' Lionel corrected her.

'Two. All sorts of buildings and people moving about saying hello to each other. I loved the town. I would like to live in a town again.' She clutched the blanket as if it were an heirloom full of nostalgia.

'The coal they come out with today, we wouldn't have used as slack. I don't know how they get away with it.' Now that he had, as he would say, 'set her up', Lionel addressed himself whole-mindedly to the work in hand.

'Yes. He had just come back from the day shift. That's what I always remember. The street. There was a gas lamp, the man used to light the mantle with that long pole. We used to watch him and he'd say he was laying a light-egg on the lamp. We thought it was a light-egg for years. We were playing Stuck-in-the-Mud. I was frightened because the bigger ones wanted to play Hide-and-Seek and I didn't want to stop playing with them. Then Father came out of the dark, just – appeared – and took my hands so that I walked up his legs and then he tumbled me over backwards and forwards and before I knew where I was I was high on his shoulders with my knickers black as soot. Up and up. Head over heels. I felt like the Queen of Sheba.' She paused. 'And I never saw him alive again.'

Lionel glanced at her. The memory had transfigured her. She looked years younger than her age, glowing with a sensitivity to life that moved him to wonder. She was the sort of woman, he had once heard himself saying, you could go to war for: and she was the sort of woman who would wither at a touch, like killing a butterfly by brushing the dust off its wings when you caught it. Just that one memory and look at her: in the grey room she seemed to make a point of light.

'Never forget to make a wigwam with your sticks,' he announced, very sternly, as if reprimanding himself for neglecting his duty. 'That's what gives it air. Then lay on your smallest bits of coal first.' He did as he instructed. 'They send the best stuff abroad.'

'Of course! Gareth!' Elaine's relief at solving the immediate problem was great. 'Jimmie's room, Mother's, mine, Marianne's, Alan's, Miss Wilks in Gareth's room – that's six; Gareth would have slept down here because of Miss Wilks. Do you like her?'

'She seems a decent enough body,' Lionel said cautiously. He sensed Elaine's anxiety and trod lightly. The fire was now fully prepared and he eyed it appraisingly.

'She's very clever.' Elaine spoke fervently as if rushing to the defence of Helen Wilks. '*Very* clever. Jimmie says she's halved his work in the week she's been here.'

'I don't know what your dad would have said about being married to a Labour MP and living in a vicarage! Chapel and Liberal was dead set against Church and Labour in his day. Mind you, he would have liked Jimmie. You can't but.'

Thoroughly poised, Lionel struck a match.

'Only one match,' he said, and turned to Elaine to make sure she was watching. Both of them enjoyed this little performance.

She had taken out a cigarette.

'Doesn't count,' he muttered as he hoisted himself up arthritically and hobbled across to feed her tobacco.

'What else could Mother do?' Elaine had seized on the reference to her father. Any time Lionel wanted her complete attention he had just to begin talking about her father. 'She had to find somewhere to live. Alan was alive then.' Alan, Elaine's younger brother, had died at the age of eight, a couple of years after they had come to the vicarage. A sore throat, a bad cough, the local doctor had eventually climbed up to the hamlet and after a close look at the small boy's eyeballs and tongue, pronounced 'a heavy cold' and aspirin. The boy had died the night after the visit. The doctor had spoken gravely of 'silent pneumonia'. Oddly enough it was one of the rare occasions on which Canon Johnston had lost his temper. He had loved Alan. Jimmie was away at school and the vagaries of a small boy for whom he had only secondary responsibility, entranced him. And Alan's townee-brightness, his thick accent, his nimbleness and loving openness had beguiled and delighted the old clergyman, who came to dote on him. He had thrown the doctor out of the house. Elaine remembered that, clearly. She remembered how for years she had held imaginary conversations with the empty bed which had been Alan's. Mostly, though, she remembered the sound of crying from the next room as her mother, still quite young and attractive, tried to face up to a life without a husband lost in the pits, a son lost through ignorance, a job away from her old friends and relations, and a daughter whose health and moods switched alarmingly wildly. Canon Johnston had persuaded her to stay on until she had thought things through; and then Mrs. Burns had made a settlement within herself and she became the housekeeper, soon the fixture, the mainstay, visiting the pit-town less and less often, gradually becoming glad to be out in the country, using routine to numb the hurt. 'Jimmie's father was very kind to us all.' Elaine recited this, even now, as a schoolgirl might. 'Although she was the housekeeper he let her have the attics for us two.' She laughed. 'Alan and I used to wait for him to go off – BANG! He was a *cannon*! Bang! Alan used to be able to do anything with him. I was a bit scared of him.'

She laughed, happy again, and once more began to fold up the blanket. Lionel looked at his fire, burning up steadily.

'Open the door, Lionel.' Mrs. Burn's voice jumped into action.

'Open the door, Richard,' he sang as he hurried to do her bidding, 'Open-the-door and let me in! Open-the-door-Richard! Richard, why don't you open that door? Morning, Mrs. Burns.' He enjoyed these formal touches.

Elaine's mother came in from the door which led to the kitchen, pushing the trolley before her, a little bent over with the effort. Lionel's age, she was thin and her grey hair was thick. She dressed her age but the clothes did not seem those of an old person because her movements were not those of an old person. She had always been active and hard-working and the force of habit continued. Up at 5.30, finding work for herself in the large kitchen or in the laundry-room or, failing that, in her own room out of which came an endless line of well-sewn patchwork quilts which she did – one of her few boasts – 'with her own eyesight'. She talked rather broadly, like Lionel, but also like Lionel she banished dialect words from her speech except for a few relaxed occasions with children or the privacy of old childhood friends.

To her generation, the words of her countryside were the marks of inferiority and the accent of her region was uncouth and the stigma of ignorance. Elaine took her features from her mother, but the older woman's dominating self-possessedness had found no place in her daughter's make-up. Elaine braced herself. Her mother had seen her in the garden and there would be trouble over that.

'There's tea, toast, marmalade and raspberry jam.' Mrs. Burns looked at the blankets, the disorganised furniture, Lionel's buckets beside the fire. 'How can anybody be expected to live in a mess like this? No man could. It makes me ill to look at it.' Such disorder truly upset her: she began to tidy up.

'I was just about to tidy up,' Elaine said, wishing her mother would tell her off and get it over with. She found it hard to bear the exercise of delayed accusation which her mother practised so well.

'I'll do it. You'll make it worse. Drink some tea.'

'We could go to the kitchen.'

'It's frozen. They never spend any money on a kitchen. Not when they have help living in.'

'Jimmie likes the old flagstones.'

'Jimmie doesn't have to paddle about on the old flagstones.' Mrs. Burns was devoted to the son of her former employer who had become her son-in-law. She would have no word said against him – save by herself. 'Jimmie's like all men. When he's comfortable he thinks the world's comfortable. He should work in that kitchen a few mornings. Chilblains are supposed to be out of fashion. Drink up that tea! Running about naked in a garden!' The old woman could hold it in no longer: such a mixture of impropriety and carelessness was unbearable.

She regretted the harshness of her tone but even her best resolutions could not dissolve the vexation she felt. And invalids, like children, she believed, needed to be brought sharply to their senses now and then.

'The sun woke me up. That's the beauty of living out here, Jimmie always says –'

'He says nothing about running about like a gipsy in a storm. And after all that fuss over you yesterday. Dear me, Elaine.'

'No one can see.'

'Farmers can always see.' Mrs. Burns spoke grimly. For over forty years she had enjoyed an unyielding battle of wits and manners with the local hill farmers. She had been hired on hill farms between the ages of fourteen and eighteen and neither forgotten nor forgiven the bitter life enforced on her then. 'Farmers see everything,' she concluded. To Lionel she said, '*You'll* be wanting a cup, I suppose.'

'I don't mind if I do. Three spoonfuls. No milk. Nice and strong. I could get used to this, you know, Betty.' He grinned bashfully, the youthful expression taking his old face by surprise and distorting it wildly.

Elaine smiled to herself and turned away. Lionel's flirtation with her mother was so undisguised and so hopeless that it had become a continuing comedy. As he explained, the wages Jimmie paid him for his work about the place were useful enough, a fair addition to his pension, but by the time you allowed for the expense of travel – he came up from the town on a two-stroke motorbike, begoggled, helmeted and as leather-wadded as a Samurai warrior – he could probably make just as much nearer home. 'It's Betty draws me here,' Lionel would say shyly, '*I* saw her first, you know. Me and her Josh were out for a walk after morning shift, just going down to t'Ellen to see if there was any trout about, and there she was, standing in the middle of a field, cursing the sky black and blue because she'd dropped a bucket of pig-swill. She didn't look fit enough to carry it. Frail and ladylike and lovely she was, I'm telling you. I saw her *first*. But Josh has the gift of the gab, see. Before you could say Jack Robinson, he's lowped over the fence, pranced up to her and shoved the stuff back into the bucket. Next thing you know she's let him carry the blessed bucket and in a couple of shakes they're engaged.' Lionel had married later and his marriage had been 'steady enough', he said, 'not many frills'. Three children, all left the county; a widower now, he had reverted to his adolescent crush and was genuinely puzzled that she spurned him. 'Don't be silly, Lionel,' Mrs. Burns would say, firmly. 'We're too old for that.' He asked her to go to the pictures at Carlisle and had been offended when she burst out laughing. Later she had said that she was sorry to hurt his feelings. 'But two old-age pensioners in the ABC at Carlisle can't be trusted, Lionel,' she said. She had always seen him as her husband's willing disciple and felt no more for him now than then. His persistence touched her only occasionally. She thought he ought to have more sense. Elaine watched over his manoeuvres with happy understanding, for the rebuffs did not hurt him for long nor did they impair his affection. Whereas the realisation of his wishes might have done both. Her mother could be very demanding. Perhaps, Elaine sometimes thought, Lionel merely enjoyed the flirting and courting; for he too could be intimidated by Mrs. Burns.

'There's something I want to talk to her about,' the old woman said, authoritatively.

'Comprenez! That's what they used to say in France. Comprenez! Her dad and me dug for coal in paper suits in France. She likes to hear about the old days.'

'I'm here,' Elaine murmured and put her hands to her ears. The blanket slid to the floor. 'I'm fifty years old.'

'She doesn't look it, does she?' Lionel put down his cup with a great smacking of lips. 'Quick march!' He went to the fire, put on some coal, piece by piece, picked up his buckets and went out looking severe, a man with things on his mind.

Elaine put the copper-beech twigs in the big vase on the inlaid mahogany side-table. She did it nervously and water spilled out of the vase. She was aware that her mother had been lenient about the escapade in the garden and suspected that there was more serious wrath to come.

'I found these twigs on the ground,' she said. 'I suppose one of the children tore them off.' There were four young teen-aged children from the farms who occasionally dared each other to 'raid' the vicarage garden.

'It was me,' her mother said. 'Don't blame them.'

'Why?' Elaine saw the white-ended twigs as wounded. It was a crazy exaggeration – she was aware of that – but her nature was such that she felt the ripped-off wood to be bleeding to death: the water in the vase was simply a stay of extinction.

'I needed some for the church.'

'I can understand that. But why didn't you take these?'

'They were too long.' Mrs. Burns shook her head in annoyance. 'There's more to worry about than that, Elaine. It's not right to make such a fuss about such things when there's so much else to worry about.' Elaine's moods could still baffle the older woman.

'Is there?' Elaine stood back to look at the arrangement. How grand the rich dark copper leaves looked, she thought. How did they retain that shining deep copper colour?

Her mother came up to her, took three pill-boxes from her pocket and held them out. 'These were on the floor of the toilet. The pills were all gone.'

'The boxes wouldn't flush down!' Elaine reared like a frightened colt. She talked rapidly. 'They bobbed around like corks. I pulled the chain three times and then I felt guilty about using all that water. The pills went down first time. "Take with water." ' She laughed – that shrill laugh which alerted and grated on her mother. 'That's what it says. So I did. *Whoosh!* Gareth sometimes makes noises like that on his programme.'

'Jimmie sees you get the best treatment. He always has. The very best.'

Mrs. Burns's fierceness of manner soon crumbled in front of what she saw as her daughter's illness or hopelessness – the days when she could distinguish clearly seemed light-years past. She had never been sure how sick Elaine was, how serious it was, whether her character was different or deficient; the whole terrible business had confused things utterly never to allow them the time to be resolved. But she did know when Elaine wanted help. Her strictness was a response to that. Sometimes, though, it was hard for her not to take her daughter in her arms and cradle her. The doctor had told her that would do more harm than good. She obeyed his instructions. Now, to conceal her agitation, she moved about the room shifting the position of all the smaller movable objects which came within reach, as if re-estab- lishing some perfect order in the place. What did she want going out and trying to catch double pneumonia for? She should be in a hospital.

'They wanted to turn the vicarage into a hospital during the war,' Elaine said. Mrs. Burns, as if caught like a thief, dropped the clean ashtray she had been pointlessly cleaning. She was convinced that there were times when Elaine had second sight. 'I'll pick that up.' Elaine was at her feet. She knelt and held up the ashtray to her mother, who looked down on her in great perturbation. 'It isn't broken,' Elaine said. 'It's Highland glass or something. I can never remem- ber.' She stood up, her eyes bright with pleasure from the small act of usefulness. 'Don't you remember? A man came from the Ministry. Not *your* Minithry – he had a lisp – don't you remember? He said that was why he had been turned down for the army. He blushed a lot. Don't you remember? He talked about beekeeping. He kept bees somewhere – further south – I forget. He hoped this house might make "a convalescent home for officers and gentlemen": those were his words.'

'I wish they had taken it. There's not a modern thing in it.'

'You'd hate to move.' She smiled. 'Anyway, when he'd looked through he said it was too small. You *would*, you'd hate to move.'

'I would not.'

'Remember how you acted when I wanted to move?'

'You never wanted to move.'

'Yes I did.' Elaine clipped out the three words clearly and decisively. 'When Mrs. Johnston died. You wouldn't.' Elaine was speaking the truth and, reluctantly, her mother backed down.

'There weren't those modern bungalows then,' Mrs. Burns remembered. 'Jimmie looked after his mother well, didn't he? Sleeping outside her room every night on that camp bed. Johnstons here for years. Not that that matters nowadays. He was a good son to her.' She had wanted to find in Jimmie so much that she had lost in her husband and her son – but Jimmie was opaque to her: class, character and a deep difference of nature made it impossible for Mrs. Burns to love Jimmie as she would have wished. But she respected him profoundly. 'He loved his mother,' she said.

'She was a remarkable woman.' Elaine spoke dutifully.

'It was understandable she didn't take to you.'

'I liked her.'

'Did you?' Betty smiled sympathetically at her daughter. 'She could be an old minx. You had to stand up to her. That's something you've never managed.' She waved the empty pill-boxes at her ear as if listening to the rattle of the absent pills. 'I expect Dr. Tom will have plenty more where these came from.'

'I won't take them, Mother.'

'He'll make you and that's that. Doctors have the power.' She looked around the room. 'It's a bit better I suppose.' Then she was on her way, once again about that endless traipse from job to job which filled but only partly fulfilled her day. 'Can't waste time talking. I'd better see to Alan's breakfast. He likes me to take it to him.' It was for her sake that Elaine had suggested the name to Marianne, who had accepted it willingly.

'Let me open the door for you,' Elaine said.

'I can manage. You're not well.'

Elaine went past her and held the door open. As her mother went out she murmured 'That Gareth!' but said no more and Elaine did not divine her meaning.

She went to the fire which was blazing now. The brandy and the tea had taken the cold out of her but still she felt restless, full of new energy without the pills.

Treading heavily on the soft pedal she began to play the piano, practising Jimmie's favourite Beethoven sonata. It would be a nice surprise if she could play if for him one night when he came back tired. Then she pictured yet again his embrace with Helen and her eyes blurred over. But she forced herself to play on. Jimmie must not be upset now when the election was so close. That was her excuse. But she knew it to be an excuse only, for the thought of facing up to the consequences of Jimmie's possible infidelity or, worst of all, desertion, had shocked her deeply and she felt that she was fighting for her existence.

Chapter Five

Gareth was woken up by the sound of hail outside and his son, Alan, inside, pretending to be a soldier, charging up and down the corridor on the floor below. He was torn between the desire to go and tell the child to be quiet and the realisation that if he revealed himself the boy would plague him mercilessly. He stayed where he was.

He knew this attic so well. Elaine had told him that it had been her room as a little girl. She had shared it with her brother and she had confided to Gareth that it was the happiest room in the house. He knew that she meant it was the only happy room in the house but had restrained himself at that stage. That stage was past now.

It had been his hideout. He had sneaked up here to get off the eternal round of odd-jobs his grandmother found for him. He had read his way through painful adolescent vacations in this slope-roofed top room. He had imagined himself to be every sort of hero in novels and poems and history in the cell-like austerity of the attic. Its height had always impressed him. From the little window you could see clear across to Scotland and he would make plan after plan to foil the Border reivers and resurrect old battles on the Solway Moss. If there was one space on earth where he could feel in contact with his former selves, it was here. It was his only indulgence in the house.

Even now it could set him to pastoral, placid dreaming.

The hail would have sent the sheep to the walls, he thought, and the cows to the gates hoping to be brought in. His grandmother would be cooking one breakfast and serving another, pacing out her treadmill. Elaine would be in her bedroom or perhaps already downstairs, seeking to avoid contact and yet longing for it, irresolute but somehow still whole, waiting, Gareth thought, like someone in a fairy story, to be kissed into life. Lionel would be making fires in the house and, this season, later, in the garden. Jimmie would be coming in from his constitutional with hiking heartiness – there indeed he was! – the big oak front door banged like a castle bolt and the imperial 'Good Morning!' reached even up to these rafters. Alan would scamper down to greet him like a hamster. And there he went: Gareth resented Jimmie's easy way with *his* son.

Outside the farmers would be past the first milking, about their fields, looking at the walls and fences, ferrying feed to the higher fell-land, weighing up what they could carry through the winter and what they must sell. In the towns the factory would have gulped down the morning shift at six, the shops would be open and the schools, later the banks and council offices and solicitors. It had always been cosy in the attic. The world came into the attic. If he wanted to give up, his world was the attic ready and waiting – nothing harsh or questioning here: if only he would accept the past, all could be well. Sweet, pungent, smelling of apples, safe against the weather, even hail, the day's work being done all around, his own past orderly, his present contented. Brer Rabbit's territory; wet seaside holidays; contented commuters – Beware!

The cosiness was the plague. It was oppressive, corrosive, the poisoned charm of the English, he thought, and he got to his feet to get out of it. There was nothing for him here. All that had to be destroyed. They bled him, these memories, these certainties, these cosy-cosy comfortable images, like leeches, black sticky slugs stuck sucking on the skin. Salt – bitterness – needed to rub them off. There were scores to be settled. The attic was a trap.

He went down the back stairs to avoid Alan and opened the door of the living-room very gently so that he could withdraw if he heard anyone he did not wish to meet. That, at the moment, was almost everyone. Except – as he heard the soft, hesitant piano – his mother. Gareth moved in very quietly and went across the room with care. The sun had come out again and shafts of it caught her as it appeared and then disappeared again through the scurrying clouds. She sat in her dressing-gown, her wavy blonde hair down her back, exactly, Gareth recognised it, like someone in an English film of the forties. If he had not been concentrating so hard on being unheard, he could have brought the actress to mind.

He stretched out, put his hands around her eyes and instantly regretted it. She reacted violently, squirming horribly under his touch.

'I'm sorry, Jimmie. I know I shouldn't have gone out. It was the sun. Half-dressed – it was the sun.'

'Hey. Hello.' He bent to kiss her hair but she twisted her head and his mouth bumped her brow. 'Hello – hello.'

'Oh!' She pretended it had hurt a little, to give herself time.

'It's me.'

'Jimmie sometimes does that. Well!' She breathed out in relief, he thought. 'How lovely to see you. Kiss?' She kissed him and then she stood up and, as usual, to his embarrassment (but this time he was determined not to let it annoy him), she looked at him without speaking and without wanting him to speak. Held his hands and gazed on him for an unnerving procession of seconds. Looked through him, he thought, to his childhood.

'You look tired,' she said, eventually. Her full attention was so concentrated that even Gareth wilted. She had the

58

power that belongs to a few very good, naïve, even pure people: power which makes you want to turn away, a little ashamed. Gareth did not turn away but he broke the silence abruptly.

'*You* look lovely.'

'Don't make it sound like pity. Have you a cigarette?'

' "Son gives mother fatal cancer fix – shock horror probe." '

'I like these French ones; I don't like to ask for them at Mr. Tomlinson's. He always puts Benson & Hedges on the counter whenever I walk in.' She laughed. 'A bit like a dog bringing back a stick you've thrown into a pond. It would be so unfair if you said – "NOT MY STICK! GO BACK!" ' She laughed again, gently, pleased with herself. 'You always make me feel better. Mmm.' She drew in the smoke deeply. 'Miss Wilks only smokes Menthols. I can't stand them.'

'Miss Wilks?'

'Helen Wilks. She came about a week ago. She stays with us because Jimmie can't afford to put her up in a hotel.' (And he kissed her, she wanted to add: he loves her: he stopped loving me years ago, years, years ago.)

'I see. What more of Miss Wilks?' asked Gareth. The co-incidence would be so extraordinary that it had to be no coincidence. Of course it was Helen, he thought confidently. So she'd turned up again. Helen Wilks, return of the screw, he thought, and smiled.

'Jimmie advertised for a researcher about a month ago. She wanted to do this book. She's writing something. She had a grant – that's right – at Lancaster University, to do with Electoral Reform. I remember that. So she stayed on because she wanted the experience of an election. Well?' Elaine demanded. She had sensed that Gareth knew this young woman.

'What do you want to know?'

'Oh, anything and everything as a matter of fact,' Elaine said, clumsily aping carelessness. Gareth was too absorbed in his own recollections and surprise to be aware of it. 'We've never actually talked much about her – past.'

'She was at Oxford when I was up,' he said, briskly, deciding that was the best cover. Appear to tell all. 'Very clever. Read History. Did some acting – I met her when we did *The Tempest*. What else? Red-hot Socialist then – father worked on an assembly line in the Midlands and she was half-ashamed of it. We probably teased her too much about that. The middle classes have no idea how vicious their so-called teasing is to those who did not go to public school. Still, she seemed tough. She was always taking up lame ducks. She joined the BBC of course, and the last I heard she had been rather ill. Very ill.' Tough on the top, he thought, soft inside.

'Poor woman.' Elaine's relief at being able to be sympathetic to someone she was already ashamed of disliking gave the expression a force of concern which Gareth noted. 'I didn't know she'd been ill.'

'No reason why you should unless she volunteered the information.' Gareth said no more. Helen's severe nervous breakdown was still too raw on his conscience.

'She's very self-contained. I like that about her.'

'She always tried to be independent.'

'Jimmie will be so pleased you've come!' Without knowing why, Elaine was a little cheered. 'He's worried about this election. More than I've ever known him to be. And he *must* win,' she added with adopted passion. 'If he loses, he's unemployed.' She tried to look severe, but instead she smiled, guiltily.

'You're quoting,' Gareth said, but only lightly reproving her. 'You can leave him to speak his own lines, you know.'

'He'll be delighted you've come to help, though. That's true.'

'Marianne phoned.'

'Yes?'

'Don't pretend, Mother. About you. Why didn't *he*?'

'Your father?' Elaine emphasised the word 'father': she had begun to do so from the instant she had got scent of Gareth's disaffection with his step-father. But her defensiveness only seemed to increase his aggression and she shuddered almost visibly when he retorted, 'Who is not my father.'

'He was as good as a father.' She quailed before his angry bitterness but she was determined to continue to be the peace-maker.

'GOOD! How are you?'

'All right. Can't you see? Jimmie understood – it wasn't serious.'

'Marianne thought it was.'

'Perhaps she wanted to see you, kind sir!' Elaine curtsied, coquettishly, a Southern lady, belle of the ball.

'Mother!'

'There was thunder and lightning last night. You must have driven through the storm. Just like you.' She touched his cheek tenderly and withdrew her hand only when he shook his head sadly. Again he thought her gesture was imitated, filmic, as if it came, frozen, from her youthful past. Again he repressed his unease. 'The lane outside was a swamp,' she said, 'we'll never get it re-surfaced now with the cuts, Jimmie says. Just like him to leave his own lane until it's too late, isn't it? My two men. So alike.'

'Marianne told me you blacked out.'

'It wasn't important, Gareth. Marianne hasn't seen me when I've – had a little turn before – believe me,' she was firm, 'it was not serious. Would I be up and about if it had been? Dr. Tom didn't even come himself. Jimmie did it all on the phone. Believe me?'

'I believe you.'

'Hooray! Now. The important thing. Your radio programmes. I know you think we're all disappointed and let down by it – you *do*! – Jimmie *says* you do – but I *love* them. Honestly. I had no education. I liked Bing Crosby and Frank

Sinatra before I married Jimmie – and Ambrose – lovely Ambrose! And you sound so full of *life*! I like you on the radio. So. Who's doing it this morning? You mustn't neglect it for me.' Her play-acting sternness moved him.

'I recorded a couple yesterday to see the week out ... that's why I was so late.' He smiled: it was her smile that came to his face this time, without the guile and innuendo which coloured his usual self-conscious expressions of feeling. 'So! You had no education, you *liked* Bing Crosby – I love it!' He took her by the shoulders and kissed her on both cheeks, South American Generalissimo style. 'Eez mucho ap-preezeeate! Sank you! Sank you! Olé!' In his normal voice: 'Then I'm taking two or three weeks off. I need a break. Nobody's worried.'

'That will be just right for Jimmie. You two used to be such friends. You'll come around to his side in the end. You'll see. He'll convince you.'

'I'm glad you like the programmes. That means a lot to me.'

Elaine nodded and then turned and walked from him towards the lectern. She paused beside the eagle and rubbed her right forefinger up and down its polished chest, as if hesitating before a grand and grandiloquent announcement. Once more Gareth pushed back the irritation which rose up so rapidly and so disconcertingly. But why did everything have to be pointed so dramatically? The room, he thought, this room makes players of us all. Why did she not just *say* what was on her mind without all this posing? His short fuse of critical temper threw him off balance. He ought to be more in control. Perhaps, he reassured himself, it was the preoccupation with the struggle to come which was debili-tating his present energies. That could be it.

'Gareth,' Elaine began, poignantly and ominously. 'I can't any longer stay as I am.' She paused. Gareth felt that a response was expected but he was too unsure of her direction to give it. 'I'm going to cure myself. I have to. If I don't I'll just go through the rest of my life like some of the people I saw when Dr. Tom took me to that awful hospital just before summer. They took pills. Every mealtime, every hour, day and night, different pills, pills to help other pills, pills to balance pills, pills on pills – they had no life of their own – I can't do that! No, let me finish. Please.' He had begun to move towards her, ready to support the collapse of this effort which, he thought, was straining her resources enormously. 'And I want to get out and meet people,' she went on, showing more tenacity than he had anticipated. 'It's too lonely for me here. The farmers' wives are nice but they're too busy. And in this house we're bound to get on each other's nerves when we're all here. And when you're both away I just wait. It's no good. I want to work in a flower shop. I always wanted to do that. When I left school I wanted to do that but they said there was work for me here and Jimmie's mother needed help. Then when we got married Jimmie said he didn't want his wife in a shop. But I could learn to do it. Couldn't I? I could learn to do it, and be useful, and meet people. Couldn't I, Gareth? Help me. Oh, please.'

She was in his arms, he was absorbing her sad-happy crying, telling her yes, he would help, it was what he had longed to hear, of course she could learn to work in a flower shop, there was time, she could, of course she could live without pills – son and mother they were bound to each other, giving and gaining strength in this rare revelation of need and want.

Jimmie bounded in like a lolloping hound eager for the chase and they sprang apart like illicit lovers.

Chapter Six

Gareth could have murdered Jimmie, he thought. And would have done if he could have thought of the perfect crime. Over the past few years he had fantasised about it so often and in such detail that Jimmie's presence had the shock of an act of resurrection. He felt violently, savagely murderous towards the man he had been deceived into calling 'father' for so many years, years as lost to his new self as life before birth. Nothing that Jimmie said could lessen the intensity of the younger man's feeling. Everything once loved was now as passionately hated. When Jimmie was being reasonable and fair, Gareth felt himself loathe what he saw as the face of a hypocritical and patronising poseur, willing to use any tactic to *appear* reasonable and fair: for Gareth would not grant his once-called father any genuine feelings at all. Nothing was authentic about this man and the mere sight of him set off a pain inside Gareth's head as oppressive as migraine, but he endured it, and forced himself to wait; he repressed it, apparently 'over' the time of outburst and fury which had marked the revelation that 'someone else' – only most vaguely defined as 'a soldier', and left vague 'to spare Elaine's feelings' – was his real father. He had been too shocked to demand to know who this 'someone else' was and in truth he did not admit to himself that he wanted to know. For as much as he hated Jimmie, he hated the other man as much or more. Besides, he told himself, Elaine needed to be allowed to tell him of her own free will. Gareth had given her the opportunity, twice, but she had not taken it. And so the concentration of bitterness and the wounded lust for vengeance was funnelled all on Jimmie. But Gareth repressed it now. It had to wait. Soon it would come. It had to be done properly. A slow burn. It was under way. He must be patient. For the next few hours he must even seem to be prepared to be compliant. Act the part of the surly but fundamentally 'good' son: the rebel without a cause who would grow to know that Pop and Momma were fine folks underneath it all. The knife would go in very soon now.

'Morning old chap! De-*lighted* you could make it.' Jimmie beamed his public grin on Gareth, who grimaced tightly in return and wondered what he had done to deserve it. Jimmie's muscular Christian heartiness spilled into his private life only when he was very nervous, but Gareth dismissed any excuses or explanations, preferring to blame Jimmie. He pulled out a cigarette and noted, some paces behind Jimmie, at the entrance to the room, Helen. She was looking straight at him. He returned her glance but made no other sign. She neither. 'As for you, young lady,' Jimmie had put an arm around Elaine's shoulders and she shivered and then clutched tightly at his fingers, pecked his cheek, quelled her panic, 'you should be in bed.' He pulled her into his shoulder protectively but his manner was censuring. In public he found it totally impossible to be delicate or tender with his wife.

'I was just going. It wasn't Gareth's fault. I talked – we were talking, weren't we?'

Gareth wanted to shout out as he saw his mother's confidence scatter all over the room, her insecurity scuttle over her face like the clouds across the sky. He loathed the man who had made her like this: the very sight of Jimmie had made him too sick to speak. His resentment had become all but uncontrollable.

'Gareth knows Miss Wilks,' Elaine announced, seeking a diversion.

Jimmie watched as the two younger people contrived a cool greeting. Oxford, the BBC, a few brief facts were explained quickly.

'You kept it all dark,' Jimmie said to Helen, almost succeeding in keeping the note of reproach out of his voice. Clearly they knew each other very well.

'It didn't seem important,' she replied. 'You bump into hundreds of people. Besides, I certainly didn't expect Gareth to turn up here – not with his radio programme.' The explanation was added hurriedly and clumsily. She had been about to say that she had not expected Gareth to come and support Jimmie. This unsaid explanation hung potently in the silence.

'Oh, old Gareth's like a bad penny, aren't you, old chap?' Jimmie said, affecting cheerful matiness.

'No,' Elaine protested. 'He's the friend in need. A friend in need is a friend indeed.' Jimmie saw how much his wife *wanted* to believe that Gareth and he would resolve their differences: not for the first time he wondered how successfully she convinced herself.

'Yes.' Jimmie made an effort and once more focused his attention on his wife. 'Bed, little lady,' he announced. 'Up Timber Hill, down Sheet Lane, and into the Blanket Shop! Dr. Tom said you had to rest as much as you possibly could. Come on now, I'll help you up the dancers.'

'Why shouldn't she stay here – she can rest here – if she wants to?' Gareth's challenge was unmistakable. Elaine looked from one to the other and back again. Jimmie was taller, broader, elegant and attractive in his hard-worn tweed suit. Gareth, of average height, thin, dark, somehow battle-clad in the clinging denim, always tense and tight coiled even when as now there was a pretence of affability. Helen took out a Menthol: she had gone over to the window to look out on to the garden. The sun was struggling to come through.

'Very well.' Jimmie dropped Elaine's arm and addressed

her as if interviewing her. 'Do you want to stay down here –
or will you do as the doctor advised?'

'Loaded.' Gareth rapped out his disapproval.

'But accurate.'

'I don't know.' Elaine stood stiffly eager, determined to try
her hardest. 'I'd like to . . .'

'Yes.' Gareth's voice was soothing, helpful. 'What do you
really want to do?'

'I'd like to get dressed . . . and then come downstairs for
breakfast . . . just like everybody else . . . but first I'd like a
bath.'

'Good for you,' Gareth said and she gave him that smile
which entranced all who benefited from it and gave her such
a guileless and transparent expression that you could feel the
goodness and sweetness of the woman directly, leaping over
the sad restrictions which beset her life. Jimmie felt a surge
of jealousy: although he was more aware of the subtleties of
Elaine's moods than Gareth was, his shyness meant that
he had never *felt* as close to Elaine as Gareth could.
Gareth noticed this and, sure again of his rule over her,
relaxed.

'Water won't be hot again for another half-hour or so, I'm
afraid.' Jimmie regretted that petty sentence the instance it
was out. Gareth grinned.

'Offside!' Gareth blew an imaginary whistle. He pointed
to Elaine. 'Free kick.' His satisfaction at this small victory
over his step-father was embarrassing.

Elaine thought it wise to move out. 'I'll go upstairs
anyway,' she said. She paused and looked searchingly at
Gareth. 'We made a bargain, didn't we?'

'We did,' Gareth said. 'We did indeed.'

'It's only fun – not important,' she explained to Jimmie,
who nodded briskly, once more in command of himself.

'I'll provide the escort. Up we go.'

He patted her bottom to shepherd her out. Gareth felt a
twist of anger knot in his stomach. When they were clear of

the room he turned to Helen and said, calmly, 'I loathe that man.'

'He speaks well of you,' Helen said. 'Not that you crop up much, you'll be distressed to learn.' She screwed out her cigarette slowly, deliberately, into the ashtray. It was important to keep calm.

'Tyranny dressed up as Charity aping Affection.'

'You should make that into a motto for a Christmas cracker.'

'It *is* a bit Imperial Somerset Maugham,' he admitted. 'When Epigrams were power and black was bad.'

'Jimmie's no tyrant. You exaggerate.' She took slow breaths as the doctor had told her: even three or four years after the breakdown she could still, when occasion demanded, call back his simple, useful aids to self-control.

'But then,' he bowed, once more assuming the theatricalities which he had so recently employed with Marianne, 'I always did.'

'But then you always did.' Helen spoke flatly, unresponsive to his bid for play.

Helen was about thirty. She had a fair figure and pleasant features, but she could not be called beautiful, pretty or even the hold-all 'attractive'. Yet there was the feeling that she might become so if she tried. She dressed badly, presenting herself now in a margarine-yellow smock which could have served for one of Shakespeare's mechanicals. Her hair was centrally parted and drawn back tightly and plainly, in imitation of Charlotte Brontë, but the square pale blunt-featured face did not suit it; let loose, cut short, given some waves, the long brown hair would have framed and made a fine contrast to the strong features. Her face was further spoiled by make-up. Where there should have been none there was too much and where there should have been a little there was one. Her eyes, which were plain brown, the lashes and brows rather fawn and wispy, would have benefited from attention: they were left untouched. Her mouth, which was rather thin, was smeared with a garish modish lipstick where the lightest dab was called for. And her tights, Gareth had noted immediately and groaned, above the clonking Old Mother Hubbard grey suedette shoes, were lime green.

Yet there was no mistaking two things. Her intelligence and the stress she was still under. Both were held close, reined in, but sharply, even rawly, evident.

'Well. Shouldn't we rush into each other's arms?' Gareth teased her with his sprightliness: it was a mockery. But she did not rise to it. 'Alms for oblivion? No? Sorry. I mean – how are you?'

'I knew you'd say that. "How are you?" and "Sorry." They are the two attitudes inside which you don't give a damn how anybody else is and feel sorry only for yourself.' She spoke vehemently.

'The same old Helen.'

'I didn't mean to say that.'

'Sounded to me as if you'd been working on it for years.'

'Don't flatter yourself.'

'Do you want to brand it on to my forehead?'

'I'd no idea you'd come here.'

'I did live here, once.'

'You know what I'm saying. Have you a light?'

'Lauren Bacall? Play it again?'

Helen walked over to the fire, took a spill from the jar Jimmie kept for his pipe and watched Gareth let the match he had lit burn down to his thumb and forefinger without flinching.

' "The point is not to mind that it hurts",' he said. 'Something like that.'

Helen lit her cigarette, took a deep breath and turned to, him calmly.

'I just want you to be absolutely clear in your mind that I did not come here to lay myself across your path. That took some saying.' He did not respond. She recognised the trick.

Arbitrary silences generally guaranteed to unnerve the opposition. 'Why did *you* come?' she asked; it had to be her who broke the silence; she recognised his old game and got it over with.

'One thing and another. Let's say – for Elaine.'

'She isn't well.' Helen spoke very quietly. In Elaine she saw so many of her own former symptoms.

'Why did *you* come?'

'For my book. If it ever makes a book. And Jimmie wasn't only a good subject, he needs help. The election is a bonus. I only needed everyday life in a constituency. Jimmie's is usefully representative. And handy for Lancaster.' The explanation was like an excuse.

'So the academic life got you in the end. The Ph.D. Brigade: poor old you.'

'I don't want to talk about it.'

Gareth produced his hip flask and held it up like a pack of trick cards. 'An eye-opener? You look a bit down.'

'I don't feel the need, thanks.' Her awkwardness made her sound prudish. She would live with that. It was one way through and Gareth's unexpected arrival had forced her back to her survival tactics.

'The *need*, eh? You've caught Jimmie's manner quickly enough.' He drew a good mouthful from the flask and swallowed it slowly. 'Good stuff. Tell me – you're the scholar – isn't there a polite and painless Greek pronoun for a woman who moves from the son to the father? You know – Phaedra or Lysistrata – all those classical dames whose high-sounding names are useful to cover up the muckiest human weaknesses – which one went from son to let-us-say-for-the-sake-of-argument – father?'

'I haven't moved anywhere.'

'Oh. I see. Sorry.'

He raised the flask and took another drink, clearly disbelieving her. Even so, she would not be stirred to engage him. Once he had drawn you, she knew, he could and would attempt to move you wherever suited him and just as it suited him. She could not afford that. It had taken her years to get him out of her system. Years which were mixed up with illness and indecision about her life and the struggle to help her badly-off parents. She was no longer tough.

'Is that a ritual?' she asked as he screwed on the cap and shoved the flask back in his pocket. She could have bitten her tongue. She had given him a lead.

'Well now. "Ritual." ' He looked up at the ceiling and winked. 'You get in on everything, don't you? Now then – a "ritual".' He paused again pseudo-thoughtfully. 'Only academics could use that word before breakfast these days. Let's see. Yes, I believe it may well be.' He put on the old upper-class 'thinking man' voice made famous by highbrow BBC radio programmes in the forties and fifties. 'It all depends, of course, on what you mean by ritual. It's nearer a ceremony or – wait a minute!' He whipped out the flask and opened it – 'a sacrament. Yes.' He sipped. 'You see, I turn this whisky into water. Trans-substantiation. Oh dear, Helen.'

'You're still as twisted as a corkscrew.'

'Eeh, lass!' Her neutral English tone had lapsed into the flat Midlands accent of her childhood. Gareth naturally jumped on it. 'That lets you off takin' me straight, then, don't it. Clever dick. You say somebody's not normal. So everything they say is of no account.' He dropped the accent and spoke in his own voice. 'Bloody impertinent, really.'

'We *are* on our high horse today. Your father—'

'Who art in heaven, or wherever – proceed.'

'Jimmie doesn't know about us.' Helen spoke warningly, her voice harsh and tense. 'There's no reason why he should.'

'I won't give you away.'

'I didn't mean that. *And* you know it.'

'Do I? Let it pass. We're good at keeping secrets in the old vicarage.' He looked at the ceiling. 'Aren't we? Don't give much away, do we? *You* spend half your time keeping things dark, don't you?'

71

He looked at Helen for a reaction but she refused him one. She had stayed beside the fire, sitting on the padded fender, warming herself like a waif, he thought. He wanted to rip the hair out of that stupid style, pull off the folksy clothes and ram into life the constrained and constricted huddle so abjectedly avoiding contact. He had done that once: and both of them had loved it – for a while.

'Let's have a screw,' he said, bluntly. 'You look as if you need one.'

'Marianne's very pretty,' she said, without acknowledging his remark.

'Nice one, Helen.'

'I like little Alan too.'

'He was after your time. Not that it matters. Not that time matters in that business – it *is* a business, isn't it? – does it? *When* is unimportant. *Who* is what matters. Oh God – listen to the man. Yawn.'

'It *is* none of my business,' she agreed, gravely.

'Cor-rect! Baby!'

'Jimmy thinks you'll marry her, eventually. He thinks that inside all this – this show, you're a strict conformist.'

'What do you think?'

'I don't comment.'

'Good,' he said. 'Why did we stop making it in bed?' He sat tilted back on an elegant ladder-backed chair, one leather-booted foot poised on the edge of the table, rocking himself as in a cradle. And flaunting himself at her. 'You were good. Very good.'

'Was I?' She trapped her mouth shut, resenting that she had been drawn. His arrogance was intolerable, she thought. And yet she stayed. 'I don't know,' she said quietly. 'I don't know why it stopped.'

'Yes you do! And I know you know! And you know I know you know! So, Miss, we understand each other! Very well, we misunderstand each other! Don't lie, Helen! Leave that to the rats.' His anger surprised him: he was more keyed up than he had anticipated. The whole deception was harder than he had thought.

'You were unfaithful,' she said, very sadly.

'True!' He slapped his hand on the table. 'True!'

'And you told me.' Helen spoke painfully now and slowly, dragged back into a struggle with him as if they had been apart for five days, not five years.

'You asked.'

'Yes. I did.'

'Truth outed,' Gareth said.

'Lies would have helped, then.'

'Truth routed? Oho! Don't weaken. Not that bull from you. You *are* somebody.'

'I couldn't take it.' She paused. It was useless trying to pretend she could be detached from him. The years they had been apart collapsed like a house of cards and before her once more was the infinite present confusion of her feelings for him, for herself, for what was important and what was merely necessary. 'You were such a bastard, Gareth. You could be – you could be very good and – *right* – but then, such a horrible, horrible cruel man.'

'So you said.'

'As if there was something – not just the infidelity – something destructive.' She spoke as intimately as if he had never left her, as intensely as if they were safely alone, despite all her urgently summoned intentions at the first sight of him, once more absorbed in the conflict they had had where once she had said she would be happy to escape with her life. 'More than destructive even,' she went on, for over the years she had returned to it again and again, this fierce affair which had blown up in her face and destroyed so much, 'it was as if there was a feeling of Evil about – outside yourself even, as if you were possessed and couldn't resist it yourself, something a bit mad and so violent, so violent – yes, evil. It was as if—'

'Shut up! SHUT YOUR MOUTH!' The words were slurred,

low, full of vicious anger. She was frightened by them.

He swung the chair on to its four legs and jumped up. For a few moments he stood there and it was as if all the darkness in the room was gathered into him. He felt a rush of tidal anarchic sick fury pour into him and Helen in her light dress felt herself cower away, afraid to run for fear of provoking him to action, afraid to be there, wanting to evade the malignant force which came unmistakably from his tensely quivering figure. And yet she loved him.

Jimmie banged warningly on the door and Gareth felt suddenly weak as if a spine-breaking load had been slashed free from his shoulders. There was a trickle of nausea in his throat. Helen waved at Jimmie as if he were a friendly ship passing a shipwreck. He waved back, his hand flushed with letters.

'Talking about old times, then?' Jimmie twinkled at his deliberate tactlessness. He had taken some minutes alone in his room to pull himself together. 'Now then. *Au travail!* Helen, would you remind me to slip in Tom's for a prescription for a new complement of pills when we pass through Thurston?'

'Yes. Of course.' Helen brought out a small notebook-file from the kangaroo pouch which adorned the front of her smock.

'She appears to have mislaid every blessed box he sent her. And she insists on getting dressed and coming down. I thought she'd better do that. For her own sake and to allay old Gareth's fears about the totalitarian face of central government – i.e. somebody who cares most taking charge. Once we get the pills she'll be settled again.'

'What the heart can't feel, the head can't know,' Gareth said loudly as he walked across to the fire, causing Helen, as if bound to him by a system of pulleys and balances, to get up and move across towards the side-table she could use as a desk. 'Oh brave new world, that . . . never mind.'

'Could you tell Bill I'll be in for morning surgery nearer

74

ten-thirty than ten and rearrange the morning schedule?' Jimmie had decided to press on as if everything was fine: it was, he had found, the only way to cope with deep problems in a short time.

Clearly pleased to be employed, Helen went across to the phone which was in the far corner. While she dialled the agent and spoke she kept her back to the two of them, glad to be out of it.

'So Mother's full of pills and you're off to surgery,' Gareth said, scornfully.

Jimmie was slitting open his letters. There grew in front of him a neatly peeled pile which he would then go through with care and speed, numbering, dating and fully answering every single one.

'It's a curious usage, isn't it?' he agreed, as if engaging in a civilised chat. 'Like unions and their chapels. There are similarities to doctors of course. People only come to MPs and doctors when they're in trouble.'

'Which you've often helped to bring about.'

'Touché. And I'm afraid we MPs are a bit glib, assuming that we can cure all when in fact we can usually only tinker about.' Deliberately he spoke on the most trivial level, not entirely unaware that this was what most annoyed the younger man.

'And they have to take the tablets you hand down,' Gareth said, lightly. 'Was Moses a doctor? Or just the Christian Nationalist Member for Canaan?'

Jimmie moved across to the lectern where he kept his House of Commons notepaper. He found that business letters were faster dealt with when he was standing up. In further justification he would instance the number of writers who had preferred to write on their feet rather than their behinds. Neither explanation held conviction. The fact was that he enjoyed standing at the lectern as his father had so often stood at it to read the lessons and practise his sermons. It was, people thought, a harmless affectation. And it brought his lighter work into the living-room where, usually, he could chat away to Elaine.

Jimmie's last encounters with Gareth, infrequent and well-spaced over the last three or four years, had generally been bitter. He was perfectly aware already that Gareth was once again shaping for an opening in order to raise what appeared to the younger man to be the mountain of grievances which divided them. Jimmie wished to delay the inevitable row and yet he could not resist teasing Gareth by pretending to believe what he knew to be the complete opposite of his motives. 'I'm terribly pleased you've turned up to help,' he began, peering over the half spectacles he wore for such escriptorial occasions. He put his hands on the edges of the wings of the brass eagle and leaned forward in that churchly manner which he knew irritated Gareth greatly. 'Believe me, old chap' (the 'old chap', too, amounted to a deliberate provocation, invoking, as it did to Gareth, all the chummy old-school bonhomie he so fiercely disowned) 'we need every bit of help, every possible hand on deck this time. Eighteen hundred is just not enough – not with the Tories taking all those by-elections. They could annihilate us.' The contemplation of this possibility, which seemed to him to be present and very likely, doused his spirits and he lost interest in teasing the bedenimed tyro glowering at him from the comfort of a chesterfield. 'There are some who think that the best that could be hoped for is exactly that – the annihilation of the Labour Party.' Gareth opened calmly. He was not ready yet. The plan was to wait. He could cross swords, but he was not to go in for the kill, not yet. He had worked too hard at it to spoil it for the sake of a few easy points. Nevertheless some response was called for: it would be out of character and suspect for him to allow what he thought of as Jimmie's soft-brained lamentations to pass by without a cat-call or two.

'There are those who believe in the annihilation of anything and everything,' Jimmie said, evenly, not interrupting his work, replying to every letter on about one and a half sides of the official notepaper. He always thought that one side was not evidence of sufficient care. It was time to put a mild shot across Gareth's bow. 'There's an enormous pretence of intellectual torment, in fact it's facile despair, especially in a democracy such as ours – all the jargon and chatter of the Far Left is toytown Marxism. The Left is a tiresome joke in this country.'

'The Labour Party's a mess,' Gareth asserted, easily. 'It's not socialist. It's not representative of the people. It's not even representative of the Unions – the Unions don't need it, the people don't want it and the socialists aren't in it. All it's done is to push forward the Liberal improvements of the Lloyd-George/Asquith lot. A useful tradition with some useful reforms to its credit. But it's over. The Labour Party has nothing more to offer except an ability to carry out conservative policies.'

Jimmie replied unemotionally and without pausing in his work. He had despaired of Gareth long ago but an ineradicable sense of duty and decency made him try afresh every time, however awkwardly, however badly. He had done the man great harm, he now realised, by keeping the truth of his birth back from him. The least he could do now was to enter into an argument, however bored he felt with what he thought of as Gareth's futile opinions.

'The central principles of the Labour Party are the only notions which will prevent this country being bamboozled into another and worse bout of red-necked capitalist vandalism with the poor paying first but everyone paying later, or – or, let me finish – the crypto-fascism of the Far Left and the Far Right, the National Front and the SLL or the IS – whatever the Trotskyists call themselves now.' He waved a piece of paper in his left hand. 'Fairly typical letter here from a woman who doesn't want to move out of a slum property, condemned, because (a) she likes it and (b) the rent's low. The Far Right would knock the house down. The

Far Left would terrorise her by turning her into a Cause.'

'You, of course, will mount your white horse.'

'I'll look into it, yes.'

'How pathetic!' Gareth snapped and was silent. He had to control himself. He looked to Helen for support. Her face to the wall, she was murmuring into the phone and methodically taking notes.

Jimmie noticed the self-restraint and took it to be a resolution on the younger man's part to be more reasonable. He welcomed it and was a little ashamed of the way in which he had set him off. If Gareth were trying to be temperate then Charity dictated that a helping hand should be held out.

Sunlight warmed the large room again: the ample space, well stocked with good furniture, seemed a peaceful forum. There was good taste here and a tradition of discussion. The sounds from the rest of the house and the occasional cry from outside contributed to the security Jimmie could still draw from this room in which his parents had lived out so much of their lives. He sensed that Gareth *was* making an effort. It would be churlish not to seek out the good to build on it.

He changed the subject. 'I'm expecting Harold tomorrow morning. He's been asking about you. He's keen to talk to you again.'

'That I doubt.'

'Oh he is. He's always liked you, you know. When you were a boy he bought you the most magnificent presents. Quite vulgar, really.' Jimmie had given Gareth a perfect opening which was gleefully taken.

'Tut-tut. Your class is showing.' But it was said apparently without a barb, Jimmie noted, even with amusement. Gareth was trying. But why? Jimmie could still not give him the benefit of the doubt.

'No, not a bit.' Jimmie was touchy about his 'class': indisputably middle- to upper-middle class himself with 'sound' institutions behind and about him, he genuinely detested the class differences which still stratified British society. He considered them to be seriously damaging to the moral and economic health of the country. Yet he was always aware of his own privileged position in the existing pecking order. 'Harold's looking after himself these days,' Jimmie said, as if this upgraded his old friend or at least redeemed his own slip by showing how authentic and close his interest in Harold was. Harold had come from the 'lower reaches' of the working classes. 'Cuts down on drink – well, a little. And cigars only – those Romeo y Julieta jobs, hellishly dear. And he has been known to put in nine holes before lunch.'

'Golf, I hope,' Gareth murmured, avoiding the use of a camp tone just in time. Jimmie did not catch it.

'He's a man and a half, all right.' Jimmie grinned at some private recollection. 'He *did* used to be a ladies' man – he wouldn't deny it. A bit of a satyr, really. I wondered where he got the energy. It's amazing, isn't it, the way in which societies organise themselves. I mean, Harold and I, almost to the month the same age, brought up within five miles of each other – lots in common – and yet such is the way we are that it took a war to bring us together – and in North Africa! Tough as old boots, he was. Sort of chap who ran the outfit, Sergeant Major to the collarstud. He could get you anywhere and anything. I value him. We disagree. But I cherish him.'

'I like him as well. He's a gangster.'

'You're unfair.' Jimmie glanced at Gareth intently, but the younger man gave no sign.

'You're too soft on him.'

Helen put down the phone but stayed apart from them. She sat where she was, hunched over her notebook as if hoarding it – Gareth knew the attitude well – and went about some private business of transferring information from one page to another. She had heard every syllable of the conversation. The phone call to Bill, Jimmie's agent, had proceeded like a police report; already she found it so well established in its stages and its pace that she could put her mind on automatic pilot and deal with the familiar landmarks of the day quite adequately. More than Jimmie, she had sensed that Gareth was repressing and concealing his true feelings and she wondered why. More than Gareth, she realised that Jimmie had anticipated antagonism and was prepared to meet it head on, even to tease it out. The two men seemed so full of bad feeling, misunderstanding and ignorance of each other. She could not bear to watch them.

Her face to the wall, she could visualise Jimmie's elegant slouched stance at the lectern, the rather dandified half glasses and the slightly juvenile flop of grey hair over the face, still well-shaped and full of the benevolent anxiety that concealed, she knew now, a complex of unhappiness and painful doubt. And Gareth she could see, too, crouched in some self-hugging attitude, his eyes flickering about like a lizard's tongue, something cold and, yes, even reptilian compared with the stork-like open-faced chumpiness of Jimmie looking down at him over the brass eagle. Gareth always restless, kept thin by the nervous energy which enabled him to work, drink and play so much harder than anyone she had ever met. His body tight and muscular with hard, pushing exercise. Gareth hidden behind the flutter of movements which seemed to tell all. Inside there was, Helen thought, a space like that between the outer and inner casing of a vacuum flask, and at the centre, there was something still and self-contained about Gareth, watchful and calculating, and yet, as she had seen once or twice, quite childlike and childishly hurt. Whereas Jimmie appeared to wear his heart on his sleeve and his thoughts on his face. His easy size and innate athleticism rather mocked the strenuous fitness of the younger man but there was a seediness round the edges of Jimmie which Gareth, she felt, would never tolerate.

Most of all, Jimmie was open. Open to ideas and people and their problems as individuals. He was totally without Gareth's social skills to discern and dart about between different persons, a blunderer compared with Gareth's swift knowingness, but patently honest, decent, puzzled, a man of principle; a good man. You would give your allegiance to Jimmie, she thought, and indeed she had already done so, after a fashion. But you could give your life for Gareth – and she had all but done that, too. So unlike. In every sense so unalike, she thought. But held together as if they had been tied together with chains. Helen suspected too, and rightly, that she was an audience – in large part to Gareth, in some part to Jimmie. It was not a duel, nor was it a battle of wits, but they were definitely testing each other out and she was the lady whose favours each of them sought. The rôle excited her but she could not accept it. It did not belong to her. Her job was her life now and that could not change. She strove to appear oblivious of the men who had once, she knew, and in this room, been able to talk as warmly as any father and son.

'Do you really think you could lose your seat?' Gareth's question was so straightforward that Jimmie dropped his guard.

'Yes. For a number of reasons I won't bore you with. Some our fault, some bad luck, some the fault of others. But yes, this seat is vulnerable.'

'So you think you could lose?'

'I'm afraid so. The constituency isn't solid-core Labour. It's gone Tory before. It was Liberal back in the old days. Yes. I could lose.'

'Then what would you do?'

'Look for a job. Fifty-seven and nowhere to go.'

'You must have something saved up.'

'My salary, Gareth, is, I would guess, about a half of what you get for – expertly I grant you – talking between gramophone records on a popular radio programme. My wife does not work. We have others here too. I have to keep up a small flat in London. MPs are possibly the only persons left in the United Kingdom whose expenses are scrutinised to the ultimate penny. I count myself lucky to be manageably over-drawn.'

'You must have something tucked away.' Gareth pressed the point with a concern which touched the older man.

It intrigued Gareth to know that Jimmie himself was so financially vulnerable. It was useful to know that.

'No. No nest egg.' Jimmie smiled ruefully; another of those boyish expressions which did him no good with the heavies in the Party.

'No crock of gold either?'

'You know that the extremists are putting up a candidate here of course?'

'The National Front?' Gareth asked innocently.

'No, no. They'd get no change here. As you know. The Left. The Workers Revolutionary Party they call themselves nowadays. That clutch of hare-brained thespians, disaffected television producers and sadly gullible apprentices. A chap called Weston's their man.'

'They never poll more than two or three hundred votes,' Gareth said, carelessly.

'It's still awkward. They make the whole thing nasty.'

'It's a nasty business.'

'It need not be. It hasn't been in this country for quite a long time. Not since Mosley in the thirties.'

'It hasn't *seemed* to be,' Gareth said. 'Things have been under control.'

'All civilised men have disliked mobs and vandals, Gareth, and this extreme Left seems to me to encourage both.'

'The Terror of the Middle Classes?'

'If you like.'

'The Conscience that came in from the Cold? That's how they see themselves, you know. After all, your nice centrist Labour Party began as a bunch of wild men who were thought of by the Good Old Jimmies of their day to be no better than criminals and degenerates. History tints up the successful.'

'This lot is merely destructive – and hysterical.' Jimmie spoke fiercely. There is no comparison, not for a moment, with the early founders of the Labour Party – none, except in the poorly furnished brains of those deluded enough to believe that all opposition is necessarily virtuous and the more extreme the opposition the more virtuous. Poor stuff.'

'You're nettled! I bet you *really* think there's something *in* what Weston says. That would be just like you! Fair to the bitter end.'

'That, old chap,' Jimmie said, grinning hugely, 'is the nicest thing anyone's said to me for months. Merci. And, incidentally, Weston is indeed – the bitter end.'

'You're a twenty-two-carat sentimentalist.'

'Still the armchair radical?'

'I try to see those who are set in authority over us for what they are, yes,' Gareth said, contemplatively, as if sucking on a well-rubbed briar pipe. 'Ego-trippers, barely constrained megalomaniacs and blundering oppressors beside whom King Kong is a model citizen. That's about it, yes.' He paused. 'Oh – and vain. Very.'

'It's all too glib, Gareth. Like Weston and his WRP gang. Destroy everything – that seems to be the grand theme of his political philosophy. Destroy the lot and *then* sit down and have a good think. Friend Weston doesn't only think too little and see too little, he hasn't even read enough. He ought to look up some of the blue-prints of those Utopias he intends to plant on the wasteland he wants to reduce us to. Thomas More's Utopia makes the Gulag Archipelago seem quite a pleasant resort. Marx's idea of Utopia was somewhere between Disneyland and Cloud Cuckoo Land – run, as usual, by the self-selected and self-perpetuating elite. If Weston wants to address himself to big questions, I'll give him one. Where are we, English, British, now? Or, much harder, but after all he's supposed to be intelligent, *who* are we? What is that identity without which nations are as lost as individuals?'

'Who cares "who are we English"?' Gareth shook his head sorrowfully. 'Really, Jimmie; who the hell cares?' He began to whistle *God Save the Queen* – deliberately getting some of the notes wrong. Jimmie spoke over it, calmly. Gareth had used the trick before and it annoyed him most to be totally ignored.

'I do. You'd dismiss that as either patriotic and regressive infantilism or mere populist fawning, I suspect. But it just won't do to wallow in easy cynicism, Gareth. Cynicism is very fashionable at the moment, but I don't have to tell you that it's the midwife of Fascism. It is important to a lot of people that in England we still have certain liberties. These are under threat all over the world *and – and – here*. Now.' Gareth broke off the whistling and sang:

'Long to – o reign over us. Go – od Save the Queen! Tarantara! We built up our liberties on the corpses of the weak and that's why they rot our guts now. Black guilt come home to roast us alive. Retribution!' He nodded at the ceiling. 'Good thinking.'

'The saddest posture of all – an intelligent man mortgaging his mind to unearned despair.'

None of them had noticed Elaine. She had come in from the back stairs: Helen and Jimmie were turned away from her and Gareth was masked by Jimmie. She had listened alertly, as if waiting for her cue, hovering, attendant. She was wearing a mauve dress, not bought recently, nor expensive but because of one or two adjustments, and because of the way she wore it, both fashionable and elegant. Her taste was as flawless as Helen's was flawed. She had brushed her hair back from her forehead, showing the full width of the delicate face. There was clever make-up, an antique coral and pearl brooch old-fashionedly at her thoat – but successful, as were the three or four cheap bangles which made up the rest of her jewellery. In the pause following Jimmie's last cumbrous pronouncement, she clapped and walked forward continuing to applaud. 'Gareth always *loved* contradicting you! You taught him that youself. My two men!' She stood between them, glancing proudly from one to the other, and then she saw Helen and caught her look and felt her head sway, but she stood firm.

It was the only way left her if she was to live a life of her own, she thought. She had felt herself come to a final decision after Jimmie had led her up the stairs and yet again made it plain she was an invalid. It was not his fault: she had indeed been very ill and he had become used to her like that. But the habit had formed so quickly and stuck so fast she had found herself labelled for life.

Many times she had tried to break out of the pattern which was partly self-induced, partly the result of genuine poor health and a true and terrible breakdown; but partly also due to the imposed view and expectations of others – especially the two who were most kind and most loving, Jimmie and her mother. And so whenever she did try to break out she would be checked, in the kindest way and for the best reasons.

But just as there comes a time in the life of some alcoholics when they realise that a unique combination of desperation, hope and circumstances gives them the chance to exercise and spend the small hoard of will they have saved up over the years, and just as in the lives of certain men and women there has come a time when a particular incident of trivial importance in itself has crystallised a longing which has been concealed and frustrated and inchoate for years – so in the life of some of those who have found themselves classified as permanent convalescents, there can come a time when a great change, even a miraculous change, seems finally possible.

As Jimmie had led her from the room, taken her away, as it were, from the adult world, comfortingly, even lovingly, but still taken her away, and as he had led her upstairs with that absurd nursery enticement 'Up Timber Hill' – Elaine had felt a cool, rather apprehensive, but perfectly clear resolution from her mind. She had to act the way she wanted to be and she had to start now. Or her life would indeed be over. Somehow she had managed to tell Jimmie this and he had not laughed at her. He had kissed her, very gently, not as a child, and said, 'Well done.' That was all. But a great surge of comfort consolidated her confidence.

Please God, she muttered inside her mind, again and again, help me, please help me, please, I know I'm not worth it, but just this last time.

Chapter Seven

Helen stood up. 'I'll go and type up these notes. There's just time.'

'Don't go.' Elaine held out her bangled arms and the sound added to the effect of a bar being thrown against Helen's escape. 'I want to come with you this morning – no, Jimmie, *please* let me finish.' Though she spoke to Jimmie, who was moving into his automatic custodial routine, it was to Gareth that the appeal was directed and his reaction stayed Jimmie's manoeuvre. '*Please*. Thank you. I never come with you. I haven't done for years. I remember when they first asked you, the very first time to *sit* – or *stand* ...' She paused. 'Which is it?' Gareth laughed delightedly; Jimmie, too, smiled at the bewilderment. 'Stand?' He nodded. 'It sounds bolder, doesn't it? You told me all about the rôle of a member's wife.' She smiled, her confidence was there; it was happening; she had made a start.

'I didn't.' Jimmie's denial was self-condemning. He groaned. 'Oh Lord ... I did.' So she was serious, he thought. God help her.

' "A Member's Wife",' Gareth repeated with the greatest relish.

'It sounded so terrifying!' Elaine began to enjoy herself. Jimmie and Gareth were amused – and they were listening. Helen was not getting on with something else, and making Elaine feel that whatever she did was unimportant. She held the stage not as the object of concern or pity, but as someone, just someone talking. Her mind flittered with restlessness and vivacity resulting from the abrupt withdrawal of her heavy diet of chemicals. She almost prickled with the sensation of a new life already budding, pushing aside the wintry bark of those dulling dosages of poison. 'It was terrifying!' she repeated rather breathlessly. 'Attending meetings, sitting on platforms, sitting on committees, sitting on councils, sitting on charities – sitting, sitting, sitting – that's where I got the sitting from! *You* had to stand. *I* had to sit! Or open things. Open carnivals, open garden fêtes, open dog shows, open baby shows, open new wings of whatever needed new wings. Or – what else? Oh yes – judge! Judge everything as far as I could see. Cucumbers, village greens, knobbly knees, beauty queens, dogs, amateur tenors – oh! It was far harder than being the MP.' Elaine had entertained herself too and was laughing as the men were, as Helen was attempting to do, at the image of her own utter incapability of taking on the doughty duties of a hard-working MP's wife.

'You very wisely refused all offers as I remember,' Jimmie said, 'thereby, in time, creating an allure, an aura, the mystery woman – far more valuable to me than another drudge. You came to represent the glamour. The Greta Garbo of the local Labour party.'

But he had gone too far: in wanting to extend her good moment he threatened to mar it. He had not got her measure. He saw that she was 'up', but that had happened before; he feared she would over-strain herself.

'No. I was the invalid, Jimmie. The sympathy vote perhaps. I've been a failure up until now. I'm sorry, Jimmie.'

The pause registered the truth of what she had said. But the energy raced life through her again. She pushed herself.

'I don't want to be like that now. That's what I mean. I'll help you properly.'

'Darling,' Jimmie was firm, 'you simply have not got the strength to walk around the place, shaking hands, standing

88

in draughty rooms, eating stale sandwiches for lunch, going around council estates in the rain. There is not the slightest chance of you being able to do that and so, please, darling, don't try to do something which will just wear you out.' Still the guardian.

Previously, that would have caused her to run away. Now she glanced at Gareth and visibly summoned up more resources to fight for the right – so long and so gradually and so fully ceded that no one could have marked her passage from someone fully taken into account to someone always accounted for – to have the primary say over her own life. Gareth nodded encouragingly but it was Jimmie who was the first to understand the battle she was taking on. And finally he appreciated it was not another flight caused by the arrival of Gareth or another bout of illness. And as soon as he saw what she wanted he wanted it for her too. Up to a point. For although his heart went out to her, there was no doubt in his mind that she remained a sick woman, diagnosed, classified, indisputably. Sick people did not one day simply rise from their beds and walk – and yet as this phrase went through his mind he smiled hugely. For of course they did! He kept the discovery to himself, not wanting to break her new, fragile resolution.

'OK, darling. With you now. Helen, would you be kind enough to take Elaine through the schedule and see what she could fit into, see where she could help.'

Elaine came and kissed him – not rapturously as he had feared but business-like, on the cheek. 'The member's wife,' she murmured in his ear and giggled. Her eyes shone with pleasure in herself and Jimmie experienced an echo of that protective passion which had first attracted him to her. It was quite extraordinary, he thought, how she could come out of the chrysalis of befogged dependence and depressed misery to be there, so *present*, so vibrant and apparently self-possessed and beautiful. Helen's youthful advantage was more than outshone by Elaine's polish and finer looks. It was as if something of the grace of Jimmie's own mother, who was what used to be referred to as 'a noted local beauty', had fused with the clarity of Elaine's own mother. Heredity and environment or, more accurately, imitation – perhaps the strongest driving force of all (and as a child Elaine had been spellbound by his awesome mother, the imperial lady of the house) – had met and matched – he could see his own mother's gestures, he could see Elaine's mother's attitudes – and yet they had not sunk down to the foundation of her character. When they existed successfully, as they did now, it was on the surface, it was an act, theatrical, pleasing and compliant but balanced precariously over what seemed to be a pit of unhappiness. Now, though, now she was flying. She waltzed across to Helen and sat down beside her at a table, as bright and alert as a new school prefect.

Taking a risk, Jimmie said, 'So you've come up to work in the election, then, have you?'

'Yes,' Gareth answered promptly. 'That's right.'

Jimmie paused and then nodded, forbidden by his code of behaviour to seek further reassurance. He went to the lectern and came back with a copy of the magazine *Private Eye*.

'Read this,' he said. 'It's in the back pages. I've marked the passage.'

Gareth nodded and took it from him. Jimmie returned to his lectern, uneasy but assuring himself that he had to return Gareth's show of solidarity – however spiced with aggression – with an act of trust. Besides, the matter pressed on him urgently. Harold should have been there this morning to discuss it. It could ruin everything for everyone. A life of honourable work, a decent reputation, the prospect of more good to be done and an old age rich in interest – all this could be destroyed by the information in the magazine which Gareth was reading so slowly! Jimmy realised how impatient he was to discuss it and find a strategy or at least comfort. He hid all this and steadily replied to a letter from an elector who was complaining about dogs fouling the pavement in her street.

To keep her hands occupied, to provide some focus of physical activity for the energy which seemed to swirl about in her, Elaine could find nothing better than the large flower vase which held the copper-beech twigs. Helen was struggling hard to keep her composure: Elaine's magically transformed appearance and spirited entrance had disturbed her. She had felt a network of intimacy and involvement growing up between Jimmie, Gareth and herself: she had begun to imagine that out of it would be resolved cares which were crippling each and all of them. Though she had been silent she had felt a third part of their company. Now Elaine had confused all that. From being a muted acquiescent invalid Elaine had leapt into a vivacity which took Helen, unaccustomed to her, completely by surprise.

Helen's manner to Elaine from the first had been sympathetic but rather formal. It was not a difficult manner to adopt now when she desperately wished to be out of the room, alone, shredding and analysing what had happened, shoring herself up against the disappointments she had come to accept were to be her inevitable lot. She needed time to think out a strategy to deal with Gareth – that was the heart of it. Or she would be in danger of being hurt, badly, again.

'Do you like our copper beech?' Elaine asked, brightly.

'I can see it from my bedroom window. It's enormous.'

'Jimmie's father used to say it was more than two hundred years old. There was some other copper beech at his university. He once took a tape measure to find out how thick the trunk was to compare it with ours! Ours lost, I think!'

'It must be ...' Helen flailed for a word: forced conversation such as this used up her resources so quickly. Why did she not have the poise or the nerve to get out for a few minutes? By what force of convention was she sitting making meaningless chatter when she ached to be alone, indeed feared not to have the time and solitude to recover her balance? It must be – what? '... lovely,' she said, 'to be able to walk out, just walk out into a garden in the middle of the countryside and bring in armfuls of nature.'

'I was born in a town,' Elaine said. Then she whispered, 'I would like to persuade Jimmie to go and live in a town. Ssshhh! There.' The arrangement was made. She sat back to admire it. 'Already dying,' she said. 'That's the pity.'

'Mrs. Johnston, I wonder if I could ...'

'*Why* don't we use each other's Christian names?' Elaine interrupted her, zealous to extend as many frontiers as possible while she felt strong. 'Especially in a house such as this! And our names are so alike!'

'I think they are the same name, originally,' Helen said, dry-mouthed, flushed, realising that she would have to stay and quell her upset.

'Are they? I suppose they are. My mother always says she picked "Elaine" up in a book. She says it rather in the way people say they've picked up a bargain at a jumble sale.' She smiled, even strong enough to joke about her mother.

'I've never thought to ask my mother why. It wasn't in the family.'

'Let's be friends. Shall we?' Elaine actually held out her hands.

Helen had no means to meet the direct appeal. She nodded. For a terrible moment she thought she might want to cry. Elaine still held out her hands and so she reached out furtively and dabbed finger-ends together. Then she turned on herself, desperate and urgent to find a reason for the violence of her feelings. It was the shock of seeing Gareth! That was the root of this unexpected turbulence. She was relieved, having identified the cause. Gareth. She nodded.

'Now then,' Elaine said in what she took to be her business-like tone, but in fact rather parodied the business-like tone of Helen herself, '*would* I be a nuisance? To Jimmie. Tell me truthfully.'

'He *does* have a rather complicated morning as it

happens.' The rôle of instructor helped to restore Helen's poise. She had been foolish to have been so easily unseated. She took control of herself, exercising that mechanism for forcing herself to do what ought to be done which had been so important in her life. 'There's the literature to check and begin to set: the surgery: a meeting with the shop stewards at the steelworks at lunchtime: speech in the Market Square at two: some canvassing after that. Then, it's the first full day of the official campaign, you see, and everybody will be out to make a good impression. There'll be the local press looking for stories, I suppose.' Helen grinned. 'I hope so. I'm new to this as well, you know.' She liked this new woman before her – much much more than the slippered invalid in a dressing-gown who had haunted the stairs and landings with such sad looks. She realised that she liked the idea of Jimmie and Elaine being married, nothing to mourn, nothing to regret. It was a great relief. She could see them together – such a handsome couple, as the saying was – well matched, almost, indeed, brother and sister in their distinct good looks and gracefulness. Now that she had put her finger on the cause of her own unease, she could think clearly. Of course Elaine must come and help. Why not? Activity was therapeutic. 'I suppose,' she said, 'if you *have* been out and about as little as you say, then *you* yourself would be the news!'

'Oh no!' Elaine's alarm was real. But the more she thought about it, the more enjoyable it promised to be. 'Oh no! I want to do something useful – licking stamps, that's what people always claim as proof of humble helpfulness, isn't it? Or answering the telephone.'

The telephone rang. The women laughed aloud. Helen nodded to Elaine who took it. 'I'll help Mrs. Burns with the coffee,' Helen said and went out. She had heard the clatter of preparations from the kitchen and knew that assistance was expected from some quarter. But mostly it gave her a chance to be alone and calm herself down.

Elaine was delighted to speak to the caller. When Jimmie, who had sat down next to Gareth, roused up to check, she merely waved and he turned back to his discussion with Gareth, immediately impervious to Elaine's laughter and prattle.

'It's what the next issue prints that's really important,' Gareth said. He folded *Private Eye* back into the quarter size which indicated that Jimmie had carried it about in his pocket. 'I had *seen* that one, as a matter of fact.'

'You know some of the people who write for it, don't you? I remember you saying once.'

'That was some time ago. The man I know broke away and went to edit his own paper.'

'Harold's supposed to be bringing the next issue across tomorrow. He's having it sent up Red Star.'

'Do you deny it?' Gareth asked this as neutrally as he could but it was as if Jimmie had been on guard for days.

'Of course.'

'You're only mentioned in passing. Although the "fading debonair political dilettante" is a bit of a dig.'

'Harold wants to slap in a writ of course. I don't agree. *Private Eye* thrives on them, doesn't it? It puts it in the news, doesn't it?'

'So you're worried?'

'Of course. Especially at this particular time. I need all my energy for this fight here, which looks like being rather dirty and very strenuous. I'm exhausted from the idiotic all-night sessions in Westminster and those interminable committees I'm seconded to, let alone the marathon commission on the regions, the – oh! – this seat is more than my job. It has to be held for the Labour movement, past and future.'

'But it is, also, your job,' Gareth murmured, and added: 'Nothing wrong with that. Convergence of interests.'

'It can be very tenacious, can't it, *Private Eye*?' Jimmie had gained no reassurance. 'Look at the way they tormented poor old Reggie Maudling. I'm convinced they broke his spirit, you know, just by keeping on keeping on. He isn't a bad chap. The Tories are certainly weaker without him and a weak Opposition is no good to anyone. They just keep *on* at people as if they want to wear them down, don't they? They helped do for poor Jeremy. They started on Jim over the Welsh business but maybe someone put a spoke in their wheel over that one. I suppose they do some good. Of course they do. I'm upset, that's all – they *have* done good things – but this viciousness ... And to speak of Harold, what is it – as the "Poulson of Cumbria" – that is ludicrous. Harold's a hard-headed contractor, no more, no less. A tough self-made businessman. A rough old diamond if you like, although he's polished up remarkably well – in fact he's one of the most sophisticated men I know now, he has this capacity to keep learning – but *sound,* sound as they come—'

'Are you trying to convince yourself?'

The door opened, Lionel pushed in the trolley as if it were a wagonette full of coal in the most arduous pit, back bent, arms full out. The dialogue stopped. Jimmie leaned forward, patted Gareth's knee, and switched on the public face which had been forgotten while he had been striving to understand what might happen, what course to take, how to survive.

'I'm *very* grateful to you for stepping into the breach, old boy,' he said. 'Very,' he repeated. 'I know we haven't been seeing eye to eye lately – still don't – I accept that! – but first things first – let's keep the Party in. That's very important, you know.' Jimmie spoke open-heartedly and Gareth felt a twinge of conscience in deceiving him so completely. 'Democratic socialism has *got* to be the answer, hasn't it?'

He was up and away to help Lionel before Gareth could summon up an appropriate reply.

Chapter Eight

'Coffee, she is served,' Lionel announced, 'on the dot of ten. I should wear a Jiminy Cricket suit and collect tips.'

Elaine put down the phone and walked across the room as Marianne, carrying a plate of biscuits, and Helen, rather self-consciously carrying a sugar bowl, came in. Lionel went across to the Victorian wall clock and noisily hoisted it down, taking it to a table and placing it there face down.

'It was Harold,' Elaine announced happily. Talking to Harold always cheered her up.

'Why didn't you tell me?' Jimmie failed to keep the annoyance out of his voice. Elaine hesitated, nervously, and though Jimmie was becoming unbearably agitated because of Harold's failure to turn up, he was able to regain total control and she nodded.

'It was for me. He wanted to know how I was.'

'I wanted to talk with him.' This was said gently.

'He'll be here the day after tomorrow,' Elaine reported. 'He's got to go to London and – somewhere in Yorkshire.'

'Where is he now?'

'I didn't ask.' Elaine looked crestfallen. 'I should have done, shouldn't I?'

'Never mind.' Jimmie exonerated her with an obvious effort and tried to push the matter out of his mind. It would not be dismissed. Harold had Jimmie's future in his hands and the longing to know where he stood, the longing to have a decision attacked Jimmie painfully. But he concealed all this from his wife.

Mrs. Burns came in fiercely.

'Where's Alan's Teddy Bear?' she demanded. 'He's lost it.'

'This clock needs one hell of a clean,' Lionel announced. He had opened the back of it and he stuck up a finger smeared with sticky dust.

'It'll have to be found,' Mrs. Burns went on grimly. Her devotion to her great-grandson was excessive even by the standards of the class and time she came from. 'He won't be a good boy until it's found.' She looked at Marianne, who was pouring the coffee. 'He won't travel without it, Marianne knows that.' Marianne, the Sacred Mother, was always referred to – out of respect: Gareth, the delinquent father, was a source of shame to the old woman and she suffered for him. To Elaine she said, 'You take that side of the room.' She turned up the cushions of the sofa, came across Marianne's brassiere, and replaced the cushion firmly. 'It's bound to be here. He has a good memory for that Teddy Bear.'

As if in competition with her, Lionel scanned the room as a sailor in a crow's-nest might scan an ocean. 'Who's been putting slack on that fire?'

He bustled across to it as if to save it from doing itself harm.

'Lionel takes unremitting revenge against his life as a coal-miner,' Jimmie said, taking a cup from Marianne and passing it on to Gareth. 'Burn! Burn! Burn the stuff!' Gareth took the cup, looked around the room and smiled: the farce, he thought, was getting into its stride.

'Funny you should say that!' Lionel bellowed his contribution from across the room. The actual distance was not far – but the amount of furniture and the number of people inspired him to turn up the volume of a voice normally loud enough to be heard through a thick wall. 'When I was a boy – I was just thinking this the other day! – I can mind of seein' a comic or maybe it was a religious tract, maybe it would be Methodist, Primitive Methodist, or – never mind – anyhow, it showed you Hell!' Mrs. Burns looked up from her search as this word blasted through the vicarage but Lionel took her attention to signify interest. 'And they were burning COAL! In Hell! Yes! Now the question I ask is this – Who dug it out? Eh? Same buggers as got burnt up I suppose! As per usual.' Marianne handed him a cup of coffee. 'This is the life.' He sank the coffee in one and handed it back to Marianne. 'Coffee breaks!' He glanced across at Mrs. Burns and caught her eye. 'I could get used to this.' Then he began to reorganise the fire, using the poker as if it were a fine screwdriver engaged on a milli-measurement engineering task. He abhorred slack.

'Sugar?' Helen held out the bowl to Gareth.

'No thanks.'

'You—' Then she bit her lip. He used to take it.

'He's sweet enough,' Marianne said. She had noticed. She took a deep breath. So that was why Gareth had come back.

'He was absolutely certain it was in here,' Mrs. Burns proclaimed, having mown through a thick swathe of territory from the trolley to the french windows. 'And he's never wrong. Not about his Teddy Bear.' Elaine continued to look assiduously and yet her lightness of touch gave her actions that smack of humour which unfailingly annoyed her mother.

'Country habits are so bracing.' Gareth glanced at his watch. 'We'll have supper about midday at this rate.' Elaine caught his eye and smiled at him: a dazzling, loving smile which brought a twinge of envy to Jimmie.

'We must be on our way,' Jimmie said. 'A long day. Shan't be back before midnight. Will we see you in the town?' This to Gareth, who affected a look of bemused disorientation.

'There are a few things . . .' Gareth took advantage of Jimmie's amenable understanding. 'You know . . .'

'Of course.' Jimmie nodded several times. 'You have to

sort yourself out, rush up here, loose ends, quite so.' He glanced again at his watch. 'We have a few minutes in hand. Wonder what the papers are predicting?'

'What time is it?' Gareth wore no watch.

'He's worried about his programme, poor thing!' Marianne said, striking out and hitting the centre of the target. Gareth pretended not to notice but it took an effort.

'Found it!' Mrs. Burns held up the Teddy Bear by one leg.

'This house,' Gareth said, as he stood up, transistor in hand, preparatory to moving away into another room, 'is more like a three-ring circus than the peaceful rural retreat of an eminent backbencher and local grandee.'

'He's never wrong, that little boy. Not about his Teddy Bear.' Mrs. Burns, coming over to take her own coffee, passed by Gareth and banged the toy animal on his chest. 'This used to be yours.' For a moment she looked at her grandson lovingly. Gareth had some of the look of her long-dead husband: that fierce, neat, quickness, the dark glance full of – what? In her husband it had been mischief, a feeling for personal liberty, a thirst for life. In Gareth it was something else: and worse.

'Of course!' Elaine looked at the transistor. 'You're on the radio. Turn it on.' She paused. 'Please.'

'I'll listen in the study,' Gareth said.

'Ten out of ten,' Jimmie said and dug his old pipe into the large leather pouch for his first fill of the day. 'Ten out of ten,' he repeated.

'I'll take this to him.' Marianne took the Teddy Bear from Mrs. Burns's grasp. 'I know the fan club likes to gather round.' Ignoring the artificial protests, she went out. Gareth sensed that she had sniffed out his old affair with Helen: he smiled to himself: more welcome complications. Marianne's intuition was very good. Better than Helen's.

Elaine took the transistor from Gareth's grasp. She was determined to have it and any resistance would have caused

99

a scene. Jimmie had scribbled a note to Helen and she went across to phone.

'I never miss,' Elaine said. To Helen: 'Do *you* listen to him?' She fiddled clumsily with the dials. 'It always takes me hours to find it.'

'I don't know how he talks so fast.' Mrs. Burns toppled stiffly into the corner of the sofa, the coffee cup held resolutely before her, and never spilt a single drop. She settled in to listen and began to stir the cup, an activity which went on for as long as there was any coffee left in the cup. 'Do they train you to do that at the BBC?'

'His grandfather could gabble.' Taking advantage of the presence of the others, Lionel sat down beside Mrs. Burns, knowing that she would not rebuff him in company. 'His grandfather could talk the hind leg off a mule, couldn't he?' He dug her ribs, gently so as not to upset her coffee. 'He talked the hind leg off you well enough, didn't he, same fella?' Lionel knew that Mrs. Burns liked him to refer to her husband: it was his shortest cut to her attention.

'Did you put some newspaper under that clock when you plonked it on that table?' she asked, and Lionel, as he himself would have said, 'felt six foot'.

'I'll do it after.'

'That's your theme song, Lionel,' she said and nodded, but smilingly.

'I'd make a clean husband,' he ventured. 'And I saw you first. Remember that.'

'The shock of it never leaves me,' the old lady answered, imperturbably. 'It made me drop my bucket of pig-swill.'

'Sssshhhh!! I think I've found it.' Elaine worked intently, completely absorbed.

Gareth appealed to Jimmie and both men shook their heads. Elaine was by now kneeling on the floor and crouched over the radio as if she were tapping out secret messages in occupied France.

Gareth's voice followed the end of a very heavy rock number:

'Flapjack Mack and "Million Dollar Baby" – another funky black sound out to make a fortune. We love them to be rich, don't we? And freaky? Yes. And, best of all, all twisted up because then we can sincerely say – they are just like *us*, we are just like them and the funny old world goes on going on round and round. Now – *your* story, the spot on the show where we bring the people out of the pamphlets and coast to coast hear on nationwide the stories most of us don't want to hear. Stand by for – the sound of life!'

A full Hammond Organ chord bulged out of the radio and then turned into the first few bars of 'Greensleeves' played in a minor key.

'Our first caller is – hello –yes?'
The woman said: 'Good morning.'
Gareth: 'Good morning. Do you want to give your name?'
The woman spoke intently, as if counting out the words from a small and precious store. The voice compelled attention. 'No. He wouldn't like that. He'd kill me if he knew about this. But you have to tell somebody. I live in a flat. Up the top. Nobody talks up there.'
Gareth: 'If it upsets you too much, we can talk after the programme. We have your number—'
The woman said: 'It's my friend's house. We don't have a phone. She wanted me to ring you. She said it would help. She listens to your programme every time. Tina, she's called.'

For the first time the voice was bright and you could imagine that perhaps it was a young woman behind the strain of the tired voice. Everyone, even Jimmie who was embarrassed by what he considered a tawdry and misguided exploitation of human frailty, waited now on the woman's confession.

'Turn the bloody thing off!' Gareth exclaimed, but Elaine shielded the radio from his inexpert assault. Clearly, it meant an enormous amount to her and for that reason as well as for the compelling lure of vanity and narcissism, Gareth was only pretending that he did not want to listen.

'I want to hear what she says!' Elaine said, almost pleadingly.

'I don't know how people have the face,' Lionel said. 'Where I came from you keep yourself to yourself.'

'Please, Lionel.' Elaine had identified raptly with the woman's pain and now lived it with her, could not bear to be distracted from this unknown abstract voice.

Gareth: 'Take your time.'

The woman went on, and now the words grew quieter, the strain came through more strongly, her disturbance was clear. 'When the third one came along, he wasn't, right, you know? You could tell. There was something about him. And he was such a lovely little thing. They had to put him on oxygen. I wouldn't let them keep him in, though. I wanted him home where he could know some love.'

'I understand,' Elaine said. Gareth shook his head almost in horror but his mother repeated the words. 'I understand. "Know some love."'

The woman said: 'He was always smiling. They say that sort smile most. He was happy.' She paused: the pause grew and they could all hear the woman straining to keep from crying.

Gareth: 'Yes? He sounds fine.'

Gareth, hearing himself, noted how unmoved he was: others would applaud his professionalism.

The woman said: 'But he's been taken away you see! And it was his Dad. I have to tell somebody. You can't tell anybody. It was hard on him. I had no time for him. We're not married – and he wants . . . It's always harder on the man. I had no time for him. He came in drunk again this night. The little boy was crying. I'd called him Frank. He hadn't been christened. I worry about that as well, now. He cried a lot. Little thin little cries. But he, this night, just picked him out of his cot and just, just, *threw him down!* So he's gone, you see. He's *dead.*'

Gareth turned off the transistor, helped a dazed Elaine to her feet and made for the door. The room was audience, jury, family – he wanted none of that any more.

'You can hear the rest in the study if you have to,' he said.

'What about me?' Mrs. Burns looked up reproachfully. 'Don't I count?'

'The poor woman,' Elaine said. 'How can she live with that man now? What will he do?' Her involvement was wholehearted, ready to rush to help.

'I would hang him.' Mrs. Burns levered herself up by using Lionel's willing shoulder. 'That's what I would do.'

'What good would that do?' Gareth asked.

'She'd just be lonelier than ever, poor thing,' Elaine reproached her mother, gently. 'What do you think, Helen?' Why had she asked Helen? She must rid herself of this fear of the younger woman: that would only make it worse.

Helen shook her head. She would have no part of it.

'Well then,' Elaine said, 'we'll go to the study.' She was at the door when she remembered. 'You'll call me to take me into town with you. Yes?'

Jimmie nodded and Lionel and Mrs. Burns followed mother and son from the room.

'Leave that clock alone,' Lionel said, feeling it incumbent to deliver a parting shot at the door. 'You know what you're like with your hands. T.T.F.N.'

Jimmie sucked at his pipe for a few moments, and looked at Helen.

'Peculiar way to waste his talents,' he said. 'Curious I can't understand either what he is attempting to prove or why he thinks it so important to try this vague populism.'

'I respect what he's trying to do,' Helen said, to Jimmie's surprise. 'I just can't bear to listen to it.' He smiled, pleased with her.

She was looking out of the window. The clouds had beaten the sun. The greyness was omnipresent. She folded her arms and hugged herself for warmth. The big room was never really warmed through until the evening. She looked at the copper beech – so enormous and domineering and old. It blocked the view. But who would ever dare to knock it down? As the sun came up it cast a cold shadow into the living-room. Yet not only this household but to some extent the whole neighbourhood was proud of its immense dark copper strength and age.

Helen grew aware of Jimmie's silence. She turned. He stood, back to the fire, gazing in her direction, unmistakably sad. She was moved by him as she had been so often over the past few days. But it must go no further, she thought.

'We'd better hit the road,' she said.

'In a moment.' He hesitated and then, guardedly, impulsively, he held out his arms. She made no move. He let them drop and nodded: she was right – it must never begin. 'What is going to happen to us all?' He paused. 'Sudden desolation.'

'Why now? Elaine's so – she's so well this morning.'

'You think so? Yes.' He took out his pipe and began to play with it. 'The trouble is, when you start to think about yourself you ...' he hesitated. He was unused to confessing before others. 'Something – I don't know what it was – when you and Elaine were chatting away over there and I was talking to Gareth. I seem to have lost that – whatever it is inside that says: *you* – that's *you*.'

'You're the most sanguine person I know.'

'Quite right!' Jimmie breathed in heartily. 'Forgive all that rubbish. Gareth, Elaine, all that business they have, mother and son, private behaviour always seems odd to strangers. You knew Gareth quite well at one time, then?' He could hold it back no longer. It would be his last lapse into jealousy: he would pray that night to help himself keep his promise.

'Yes. At Oxford.'

'You never said.'

'It never came up.' Then she lied. 'I didn't realise the connection at first, just from the name.'

'He's changed a lot, don't you find?'

'I never really knew him.'

'I see.' He was sad that she should want to lie and in that small fine feeling of first pity, the futile impetuous love he had so abruptly felt for her began to die.

'Elaine's so much better,' she said, knowing he had seen clear through her lies. 'I'm glad she'll be with us,' Helen pressed on, as much seeking information as expressing her opinion. 'She's a new woman.'

'I'm glad you think so.'

'She's making such an effort! Gareth seems to give her strength.'

Jimmie tucked his pipe into his pocket and went to collect the finished letters. 'Gareth's part of her trouble,' he said. And added, so quietly she could scarcely hear, 'A very large part.'

Beware of him, he wanted to say, beware. But such a warning would seem like a tactic to introduce intimacy and that could never happen.

It was foolishness! He stacked the letters together and tapped them on the lectern so that they made a neat parcel between his hands. That was his life and work and God knew there was plenty to get on with. If only Harold would contact him and tell him the present state of things, then he could take action, then he could decide on his course.

'We ought to be on our way,' he said.

Chapter Nine

Marianne was glad to get out of the house. She had walked
down to the village. Alan, despite his protests, had almost
kept pace with her, his short legs trotting under protest. But
it was no more than a mile and all downhill. She knew that
Jimmie would have offered her a lift but his constituency lay
in the opposite direction to her mother's house. She had
given the back tyre of Gareth's bottle-green Aston Martin a
sharp kick as she passed it by: even his car was anti-family.
Besides, Alan liked the bus: he could see over the hedges and
count the cows and spot the occasional horse or tractor.
Every step she took made her feel better. Sometimes the
vicarage was like a big fat incubus sucking out her strength.
She was very glad to get out of it.

The further down the hill she went the more relaxed she
became. It was still a strain for her up there. They were very
nice, she thought, they were lovely with Alan but it was a
strain and there was no use pretending to herself. However
much they sympathised they all felt it was her fault. However much they helped they still, she sensed, resented that
she had not been able to get him to marry her. Such crude
considerations were always skirted but in such a politic and
wordy household Marianne sensed they were there. It was
also a strain keeping up with them. Jimmie was not so bad
because she was a little bit in love with Jimmie and that
helped. He returned her unspoken affection with the gentlest
attention, soothing and untroublesome. Yet she thought that

he would never consider her much more than a rather unsuitable girl from the estate in the town whom Gareth had got into trouble. (She was mistaken about this: but the manner of Jimmie's Christian concern for her alerted long-held prejudices.) When he talked, she alternated between being abased through thinking it the eloquence of a different class of being and annoyed at what she thought was just showing off with fancy words where plain ones would do every bit as well. Before Elaine she felt either protective or, again, when, as this morning, Elaine took flight, inadequate. Mrs. Burns was always scrupulously kind to her but her loyalties were unambiguously with Alan and not with her. Marianne knew that the old woman felt herself to be perfectly capable of bringing the boy up herself – hence the encouragement she received from that quarter to get a job. And yet she knew that, judging from the reaction when she had taken part-time jobs, to take a full-time job would be to incite Mrs. Burn's wrath.

It was much simpler, in the bus, joggling down through the fell villages to Thurston, to imagine she was independent.

She preferred to visit her mother at this time of day, mid-morning. Most of her friends from school and the factory were at work and so she would not bump into them nor be obliged to drop in and see them as she would have done had she gone visiting on a Saturday afternoon or a Sunday. She was sick of their prying. Jimmie was a man of some local eminence. Gareth had become something of a small-time celebrity. Her involvement with it all was the subject of dispute and gossip. She avoided the town. She made up many fine-sounding reasons for avoiding it – growing out of it, losing contact with the old gang, not having anything to say any more, too busy with her shorthand and typing, too busy with this course of night-classes to which Jimmie had introduced her: but the principal reason she avoided the town and her old friends was that they would, sooner or later, sing out, 'Has he married you yet, then?' meaning 'Have you got him to marry you yet?' And she would have to say no. Then there would be the sniggers. She could not stand that.

In truth, also, she had grown away from her friends. With a 'daft gang', as she had called them, she had left school at the first opportunity 'to earn good money' down in the factory. She had been clever enough, her reports said, but 'lacked application'. But a few months after leaving school, the monotony of the factory made her yearn to be back. A year later when she saw former acquaintances setting their sights on colleges and even universities, she had felt sickened. A whole and immense landscape of possibilities was now denied her because of a thoughtless adolescent determination to have cash for cheap clothes and the latest shoes. She blamed herself.

And then Gareth had turned up: bold, then: different; talking to her as if she was intelligent; teaching her. She vowed that Alan would get the best possible education. And stick at it. She would make him.

The town was too soon on her. It was about a mile from the bus-stop to that part of the estate on which her mother had the maisonette. All the new estates had been put outside the borders of the old town. Hers was more distant from the town centre than most, providing yet another subject for her mother to complain about. Her mother's epics of self-pity were what had driven Marianne from the house in the first place. Her father had left her mother, herself, the town, his job and, as far as anyone knew, the face of the earth two months after she had been born. He was always produced as the first and final cause of the poor woman's lamentations but in her later, rebellious school years, Marianne had taken the side of this absent parent and loudly declared that she could see his point. Whereupon, more woe. It had to be endured though, she now realised, though not for long. She walked through the town, a bustling, satisfying world for some of her friends – for her, a dour, bleak little place, full of malice and wrapped up in layers of small-mindedness. She would not care if she never saw it again.

Her life in the vicarage had changed her much more than she cared to admit. She was bolder and stronger and she knew more. It had given her different perspectives and a sense of the potential to be had from life which school, the factory and her friends had not given her. Perhaps the single difference was that in Thurston she had not been prepared to learn: up in the hamlet she had been forced to learn and quickly.

Now, after many hesitations, she had a plan which she was about to put into operation. She had learned shorthand and typing. Her speeds were now high. She had worked as a temporary secretary several times in Thurston and the references were excellent. The tutor at the night-classes had whetted her appetite for more work and she had decided to set about trying for an Open University degree if they would accept her. Jimmie had said he would help there: she had made him promise to keep her plans a secret – especially from Gareth. She was convinced Gareth would somehow spoil them if he learnt of them. Lately she did not know whether she loved him, feared him or hated him. He was still by far the most important person in her life next to Alan, but increasingly she had felt that she must get him out of her system and lately she had begun to think that she might be able to succeed in doing that. She wanted to live her own life on her own terms and she had spent the last two years building up the courage to take a decisive step.

She wanted to move to a nearby big town. Get a job and a cheap flat. (Jimmie had said he would help there, too.) Set herself up in work. Come home at the weekends and, next year, when Alan was five – school age – take him with her. She would manage. Other women did. And she would be free.

It was midday by the time she reached her mother's. She let Alan ring the bell. They waited on the doorstep as they always did, although her mother would have seen them coming from the end of the long empty street.

She had confided some of her ambitions to Helen, who had recommended Lancaster and offered to help in every way she could. Marianne had felt that this final stroke of luck, this new friend, was just the very push she needed to get herself launched. But she had seen the look on Helen's face in front of Gareth and instantly understood that they had known each other and that it had been important to Helen. Now she regretted having given the confidence.

The door opened.

'Who's little boy are you then?' Marianne's mother asked, peering down anxiously at Alan. 'You're my little boy. Yes you are!' She ignored Marianne. Some obscure grudge must have re-surfaced over the past few days.

II. THE CAMPAIGN

Chapter Ten

(i)

Harold came out of the clinic into sunshine. He stood at the door for a couple of minutes, holding his face up to it like a boy. Its warmth was very welcome on his flushed coarse skin. It was very, very good, he thought, to feel alive. The heat seemed to rub and nuzzle into the very centre of him in a few seconds and he basked in it, a short, broad man, expensively dressed and handsomely groomed, the apparent wealth not being able to soften or dilute the self-made power of the man. He looked up and down Harley Street approvingly. Only the very best. That was how his life was going to be every minute of every day from this second on. He clinched the decision in his mind before strolling down towards his car. Yes.

He liked this part of London. He liked all the rich and grand parts of London but Harley Street with its elegance, which still defied the traffic, its solidity which resisted rash change, and its affluent expertise, pleased him particularly. It was privilege which could be paid for and Harold was all for that. In Knightsbridge and Belgravia, for example, he still had the feeling that what was best was in some way in the hands of an exclusive club, entrance to which *could* be bought (what could not?) but only, for a man, at an expense to dignity which Harold had never quite been willing to pay. He had come from below the bottom rung of the ladder and although he never denied it, he did not like being reminded of it. There were two sorts of wealthy upper-class English people, as Harold saw it. There was one lot which respected what a man did with his own life: he liked them. There was another lot still going by the rules of who your father was, what school you went to, what clubs you had, where your house was: yes, *still*; that pack bored him. He thought they were as out of touch with life as Carmelite nuns or hippies in a commune. They were protected, he thought, and, consequently, kids.

But Harley Street was all right. You wanted the best, you could pay, you got it. On the steps of the clinic, an Arab woman was sitting calmly, clothed in her black djebella, as comfortable as if she had been beside a well in the desert. As he walked down the street, the door signs carried spiky European names; yet the street was still English. The home country kept its grip. Just. So would he; as the pain dug into his gut he merely stopped and waited for it to pass. You would have thought he was smiling, even grinning, at the fine day. He mopped the sweat from his face. It passed.

Harold waved his chauffeur on and pointed. He had a mews house near by just off Wigmore Street. He would stroll along and pick up the car there. The Rolls unhurriedly drew ahead of him and Harold took pleasure in watching it swing around the corner, sleek as a seal. Twenty-nine thousand pounds on wheels.

It was so rarely that he walked. It felt like a special treat. He wanted to know he could do even such simple things. In the brisk autumn sunshine the street seemed unusually clean, handsome, comfortable. Those blue plaques on the walls to remind the curious of the great dead who had once lived there. Those limousines ready to shepherd the international sick now being examined or diagnosed or, more likely, listened to by the best-paid section of the psychoanalytic club. How many tales of horror and panic and loss, he wondered, were this very minute being spun by the twenty-five-guinea hour? And who was better for it? Harold noticed that walking gave you a chance to indulge in stray thoughts such as these. Usually he would not have let his mind dwell for an instant on what he privately considered the self-indulgence of the rich or the self-delusion of the mentally ill. The former, he considered, could be cured by work, sex or sudden poverty. The latter, poor souls – his sympathy was not feigned – were best off with pills and nursing care. Still, he was pleased that he had given the matter a thought. There was so much to think about, so much life out there to be grabbed hold of and wrung dry. So much! There for the taking. The specialists had given him some slight hope but he was not grasping at it. No. Harold Ruthwaite, he said to himself, come in Harold Ruthwaite, your time is up. But not, quite, yet.

He noticed the shops and was in a mood to buy things. He did. The presents were fancifully wrapped. He approved of that. Two were sent by messenger, one to Fulham, one to Bayswater. He took the other three with him.

When he came out of the shop, the sun had clouded over but still he did not hurry. There was all the time he needed to do what he wanted. He only regretted that it was not quite warm enough to sit down at one of those tempting little tables on the pavement and take a cup of coffee, continental style. It would have reminded him of his first hard-won trip abroad and the greedy delight he had taken in such workaday differences as the taking of coffee and cognac outside on a crowded boulevard. He wanted to re-experience all those mundane pleasures. The more sophisticated delights had been too well catered for recently although he had never been a man to worry about excess. He would have both. The plain and the purled, the ordinary and the exquisitely rare, he would once more have all there was to have. As he walked this placid London street and turned into the mews in which he lived he felt a rage for life which almost made him bellow out loud!

It was not only easy to reorganise, drastically, his work-load for the next two weeks, it gave him a kick. They had ordered him to spend two weeks relaxing. Well – in one sense he would do that. As one *urgent, pressing* and *utterly vital* meeting after another was ripped from his large leather-bound diary, he felt more and more free. His new sense of perspective was wonderfully clear. Foreign buyers, the board, a deal in Jersey, meetings with the Merchant Bank, hospitality to those who could be helpful in furthering contracts, even a necessary trip to Cologne, they all sailed away into the wastepaper basket, page after page, like paper boats launched on a river with no thought for what was written on them and only the most meagre concern about their future.

Miss Eliot had come from the office to work with him in the house. He had not wanted to have to make the effort to go into that plush arty-chunky suite of rooms which he thought rubbishy but which clients, evidently, thought to be the height of international chic efficiency. Too much glass and metal for his taste. He preferred the furniture in this little mews *pied-à-terre* – picked up for £7,500 in the sixties, now, ten years later, worth upwards of £50,000. And then there was the furniture – sixteenth- and seventeenth-century oak was what he collected and he had managed to get in just before the boom which had seen prices go up by one to two thousand per cent in the last ten years. It was bulky in the small space but it fitted. Harold was fond of pointing out that most Tudor and Stuart private houses had consisted, in the main, of small rooms in which such furniture as this had been kept. Besides, it made the place cosy. A small and excellent collection of silk Bokhara rugs also pointed out the wealth and taste of the man – or so he had once thought. Now he did not care at all how he showed himself to the world. Miss Eliot and himself sat opposite each other in what Harold called 'Harrod's best' – they had been described as 'spacious armchairs covered in Chinese silk'.

Miss Eliot had been with him for fourteen years. She was forty-two. He had taken her to bed once some years ago. In

Zurich. She had been as accomplished as he had expected. She had also been fierce. In a mistress this would have delighted him: in such a good secretary, he worried. Secretaries as good as Miss Eliot were never easy to find and never easy to keep. He had not taken her to bed again. Neither of them referred to it.

A few months later, her salary had been put up by fifty per cent. Her pension fund was exceptionally well invested and entirely paid for through one of Harold's schemes. Her salary increased handsomely every year or two. Presents at Christmas and on her birthday were lavish. She had some indication that a substantial block sum had been allotted to her in Harold's will but she did not know how much. She stayed and stayed single in a kind of luxury deep-freeze. The will and his letters to his family and his women were the only parts of his business she did not either administer or monitor. She was still, he thought, a hell of a good-looking woman, and her slim legs, crossing and uncrossing as she strove to keep alert and balanced in the spacious armchair, excited his interest in a manner which he had forbidden himself totally after that disturbing night in Zurich.

Ken, the chauffeur, brought them coffee and some sandwiches and then hurried away before the boss changed his mind. Not that he would. 'Old Ruthwaite', as Ken called him in a failed attempt to prove to himself that Harold was somehow in his grasp, 'Old Ruthwaite' was 'a hard bugger but you know where you are'. Harold had told Ken to leave the car, be available on the phone at eight o'clock every morning but consider himself free for at least a week. Ken would moonlight in a pal's taxi to pick up some extra cash – tax-free and easy.

When Harold had shorn away his next fortnight almost to nothing, he offered Miss Eliot a drink. She glanced at the clock. It was twelve-thirty. Her lunch hour had begun. She accepted.

He mixed her a tough martini, took a generous double

Scotch for himself and they tidied up all the loose ends. She gave him the small amount of office gossip that would interest him. She refused a second drink and left before one o'clock. He was sorry to see her go.

Harold phoned his bank, his solicitor and his accountant. He had stood them by to be available in the lunch hour when they would have more time. That took three-quarters of an hour. He completed the hour with two phone calls, one to Fulham, one to Bayswater, which entailed a good deal of listening, agreeing and the making of soothing noises. He doodled throughout.

Mrs. Fernham, who came every morning, had packed the things he had left out on the bed. Just before three he pushed out on to the motorway at Hendon, pointing north to the heartland of his business in Cumbria. On the passenger seat was the new *Private Eye*, carrying a story which could ruin him. It had to be stopped. The short time he had left was not going to be ruined by that lot.

When the next bout of pain came he drew on to the hard shoulder and took the pills. With Scotch.

(ii)

The wind off the sea was bitter. The water itself was even greyer than the lowering clouds. Coal flecked the stony beaches, the scum of carbon drawn up from the old workings which went out for miles under the Solway. Jimmie stamped his feet on the concrete and tried to keep his temper down. The first few days of the campaign had gone badly. Gareth had disappeared on business of his own. Elaine, bless her, he thought, whirled around in a dazzle of activity – Helen had been right: Elaine had attracted favourable attention in a local press which had been starved of her for years – but whenever Jimmie saw her, he was more worried than encouraged. Still, he kept to his word and continued to help her. Helen was proving to be what he called 'a good soldier'.

He had been able to spend no more than a few minutes in her company, which was just as well. He had managed to repress his feelings very successfully. He was good at that, he thought, rather sadly. Most of his time had been spent either organising and 'enthusing' (a word he hated) the local voluntary workers, speaking at meetings all over the constituency, or in earnest conference with Bill Atkinson, his agent. Bill was now the cause of his discomfort. They had agreed to meet at five o'clock near the entrance to the steelworks to catch the workers coming off day shift and Bill, untypically, was late.

It was a difficult constituency to manage. There was this small industrial town; there was a small market town a few miles inland, and beyond that, reaching back into the fells almost up to his own hamlet, there was a massive square mileage of underpopulated countryside which had been flung on to the seat like a large dollop of ice-cream on to a neat little arrangement of tinned fruit. The result was interesting but arduous, for the fell-land demanded more time than the town although the number of votes was far less.

It was growing dark. The flames from the steelworks shot skywards from the tall chimneys like waving flares. At one time this whole coastline had been vivid with industry. Along the coast, Whitehaven had been the third port in England. Scientists had carried out advanced experiments on the noxious gasses from the mines. Hundreds of tall-masted ships had swarmed up the Solway and down again for Ireland, Africa, America. For a brief, wild moment, it had seemed possible that this sliver of land on the edge of the lakes and the fells would be, by some crazy accident, in the van of the Industrial Revolution. But it had fallen away. And throughout this century it had fallen away further and further. Iron ore mines closing, pits shutting down, factories and firms resisting the fat temptations of grants which attempted to seduce them to the far north-west, preferring the fatter comforts of the south or the midlands.

Jimmie loved the place. It was quite irrational. Nothing about it conformed with his view of England, with the expectation of comfort, ease and civilised life which he had been taught and eagerly learnt at school and university – indeed to those of his background, this bare, grimy, forlorn industrial town was more foreign than France, more distant than Tuscany, more bizarre than the Levant. But he, truly, loved it.

Though why, as he looked around, he did not know. Perhaps it was the very intractability of the place, its challenge, its contradiction of everything he had been bred and fed for. The look of it, for a start, ought to have depressed him. The shops were what his mother would have called 'garish' or 'too common'. People in the streets always seemed demoralised, the street itself alive only with flying fish-and-chip papers. There was dereliction in the upper stories of those Victorian shops and in their crowded contemporary windows, too many 'special sales' for comfort. Around the town, the usual post-war estates stood on convenient ground, bare of centres, shops, pubs and style, he thought. The centre of the town was as scooped-out as a quarry. The rows of terraced cottages which had once sheltered the miners had been knocked down – not all, but most of them. The operation appeared to have been carried out by a runaway bulldozer with a perfect eye for the ugliest mess possible. The new light industries which had been persuaded to build around the area stood well back from the town and above it, occupying vast acres of prime land they had been given ridiculously cheaply, as superior and secure as the old white planters' houses in the Deep South in the early days when Uncle Tom kept his mouth shut and his mind on picking cotton.

On top of all this was the wear and weariness of three generations of disappointed expectations. There had been ups and downs everywhere during the century but this town had missed most of the ups. The affluence which had seeped over Britain in the fifties and sixties like a film of alluvial silt and had at best brought useful comforts and deserved necessities to so many, had only thinly covered this town: like the water which came so swiftly and so shallowly up the Solway and as swiftly withdrew. On the other hand, the unemployment which now bit into the country bit here just as hard as anywhere. Jimmie worried about the young men, straight from school on to the street corners, jackets flapping in the eternal wind, glancing up and down the few streets for occupation. He had made their employment his chief task – not without success in bringing rather more factories into this part of the world than had been expected, although there were still significantly fewer than were needed. The problems were profound: the industrial revolution had started here, heaved its detritus over the land, and fizzled out. The technological revolution lived abroad and, it appeared, refused to come and stay in Britain. Between the nineteenth-century furnace and the silent electronic humming of the twenty-first, the town stood abandoned in the present, dilapidated and, at this moment, as often, bloody cold.

Yet whenever he came to the place, Jimmie felt exhilarated. Perhaps it was because of the amount which had to be done. There was so much, the struggle would be so hard, there was no time for weakness. Or again, there was something Jimmie thought admirable, even he would say, noble, in the complete sense and pursuit of life which went on despite the undoubted grimness of the environment. Allotments flourished, and pigeons of course, and whippets and Rugby League – the culture so long nurtured and now, he had noticed, so glibly parodied by the new smart young metropolitans – but, as he well knew from the flurry of invitations which came at him every year, there were clubs, associations and groups for scores of activities. It was as if the townspeople had agreed that the bingo hall, the old cinema, the dance-hall were no more than a façade, or just the token identity of civic gregarious enjoyment. The real stuff went on in unexpected spots speckled all over and about the town – behind tight curtains a rich life for more than before. That was important to Jimmie: it was his gospel: that the majority should be well nourished so that they could live fully.

It was the people who exhilarated him. Meet them openly and they met you openly. Don't cheat and you were honestly served. Be straight and they would stick with you. He thought of them constantly in such sentences. Jimmie's life had been transformed by the people here. When he had first taken the seat in the forties, he had stepped into it as tentatively as a timid bather into the North Sea. Then he had plunged in and found a warmth and goodheartedness which he had feared might not exist outside the close comradeship of war. His own tight, involuted and complicated inner nature longed to be lapped by such open fellowship and found some peace here. Arms were thrown about his shoulders, he was teased for his accent and his manner and his clothes; he was argued with and defended, watched, bought drinks and tested, discussed, weighed up, attended to and, finally, he came to be accepted. When he lost the seat, there were men up to his house the next morning to sympathise and apologise and swear it would never happen again, as it had not. Jimmie said very little about his constituency outside his family, and little enough there now, for sentimentality was regarded as worse than slander and yet his affection contained a thick seam of sentimentality. He was not ashamed of it. It was here, he thought, that any England worth a damn in the future must come from: from those who had had to struggle, those who knew what a hard day's work meant – the speech rolled on and would have rolled on for ever had he ever let it out of his mind. The people here, he would say to himself, were as articulate in their emotions as he was in his words and at times it seemed to him the perfect matching of two dissimilar elements which stood in equal need of each other. He worked for their interests as conscientiously as any MP in England. In the full sense, he served them and they gave him his life. The awkward questions – the power of the big Unions, for example, or the Party's line on immigration – tended to be avoided. Race was not a local issue, and Jimmie's firm liberalism was rarely challenged.

Bill arrived twenty minutes late, which for Bill Atkinson, ace-agent and punctuality-fetishist, was a disaster. Yet, Jimmie noticed, as Bill trotted over the flattened waste-land which constituted the free car park, he looked rather pleased with himself. Bill had been a prop forward in professional Rugby League and was built very short, very square and very thick-muscled. He managed the neighbouring constituency as well as this, worked fifty-one weeks a year, had no direct power, took abuse and blame when local elections were lost or local issues unresolved, was the last to be praised when things went right, was paid rather less than a schoolmaster and was, generally, as happy as Father Christmas. With a magnificently broken nose.

'Sorry. Sorry.' Under one arm he carried a package of pamphlets which he put in his hands and tossed over to Jimmie as if they had been a rugby ball. Jimmie was used to this trick.

'They'll be coming out in a couple of minutes,' Jimmie said, referring to the factory workers. 'Where's the mike and the amplifier?'

'Had to leave them.' The two men talked as they walked across to the gates.

'Why?'

'Weston and his' – pause – 'hooligans were hanging about. Trying to' – pause – 'find out where I was going so they could come and bust up the meeting like they did yesterday.' Bill was a Methodist and tried very hard not to swear. He could not, however, entirely stop himself and whenever he was upset, would leave gaps for the swear-words. Eventually, when things got very bad, he filled them in. Weston's extreme so-called 'leftist' views tested him severely.

'So you gave them the slip.'

'I wish I could give them something else as easily.'

Jimmie grinned. The sight of Bill restraining himself while Weston and his few young scrawny supporters – most of whom came from London or Manchester or elsewhere – had harried him the day before had been good to watch. Bill itched to wade in and 'sort them out'. Jimmie had restrained him. Weston and his gang, longing to be set upon, beaten up, martyrised, stoned, anything, had chanted their disruptive taunts continuously and the meeting had had to be adjourned. If word got round that Weston was out to break up all of Jimmie's meetings two things could happen, neither propitious. People would stop coming, or there would be a fight and a scandal. Bill had been right to spend time dodging them this evening even if it had made him late. The extreme left could gain publicity only by leeching on to the meetings of one of the two main candidates. Jimmie, as the MP, was better news value. Also, of course, he represented all they thought most bourgeois, corrupt, reactionary – some would go further and say fascistic – about the present Labour Government. Moreover, Jimmie defended himself when attacked: he refused to pack up his tents and move on. An ideal target in a world where pusillanimity was increasingly often dignified by the jargon of 'low profile' or 'keeping your cool'.

'Well done,' Jimmie said. 'But how am I going to make myself heard? The factory noise is quite loud. My voice is like sandpaper already.'

'And the night is cold,' Bill concluded. 'That's why I brought our latest pamphlets. You just tell them to look at the pamphlets. Advertise your next meeting. Tell them to look at the pamphlets and make it snappy. They'll thank you for that on a night like this. I'll hand them out.'

Bill was fascinated by pamphlets. He was a master printer

manqué. He spent any leisure time he had fiddling about with layouts for this 'literature' as he unblushingly called the party lines he distributed. The printing machine in the front room of the small almost derelict inner-city two-storey terraced house (which Bill called 'GHQ') was, for him, something on a par with the printing presses of Fleet Street. He would make adverse comment on the big national dailies and weeklies, speaking as one printer of another. His pamphlets were his joy.

As might be expected they were DYNAMIC! They had PUNCH! They HIT YOU IN THE EYE! There was never any ambiguity whatsoever about THE MESSAGE! What was always plastered clearly across front and back was what they were trying to SELL! Smudged photographs, all of which looked as if they had been discovered in an old tea-chest which had been flooded in a long ocean voyage so that everyone on them looked like what Bill called THE ASIAN PROBLEM!, were always placed proudly in the centre and generally pointed at by black arrows.

Bill kept up a steady patter all the way to the gates but clearly there was a gobbet of big news he was holding back. Jimmie, to tease him a little, did not press. 'The Tories turned out a beautiful pamphlet for making the schools go back to being Grammar and Technical. They didn't use "Secondary" – note that. Lovely piece of work, though. They used three colours and that' – pause: his friend the Tory agent who turned into a sporting enemy on these occasions – worthy of a silent expletive – 'must have found a new way to do photographs. Very good. Anyway. We'll have to reply. I've got the figures for you. Near enough same number of A-Level passes proportionate – percentage-wise – as the old Grammar – more kids taking Os and CSE – that sort of stuff. Headmaster's very pro-comprehensive so he's helping us but he doesn't want it known. All this television stuff about comprehensives has got people worried. You'd think to hear some of them talk that schools before comprehensives were lily-white and royal blue and full of little ladies and gentlemen scholars. Half of those who moan can only read the *Sun* by moving their lips. There's that. There'll be another dirty-tricks department hand-grenade from that Liberal.' Bill never used the names of Jimmie's main opponents. Weston, irrelevant as an opponent, was such a particular nuisance that Bill was forced to use his name, which he did, venomously, as a small release of his feelings. 'He says we said we were against the council purchase of that Town-end land for a new estate.'

'We've already explained our position on that twice!' Jimmie groaned. The town council had a Labour majority and some of his worst problems came from having to defend and justify decisions which they had made and with which he totally disagreed. The complexities, innuendo, dark talk of corrupt practices, altercations and apologies which had piled up over the proposed purchase of a narrow strip of land by the sea for pensioners' bungalows already comprised a file as thick as a government bill. Jimmie had no heart for the battle. He was, indeed, secretly against the purchase. The land was part of a proposed nature reserve for sea-birds which was part of a long struggle to bring interest and life back to a coast blasted, blackened and made sterile by the mines – Jimmie had initiated the coastal rehabilitation scheme and pressed its minor but essential, modest but fundamental, claim for years. Moreover he sniffed that there *was* some dirty deed going on between a certain Labour councillor who had to remain nameless and a certain builder whose name was planted like a victorious flag on every new building plot in town. And there was no immediate money for the building, little prospect of any, and so the land would be bought and allowed to become a weed-garden. Finally and perhaps most importantly, Jimmie favoured the building up of the centre of the town and had worked hard to persuade the council and private builders to put people back in the empty middle of the place. It was, to him, almost gruesomely symptomatic of everything wrong with the country – in its ideals, its economy, its sense of itself and its provision for the future – that the one area constantly neglected was the middle, the very centre which people took for granted without yet fully realising that it was almost dead and gone. Yet he was forced to defend and even, God help him, explain and justify this purchase.

'I'm saying nothing more about that,' he added abruptly. 'You know my views. So does Hatfield and his mob. They're playing silly b's. I can't pick up the pieces for them and I won't.' Jimmie decided to stick.

This put Bill in an awkward, even a critical position, for his daily life and his effective future depended in no small measure on the continued support and goodwill of the Labour caucus on the council. But he had no hesitation in stating his own position.

'I agree with you,' he said. 'The Liberals can take a running jump.' He laughed quietly. That would be a tidy little rumpus! 'The *Star*' – the local paper – 'took a poll this morning in the High Street. Thirty-four per cent for us: thirty-six per cent for them: nobody else in it. Not nice, that, them in front.'

'We always knew we had to catch up.' Jimmie distrusted polls but was affected by them. Not nice at all.

'This meeting tonight,' Bill began – but they were up to the gates and the hooter sounded out like a lighthouse foghorn. Jimmie looked around almost desperately.

'They'll never see me,' he said, 'there's no light.'

'I even forgot the' – pause – 'orange-box,' Bill said, unhappily. 'Sorry.'

The gates swung open. Why did they have to be closed? Jimmie had asked the manager who had laughed and offered no answer.

'Tell you what,' Bill said, 'you need your voice for tonight. It's in the school and it'll be comprehensives, comprehensives all the way there and prices in the shops all the way back. And I've squeezed in a Rugby Club Supporters Club raffle and social after it – you'll have to speak there as well. So just stand here and shake hands and I'll hand out the pamphlets. They say it all.'

The men were beginning to come towards them. Jimmie resisted Bill's orders.

'I'm not a blasted presidential candidate! I *never* stand and shake hands! I don't believe in it.'

'It's freezin',' Bill said. 'Anyway. They'll forgive you. Besides,' he grinned, unable to keep in his great secret another second, and handed Jimmie his very latest pamphlet – 'Look at *that*! What about *that*!' He nodded and went across the way to distribute the latest news.

Jimmie had just time to glance at the screamingly bold headline and then the steelworkers were on him. The embarrassment was soon swept away. The men were happy to say 'hello'. Many of them wished him good luck. One or two stood aside for a word when the crowd had gone by. Out of the factory they came, the works glittering in the night lights, and on into the town's streets already lit up for the autumn evening. Hand after hand, face after face – why should they vote for him, he kept thinking. Would they vote if the business about Harold flared up? Harold was four days late – and Jimmie was almost frantic because he could not get a copy of the magazine up here. Elaine, and Gareth's unnerving presence: Harold's absence: the so longed-for steady, sensible help and support of a knowledgeable woman, Helen, who had led to the revelation of a weakness he thought he had overcome: all this and the lag in the polls, the grubbiness of the campaign, all helped to depress him. The open, decent faces coming out of the factory only depressed him more – for he felt he had let those good people down. What on earth could he do for them? Hello – Good Luck – Thank you – How are you – I'll vote for you – Thank you – You've my support again – not the wife's though! – Good Luck – Hello – Thank you.

'Extra! Extra!' Bill was shouting, enjoying his own din. 'Come on lads, everyone a winner! Read all about it! Prime Minister to come here to speak for your Labour Candidate, your present Member of Parliament, Jimmie Johnston! Prime Minister to come on whirlwind tour!'

That was Bill's news.

Chapter Eleven

Elaine had to be taken home before the evening meeting. She had a headache. She had been canvassing for most of the day. Jimmie was not surprised she was down – impressed, indeed that her initial impetus had shown little sign of collapsing. Gareth was nowhere to be seen. Helen had joined Jimmie at the meeting. Later at the Rugby Club Supporters' party, she too had begun to flake badly and by the time they arrived back at the vicarage, just before one, she was asleep on his shoulder. He paused in the drive and waited a while to enjoy the pleasant sensation of her body relaxed and reliant on his. Then, most gently, he tugged at her shoulder and she woke up and smiled. He wanted to kiss her but forbade himself.

Upstairs, looking through her bedroom window, Elaine saw the two of them enfolded together in the car and felt a pain in her chest as sharp as a cut. She went back to her bed, unwilling to watch further, already ashamed of looking for the worst even though she thought she had found it. She dared not put on the light for fear they would notice and suspect her of spying. She lit a cigarette in the dark, sat on the edge of the bed, her bare feet cold on the cold linoleum. Alone in the room where his mother had died. That fact always tormented her when she was upset.

Jimmie had noticed Harold's car parked beyond the front of the house, convenient for a simple turnabout, but he did not hurry. He felt he had waited so long now: he would delay it a moment more. It was a clear night. The stars were hard bright, Helen was happy to stand beside him, letting him hold her around the shoulders as much for support as for warmth. They looked at the other planets and said nothing. She had understood, he thought: for her too, it was over before it had begun – no more now than a brief romance in the head. But what Might Have Been?

At the foot of the stairs he gave her a business-like kiss and let her go her slow, swaying, wayward route up the stairs.

When he opened the study door, Marianne fluttered out like a bird darting out of a cage. The black hair, the lovely young breasts, the spring of mischief in her cheerfulness: a lovely woman. She pecked his cheek, danced a couple of steps and then bounded up the stairs like a boy, catching Helen at the top, another break in her stride to say again 'Good Night' and down the corridor to her bedroom.

Jimmie walked into the study: and cocked his head.

'She thinks I was flirting with her,' Harold said. 'I'd just told her she was exactly the sort of girl – tarts we used to call them in my day without any sense of a dirty second meaning – exactly the sort of tart I would have been head over heels for when I was younger. And I offered her a considerable sum of money to marry me or become my mistress – anyway spend my remaining years with me. She thought I was joking. But she was intrigued. Then you came. How are you?'

'Tired, very: hungry – no, past it: and where the hell have you been?'

'On my way? Scotch? There's just about enough. You're rather low. I'll send another couple of cases along.' Harold was red-faced, from the drink, Jimmie assumed. He looked over-strained: not unusual.

Jimmie pulled off his coat, put down his over-full and bursting briefcase and all but fell into the armchair. The two armchairs were the only comfortable seats in the study. There were three wooden ladder-backed chairs, a hard chair for his grandfather's desk — which was a large mahogany structure built at the beginning of the nineteenth century for the labours of a scholastic heavyweight wrestler — one or two side-tables, stools, library steps and on every wall, books. Jimmie's grandfather had been the collector; his father had added a big section on local history and local literature. Jimmie had added nothing. His own political books and the necessary dictionaries, encyclopaedias, thesaurus and other cribs were kept in his bedroom. He rarely worked here: he could not settle down. Harold liked this room better than any other in the house. It brought out a rather cirloquacious playfulness in him. Especially when he was a little drunk, as he was now after a tiring drive up the motorway, a foul dinner in a fashionable restaurant near Penrith and the discovery (which he should have anticipated) that his own house was only half-ready for his arrival and entirely gloomy, the gloom thickened by the incurably servile house-keeper, a friend of his dead mother's, who had made a profession of 'adoring him like her own son' — 'and,' Harold would say, 'unfortunately for me, treating me as if I were. And have you seen that poor sod?' Drink was, as often, the best cure for all that and he had taken it manfully. Jimmie took a good pull on the Scotch.

'I needed that. The beer at that Rugby Club was disgusting. Why do the nicest people always get fobbed off with the nastiest things?'

'No one else will touch them.'

'Good Scotch,' Jimmie said, raising his glass in thanks. 'Exceedingly.'

'Nothing nice about me, I agree,' Harold said. 'But there we are. Nothing nasty about the Scotch. Buggered?'

'Yes.'

'You know you work too hard, are exploited, they don't need it or deserve it or even want it. You know all that of course.'

'Of course.'

'Saves me a lot of useless chat. Another of those?'

'Please.'

Harold filled up both their glasses to the top, settled down in his seat and tossed over *Private Eye* to Jimmie.

'You'll need that Scotch. Cheers!'

Jimmie read the article quickly. He read it a second time slowly and very carefully. Then he sat back and let it drop on to his lap.

'Much, much worse. Though—' He could not hide his relief.

'*You* aren't further implicated, no.'

'*Does* anyone take it seriously?' Jimmie felt wide-awake again. 'Isn't it just the commuters' *Comic Cuts,* a kind of cheap dustbin for the droppings of tired journalists?'

'*I* take it seriously. They got Poulson. Locked him up. They got Dan Smith. Locked him up. Cunningham – as Labour a man as you, my friend – locked him up. They nosed out Slater. That was serious.'

'Yes, but they were guilty men. Their track record on the whole – on the whole, Harold – is pretty poor, isn't it? You only remember their few successes. And who cares, fundamentally, about gossip?'

'If I go, you go.'

Jimmie tossed the magazine over to Harold's lap. He could see his friend was half drunk and very worried. His own growing relief at the discovery that he had *not* been named in the current article must not be allowed to obscure the clear duties of friendship. Harold needed help. He would give it.

'Don't be such a thug, Harold. My advice is – ignore it. Have a sense of proportion – sense of humour.'

Harold read from the small print at the back of the satirical magazine. ' "In 1964, Harold Ruthwaite, still, as he informed his local newspaper, 'too bloody far from my first million', went into the fascinating game of contract bribes – a more lucrative version of his well-publicised affection for contract bridge – one of the many socially acceptable tactics he thought it necessary to employ as he crawled up the social ladder towards the pathetic respectability he had always yearned for." Sense of humour?' He smiled. 'And that is only the beginning.'

Jimmie dare not admit that the magazine often made him laugh aloud. He took a guilty pleasure in it. But, 'Swallow it – like rice paper,' he said.

'I see.' Harold held Jimmie's gaze and then, very deliberately, he tore *Private Eye* to shreds. He held out the wad of paper to Jimmie. 'You eat it, then.'

'I am trying to help.'

'Eat it!' Harold hunched himself further forward on his chair and held out the pieces of paper in cupped hands: for a second, Jimmie thought of the sacrament of bread being offered to him.

'Please **don't** do this,' he said.

Harold did not move.

'In the war,' Harold said quietly, 'in North Africa, I made a man eat his own shit once. You never got to hear of that. Officers were kept clean.' He sat back in his seat. Jimmie noticed that he was sweating heavily. 'Conduct unbecoming to an officer – if I'd been one.' He let the pieces of paper trickle through his hands on to the worn carpet. 'We'll leave somebody else to clear up the mess, shall we?'

'You're badly shaken, aren't you? More upset than I'd anticipated.'

'You just won't see it, will you?' Although he knew he had had quite enough, Harold decided to have too many. He got up to go for another; Jimmie shook his head. Harold could feel a bout of loquacity coming on him, the sort of lengthy self-justification or self-advertisement he allowed himself with no one but Jimmie. Jimmie's capacity to absorb the confessions and apologies, the secrets and miseries of others, was limitless. Harold poured himself half a tumbler of Bell's and filled up with water. He began to talk even as he walked, rather stiffly, back to his chair. 'That snobby little clique of paper bullies is going to pull me down if it can – and I'm not being pulled down by anybody, so listen, Jimmie, excuse the strong reaction, it's the sound people make when they see the nails go in. Let us begin at the beginning. Why have they dropped you? I'll tell you why – because you're one of them. I'm not. I'm a crude feller, I'm vulgar, successful and pushy. I'm a bit like all the Englishmen of the past you never actually get round to talking about, Jimmie – the sweatshop merchants and industrial swine who made us rich – the cruel bastards who scared the hell out of Foreigners from Shanghai to Amsterdam – all those unpleasant sods who fail to appear in your Peter Pan History of England. I like your speeches, Jimmie, truly I do. You can bring a lump to my throat. But to go out and *get* the lucre that makes the world go round you need a lump somewhere else. All you state-subsidised socialists pretending to be the voice of the working class – what you've done is grab the microphone! None of you has ever *made* work, *made* jobs, *made* money, come up with "the goods" – interesting word that, eh? No, you can shake your head until it rolls off, old son, but you can't ignore what I say. You'd like to ignore it. Just like your father, the great Canon, ignored all those poor little Asiatic bastards actually working in the rubber plantations where he deposited his famous inheritance and where it vanished – an Act of God, that, if ever there was one. There's a lot you like to ignore. You ignore Elaine when she talks – except maybe when she talks about her father – oh how *interesting* that the chap made brass horseshoes in his spare time. And *what* a pity he was killed by cheap pit-props. Made on an English rubber plantation, no doubt, by somebody who went on to add lustre to the land. You were probably at school with his son. What I want from you is for you to say, publicly, without making a fuss or major point, that, yes, you were and are associated with me. That's all. Just say what is in fact so. No more.' He paused, wiped his sweating brow, grinned and drank half the glass. Then he said, quietly, 'Yes, Jimmie, I am upset. I haven't climbed a mountain just to disappear down a bloody crack.'

'I shouldn't have come on to that Board,' Jimmie said releasing an anxiety which had nagged him relentlessly since the first rumours of a campaign against Harold had begun, a few weeks before.

'Too late now.'

'I thought I could be useful.' The urge to justify himself was irresistible even though he knew he ought to be helping Harold. 'I wanted to be in a better position to bring work to the area. And after all, there is nothing intrinsically wrong with Members of Parliament being employed in industry at whatever level. Not if they work at it.'

'You certainly did that, old chum.'

'Collecting directorships is disgraceful, of course. No wonder we're so badly managed with so few dunderheads acting as directors on so many Boards.'

'Couldn't agree more. But *you* put in the hours.' Harold was now pretending to be more drunk than he was. He realised he had slightly gone over the top and was forcing himself back towards sobriety. It was possible to do this although the ravages the next morning were all the greater.

'I thought we were getting some employment for the youngsters.' Jimmie spoke wistfully.

'You signed on the dotted line.' Harold waved his glass merrily. 'MP, MC, OBE – is that the right order?'

'Harold.' Jimmie hesitated. He liked and trusted Harold. He detested and, if he could, avoided personal unpleasantness even though the future cost of his evasion could be high. He simply did not like life to be a matter of people in combat, disliking each other, wanting to hurt each other. All his character was against it. It was a measure of his will and his moral strength that he faced up to such confrontations daily in his political life: but he had no heart for crossing private swords. 'Forgive me for asking this again. I realise that we've talked it through once, I know that I should be in a position to form my own opinion – though you know how baffled I am by your company language! – but it has snowballed considerably more than we anticipated. Transport House has been on the phone of course. You've seen the "no comments" spattered in the bottom inside columns of some of the papers – nothing much but there are sounds of a juggernaut beginning to creak into action and it could destroy all of us. There's immense public feeling at the moment about corruption – and I share the public's anxiety – and of course at election time it's highly inflammable. What truth is there in what they say?'

'We've been through that.' Harold was sullen. Jimmie felt the strength of the man, sitting there, indisputably powerful and alive – and dangerous.

'If you don't mind.' Jimmie, sure that he was doing the right thing and therefore sure of his ground, settled down to elicit the information he wanted. 'We'll have to go through it again.' He lit a cigarette: the pipe was too cumbersome when he was so tired. 'Putting it very crudely, what could they get you on?'

'That is putting it very crudely, old friend.'

'Sorry.' Jimmie let the pause lengthen into a silence. It was Harold's turn to speak and he waited.

'That bloody schools contract.'

'The one they mention?'

'Yes.'

'In that case you have nothing to worry about, have you?' Jimmie was almost owlish in his earnest solemnity, Harold thought, like a young – still young – schoolmaster, terribly relieved to clear up a rather unpleasant mess. 'The enquiry went into it at great length. Three new schools cracking up in a six-month stretch – it was a miracle no one was killed – but the plain fact is that the enquiry cleared your company of all charges of negligence.' He sat back, stubbed out his cigarette and reached deep into his jacket pocket for the comfort of the pipe.

'You thought the enquiry was thorough?'

'Certainly. And so did the press. They were around like vultures of course. They sifted everything. It's not a bad method, you know, of pinning down accountability.'

'It's not much good either. They never bothered to track down all the associates and subsidiaries of our company, for example. Looks as if this lot are on to that.' Harold waited for the implication of that to sink in. Somehow in that leather-lined room, all the eminent, good and merely wordy writers of previous ages tucked discreetly but enduringly on the shelves, everything warm, civilised, cosy, the rank stink of an illegal act seemed out of place – altogether impossible, simply not to be entertained. 'And if they follow their noses,' he went on, putting the glass, still half full, to one side, 'they'll be led in a circle. Back to *us*.' It was a hundredfold more complicated than that – but Harold was too tired to do more than make a gesture at the truth.

'So I *was* an accomplice.'

'If you want to look at it that way, yes, you were.'

'Why didn't you tell me at the time?'

'Would you have thanked me?'

'Yes.' Jimmie was sure about that. 'I would.'

'I doubt it. Anyway, the point's merely academic.' Harold took out a cigar and cut it neatly.

'We'll have to re-open the enquiry.'

'It's academic, Jimmie. You were an accomplice as you call it in your worried way; so was I. But neither of us could have done anything about it. Neither of us is responsible in any sane sense. What this *Private Eye* investigation can do is to stir up a lot of mud, throw a lot of shit and splatter us all with it – but when the matter is looked at calmly, then it will be generally accepted that we were not, I repeat, in any sane sense of the word, responsible. By that time, however, your reputation and mine will be zero minus quite a lot.'

Harold then patiently explained the network of companies which connected that for which Jimmie was a director with that which had been primarily responsible for the load. By the time he had finished, Jimmie was more than ever convinced of his culpability.

'We will have to re-open the enquiry,' he repeated. 'Whatever the consequences. If we suffer, then we suffer. As you say – and I believe you – in the end it may well prove academic – but that's not the point.'

'You know the point, Jimmie, do you?'

'As far as I'm concerned, yes.'

'Boy Scouts of the world unite?'

'Perhaps. The point is to find out who was responsible. Whether they deserve blame is a separate matter.'

'What happened, Jimmie,' Harold said, lighting his cigar and as it were coming alight with it, his features suddenly animated, shaking off the glazed, aloof pose which had been an effective mask to watch all the smallest nuances of Jimmie's response to his news, 'what really happened down in the small print outside your kindergarten Parliamentary committees, was a series of cock-ups, small deceits, panics, buck-passing and genuine mistakes from the quarries in Jugoslavia where some terrified Croatian foreman worried sick about his quota let the load through the factory which closed down a fortnight later, all the way along the line to those schools, ignored or shuffled on or undetected all along the line. The mix *was* at fault. The enquiry was right about that. But if you are to blame, so is President Tito.' His apparent frankness hid the real accusations: insufficient reinforcement, bribery of inspectors: it could indeed blow them all sky high.

'I shouldn't have been a director on that Board in the first place.'

'Why not? You're always on about the virtues of a mixed economy! You put your effort where your principles were. You were very useful, Jimmie. Very persuasive.' Harold smiled. Little was sweeter than uttering unimpeachable flattery which was also sarcasm. 'The civil servants love you, of course. You're on their side. One of the spenders. I'm the opposition. One of the earners. You were a big help to the area – you did what you intended to do – you got some parts of some big firms to come up here, they would never have come without your pressure, Powells were certainly tilted just that necessary bit by you – you were helpful with the Whiteheads of course – that wasn't so successful – but Flexi Limited, they were impressed by your arguments. I still think they'll come up here when the Government next decides to let them keep a bit of what they earn.'

'Yes.' Jimmie put aside his pipe. His early relief had dissolved into further anxiety. But at least he felt he could sense a way through now. 'It was silly of me to deny that I wanted to be on the Board. For all sorts of reasons as you know. One mustn't wring one's hands or wash them like Pilate.'

'*You* needn't worry over-much, old lad.' Harold drew on the cigar carefully: it was one of the very best that money could buy and he savoured every millimetre. Jimmie always refused, in case, he said, he 'got the habit'. 'I've squared it all up as far as you're concerned. There's no way they can touch you. You weren't even associated.'

'But I *was* associated.'

'No you weren't. That's official.'

This time it was Harold who waited for Jimmie to break into talk. He watched the man's face – so open. Relief, anxiety, more relief, puzzlement, indecision, relief, and finally, a rueful smile.

'You can't simply bundle away my moral obligations,' he said, eventually. 'You can't just rub them out like an old debt.'

'I just have.'

'What about yourself?'

'I've done nothing criminal.' Harold spoke in the level steady tone he used when it mattered. No bluff, no games, straight. 'Compared with the record of blundering mis-calculations and miseries brought about by, say, the Ministry of Housing or the Ministry of the Environment with which I have had dealings, I have been a one-night amateur in a brothel. If it's "official" it's immune. Our great officials sanction tower blocks that either fall down or slowly drive people insane. They get gold medals for it – they are never brought to book. They rip the heart out of some of the finest cities and towns and villages – and end up in the Honours List. They multiply and increase their own bureaucracies so that every year we have more and more doing less and less. That would be my speech, Jimmie, if I was standing in this election. You might like to use it in the next few days. It would pick up some votes.'

'You've left the point.' Jimmie's voice was firm. 'What about yourself?'

'Of course I've blotted a few lines in my day: who hasn't?'

'So. If that's all. Why are you so – clearly – worried? Who'll take any notice of this campaign against you?'

'People like me. They'll say – stand back – he might go to the wall, don't get in the way or you'll be hurt too. Most business people are comically terrified of the press, any printed gossip, any aspersion, however silly – they feel they're on the run in this society and they all act guilty before they're accused. We're all guilty, Jimmie. Only some of us get sentenced.'

'Well. That's debatable. Why *are* you so worried?'

'It's come at a bad time.'

'Bad news always does.'

'Nice one.'

Harold carefully nudged the neat fat cylinder of ash from the end of his cigar. It landed plumb in the middle of the ashtray.

'You are worried, aren't you?' Jimmie persisted.

'I want out. I want to sell up. I've been laying plans for some time. You don't sell out of my kind of business like a sweetshop. I want a price. This little duststorm could scatter the customers. Or it could put me over a barrel.'

'But if it's what you say, it'll blow itself out soon enough. A year or two.'

'Too late.' Harold spoke briskly, once more in complete control of his faculties. 'I didn't want to tell you this but I should have realised I would have to, I've just been told I've got about a year. Two or three if I take things easy but sod that. There's one more test to do, they aren't a hundred per cent sure, but they seemed pretty convinced to me. Now – hold your horses – no sympathy for Christ's sake, I don't deserve any – with one wife buried, one, thank God, divorced, one son shagged out somewhere in California, two daughters well set up with reasonable husbands, houses and all mod cons – I, Jimmie, feel like going out like a rocket. OK? I want to get my hands on the money I own and blow it up until it falls over my head and buries me six feet deep in one-hundred-pound notes. I want to travel, drink and be in the company of interesting women. I would also like a permanent and what the Yanks call personable companion. I'm on the lookout for one of those. But what I need most of all, James, is a buyer. Or two. I'm not proud. And so I need a little strategy to give me a breathing space. This' – he tapped the pile of torn *Private Eye* with his foot – 'could – in the short run – hurt me just as much as it could hurt you. And for both of us, the short run is critical. Right?'

'I'm so sorry,' Jimmie said. He felt ashamed of his selfishness. 'I'm sorry,' he repeated.

'Another Scotch?' Harold got out his seat nimbly and went across to bring the bottle over to Jimmie. 'You need it by the look of you.' He poured the whisky into the half-empty glass. 'You should go for a check-up.'

Chapter Twelve

Helen recognised in Elaine symptoms which she herself had had. After she and Gareth had split up she had suffered from something variously described and diagnosed as 'nervous exhaustion', 'severe depression' and 'a sort of breakdown'. It was not uncommon, she had been told, comfortingly, especially for young women who had strained to lift themselves out of their background and do well academically only to find that life after university would not fit into the same protected and clearly defined objectives. In her worse times – and there were times when the world seemed to crush the life out of her mind – she thought that every social and intellectual gain had been matched by an emotional loss. She felt poorer, not richer, and somehow cheated.

But the problem was – and she suspected it was Elaine's problem too – that she had by no means been sure she was 'ill' at all.

One of the ways in which Helen had held herself together during that time had been to make an effort to learn the names of flowers. Her father had had his allotment but she had been the indoor type. She had found this simple self-instruction to be one of the surest aids to sanity.

Gareth was way ahead of her up the fell. She could not keep up and also she wanted to note what she could recognise. So far she had seen golden-rod, lady's mantle, betony, white deadnettle, the berries of bird-cherry and rowan, lousewort and wild myrtle – all couched in the browning decay of fern and the last purple tinge of bracken. She had noticed a rabbit, a badger's hole and a kite soaring slowly upwind along the fell-side. The men who did hang-gliding locally came to this fell to get the benefit of that smooth upward current. It could be treacherous. In midsummer a young man had been swept up by the wind, hung, like the kite suspended, floated over the other side of the fell and then the wind had dropped. He had fallen on to the crags which faced the south side of this seemingly gentle hillside. Crags which were testing to experienced scramblers and frightening to those, like Helen, who were subject to vertigo. The drops between them were quite deep. The man had been killed instantly.

She saw Gareth now, standing on the cairn, waving wildly to her, beckoning her on like a cheerleader before a football crowd. He had noticed not one flower: his hectic pace had forewarned all the wild life which hid or whipped away before he came near.

It was the fell on the north side of which the vicarage was built. Helen could not quite see the building for it was tucked into a jut of land which constituted the first steep rise of the hill. She had never yet been to the top. Jimmie had had to set off to Carlisle at 7 a.m. in order to meet the other local Labour man and confer about the arrangements for the Prime Minister's visit. She had finished her work in an hour. Gareth, whose appearances were as random as his disappearances, had invited her for a walk.

Marianne had watched them go.

Helen had felt the eyes of the entire household on her. But Marianne was the only observer. Elaine was in the middle of what was to be her first long sleep for about a week – a marathon sixteen hours out of which she woke deeply refreshed; her determination seemed to be bringing results. Mrs. Burns was baking: it was Lionel's day off.

Helen did not begin to relax until Gareth had pushed on ahead of her and behind her the house disappeared from view. Alone on the hillside, she began to feel strong in herself. Gareth's unexpected insistence on her company had seemed as arbitrary as all his other comings and goings over the past few days. Helen was very nervous of him and so far very wary. No one, though, could resist a walk in such a place on such a day.

Cloudless, virtually windless, the morning was suspended, she felt, almost exactly at the point where summer turns to winter; a high-mid-autumn day. It was as if the planet hesitated before taking that inevitable decision. Helen loved it, the sense of peace which came to her, however derided by her friends and ignored by most of her contemporaries, the sense of religious tranquillity in landscape which had seen man on to the earth and would outlast him, rocks effortlessly older than the oldest man-shaped stone, colours, shapes and angles of vision which the finest pictures only captured in part, this unspecified, almost swooning at-one-ness which her well-trained mind would laugh to scorn, could, she had found, ensnare and enchant her completely. Whether the words to disparage it were personal or historical or psychological, whether, that is, her state of mind was dismissed as mushy, Wordsworthian or merely 'projecting', she experienced a sense of placid goodness in the width and beauty of the natural scene, and that gave her both strength and hope.

High on the cairn, Gareth did a war-dance and she moved towards him.

By the time she reached him she was quite worn out. Gareth was even more tensed-up than usual, she noticed. He squatted on the cairn like a witch-doctor, glancing at his watch, glancing at the sky. He had lost weight in the last few days. The lean darkness of the man was being eaten away, she thought, and a clenched hardness was emerging. The flask was never out of hand's reach. Yet as he smiled down at her gasping efforts to conquer the last few yards of loose and awkward rock, she felt him envelop and enliven her. If only he had not loved her so hard she could have helped him – as help was what she felt he needed. But he was still dangerous to her hard-won peace. It was as if Gareth could search out that flicker of dearest life in her mind and by his mere presence inflame it.

'There.' He jabbed out his finger like a curse. 'Not there – there – over there.'

She turned and looked. It was a wooden bench he was pointing to. She nodded but did not intend to go down and examine it. Now she was up she would stay up. She plodded on to the cairn, the small of her back aching, her legs weak from the unaccustomed strain. Gareth hopped down from the cairn, landing neatly, and picked his way swiftly down to the seat while she at last reached the very top and immediately took out a cigarette to celebrate. She had to cup her hands to light it: the breeze was quite fresh on the tops.

'Listen!' Gareth stood on the bench and bellowed up at her, a bright red and white football scarf at his throat.

'Listen!' he repeated. He meant look. She did. He began to read, peering down for every word and then flinging them up at her like stones. 'Put-here-by-his-grateful-parishioners-to-commemorate-the-late-Canon-Geoffrey-Alfrick-Townley-Johnston-who-used-to-climb-upon-this - hill - to - commune-with-nature-and-be-nearer-his-God.' He laughed with pantomime fiendish glee. '*His* God! *His*! Isn't it priceless? *His*.' He was delighted with it.

He loped up to her. Helen wondered how hard he had been pushing himself and for what. She had plenty of time for such wondering. Gareth was in an unmistakable mood of grandiloquent egocentricity. She was his audience as she had been so often in the past: and she felt herself yielding.

'A happy vicar I might have been,' he chanted, 'a hundred years ago, to preach upon eternal gloom, and watch my walnuts grow. Know it? No? George – *Road-to-Wigan-Pier* and *Socialism-Without-Tears* – Orwell. Outside every upper-class radical is a conformist screaming to get in again. Sit you down.' He looked at his watch. 'Miracles happen on

148

this spot. Where you sit once sat a King and saw before him as you do the Promised Land. There is time for the full pageant, there is time for the panoptic presentation of the land of Britain as seen from this cairn. There is time, in short, dear heart, for my performance.'

'Clot.'

'Flatter me not.'

'Why can't you just be quiet and look?'

'A good question. Next question.'

'Can I look quietly before you begin your guided tour?'

'You can. And don't disparage the guided tour. All of us up here do it as naturally as the citizens of London turn into walking street-maps in July and August. But I will be silent while you imbibe one impulse from a vernal whatsit.'

He sat and glared at his watch.

Helen was only partly successful in ignoring him. Her eyes merely skimmed the view but that was enough to cause her to draw in her breath in appreciation. Before her, to the south, was the short, ragged patch of Bassenthwaite in the valley bottom flanked on the left by the fine smooth force of Skiddaw rising up gigantically from the Caldbeck fells like a great whale heaving itself above the surface. On this bright day, its sides glowed deep brown, the bracken smooth and clean, small trickles of snow in the high crevices, Ullock's point sharp below and straight in front of her. Beyond that she saw that magical enfolding of valleys, from Borrowdale and over down to where she could notice (but not name) Great Gable, Scafell and even the cone of Helvellyn, the interconnecting spokes of fell all working towards that point which stood, as many had noticed, like a hub at the centre of this ice-age complex. As she turned west and over Bassenthwaite fells there was the sea, a glittering cream colour, as still as a mirror, flashing the slight haze in the sky back at the sky. And from there as she turned it was hills, the hills of Solway, Criffel, hills of the Scottish Lowlands and, still turning, hills of the Pennines until she came back again over

Blencathra to the massive snug shape of Skiddaw. In the valley to the north she could pick out one or two of the villages and the sun lit up the fields so brightly they looked, she thought, like painted fields, so neat and regulated, so toy-like tidy – the hedges flattened to thick pencil lines, the patchwork shapes gaining an easy regularity with the effect of distance. The dips and slopes, the swamps and falls all smoothed away as time smooths a memory. She could have looked and enjoyed the act of looking for much longer, en-joyed her own indulgence in this panorama at once spec-tacular and modest, homely and grand, a place to gaze on and a spot to live in.

Gareth, though, was in charge. He took a quick drink. 'Time's up!' he announced cheerfully, interrupting her. 'You, I notice from that dreary dreamy look, have gobbled up the view. You should have bought a little Claude glass to help you. Or a sketch-pad to note down the picturesque. Or you would have done, once over. Now it's better to buy a postcard. I agree. Now then.' He scrambled up the cairn and squatted on it, goblin-like, his face only a few inches from her own. He tried to kiss her; she pulled back. His breath was whisky-proofed. 'That is the surface. What about the heart of the matter? This is my story, this is my song. Aaaiieee!'

Slowly he rose up and extended his arms, throwing back his head to look at the sky. Indeed he did look like a wild thing, she thought, and fought to subdue the old feelings which his tauntingly flamboyant and hugely affected actions quite unfairly released. He stood still and taut. He turned in a full circle and then came to a stop.

'Now hear this,' he began. 'Imagine a giant compass. A Sci-Fi post-Wellsian monstrous Cape Canaveral compass with its bodkin pronged in here,' he pointed down to the top of the cairn, plumb below his body. 'Deep in here, deep in the rock which might be the rock that stretches out to what might have been Atlantis. And that is so. So. In your im-agination, draw, with the compass, a mighty circle, draw, with this stupendous compass, that miraculous never-ending straight line, that symbol of symbols, the circle, and look – look' – he pointed and indeed melodramatised everything he could, 'reaching out to the nethermost and uttermost parts of the realm, to the honking gulls of Orkney, to the black cruel rocks of Cornwall, to the friendly silt of Old Father Thames at Tilbury and up to the Wash – draw then this mighty circle and you will find upon this very spot, on this ancient pile once crowned (true, this) by a rare prehistoric pile levelled thirty years ago in error by a company of Boy Scouts out to Tidy Up The Hills For Britain – you, here on this spot eerily named Catlands – Cat-lands, mark that, and remember that just down in Carlisle yonder was Arthur's finest and final court and Merlin's best and last hour – see the raven swirl – what dies? – yes – so – put in the compass, draw the circle and you will find that you, here, are in the very middle of these islands, the centre, the very plexus of Britain. And listen – listen around these visible bare kingdoms. What you can see speaks to you. North over the tongue-tied Solway Firth to the swelling hills of the sensuous Burns, hear him? East – there, to the Lowlands and laalands of Hogg and Scott and reivers making up lies for ballads for scholars for learned books of lies on lies and listen! Down there – over the sullen Pennines, deep in the sex-held earth-hug implant of the inturned passion of the three wild moon-lit sisters Brontë and Lawrence, D. H., their sun and natural heir – you hear? – South, in and out those mountains like the echo of a Stone Age Zeus – Wordsworth. Wordsworth indeed – what, you may ask, are they? Still, so, now, here, encircled by British spirits who have turned tongues into print and print back into tongues, dead mouths moan on and look! West – where the land is bright to – *there* – you can see it! Symbolic beyond all toleration or sense of taste, proportion or credibility – the Isle of Man. *Man!* But wait!' Gareth's mock show had wound him up to full pitch – that was what she had loved, Helen knew, and still could – this abandoned, even mad, leap from himself into caricature he would seem to believe in totally, this compulsive performing. And now, as he looked carefully at his watch and at the sky, one finger to his lips like a soldier urging his fellows to keep utterly quiet, crouched on the cairn, she did indeed wait and wonder what he had ready, what surprise he was going to pull. He began again very softly. 'And each morning, from East Anglia – oh Anglia, not Angels but Angels One Five – from the fen-sucked bogs east of Ipswich, at this minute precisely, our masters send out young aerial gladiators,' he sprang up, looking at the sky, 'technologically trained to correct all the frailities of Icarus, Super-Icarians in tiny jets practising low-level flying for the day when we shall bomb the world to extinction, streaking low level across England, waking children, disturbing schools, driving cows and sheep to panic, over the heavy shires, over the fallow fields of the old industrial valleys, across the bone of rock and emerald greensward – here they come! See them!' Four Phantom jets came screaming out of the east, as Gareth had said, flying so low that Helen ducked. Gareth shouted wildly at them. 'All hail! All hail! White man's magic works juju again. Tarzan rules, OK? Bound for the *Isle* of-Man!'

These last words were drowned by the rip of sound which tore apart the silence and let in a brutal injection of man-made noise which burst several small, tender, minor but irreplaceable threads of vein around the eardrums of the two humans a few score feet below. Gareth saluted the first two planes. He dropped on one knee like the mad hero in a war film and machine-gunned the second two. Then they were gone and it was silent. They paused.

'Pretty good timing,' Helen said.

Gareth jumped down, stood beside her, dropped all – as far as she could tell – pretences and poses, put his arm about her shoulders and kissed her cheek.

'It is very good to see you,' he said. 'To see you, very good. And you still taste exactly the same. Appley.'

'Do you talk like your radio programme *all* the time now?'

'You always knew how to hurt a guy! But true, Oh Queen. One of the reasons I've just packed it in. Letter posted. First Class Mail. Like me.'

'Your mother will be very disappointed.'

'Bullseye again! You always said you knew me better than I know myself. I'll miss the programme for her sake. In a way which I'm sure you'll understand, that programme was the best way I could find of talking to her.'

'It's a pity you've given up before you've made your point.'

Gareth kissed her smackingly on the cheek.

'The time for that is past.' Gareth moved away and began to pick up the smaller stones and throw them aimlessly down towards the crags where they bounced and ricocheted.

'For helping people?' she asked – and he smiled in recognition of her Sunday-School ma'am seriousness beneath which, he knew, was someone as passionate as he had ever met.

'Helping people – Holy Jimmie's way – is castrating them. Employing them, letting them loose after loot – Harold's great solution – always ends up as exploiting them. Give them back their own lives and let them make what they will.'

'In your party of one.'

'Oh, I've branched out lately.'

Helen hesitated. She was afraid to reveal her true feelings but saw little merit in continuing to conceal them in this private exchange which Gareth, she knew, could keep up for hours if he thought it served his purpose.

'It *is* nice to see you, yes. But I won't,' she said firmly.

'You always saw through me, didn't you?'

'Like a one-way mirror.'

'No reflection on your taste.'

'I always feel that I should do what that man did in the Cocteau film we once saw,' Helen said. 'He walked through that mirror, walk through you and find out what's really going on inside you.'

'Even less than you see. Still the doubting Helen.'

'Oh yes. More doubts. That's about all the progress I can report.'

'If you want something,' Gareth said, 'I told you. Go for it and hold on to it.'

'You told me that.'

'Even if it does things you don't approve of – that's not your business. If you've got what you want – be content. Let the rest just happen.'

'You told me that as well.'

'So you won't.' He coarsened his tone. 'Open-air screwing is good for the complex.'

'Let's go back. I am in Jimmie's employment after all. Or the State's. Or both. I've work to do.'

'Oh dear. I've led you off. And I'd only hoped to lead you astray. Poor Tom.'

'Will you tell your mother about the radio programme?'

'Eventually.'

'She relies on it. You know that.'

'No she doesn't. *No she doesn't!*'

'Still as lost.'

'Another lame duck for you? Her? Me? Not me. Things are on the move, Helen; the show's on the road now. Let's go.'

He was angry with her. She thought it was genuine and she guessed it was because he was worried about Elaine. Anything to do with Elaine, mention of anything which would upset her, upset him. She had noticed that before, but over the past few days it had been unusually clear.

She decided that she would tell the truth. The strain of not doing so was too great. The day was perfect. The view and her feelings on going up the hill surely signified well. And what was the point in lying to herself? However much she distrusted him, felt betrayed, thought him bad and cruel, she was aroused by him and she went across and kissed him.

'Of course I came here hoping I'd see you,' she said, wanting to please him again as she had once done. 'I should never have left you.'

'True confessions?'

'Yes.'

'Well? On this bare rock?'

'No.' Sex had not to be that easy this time. For him it might be no more than the generous seal on a friendship. For her it mattered deeply and fundamentally. 'No,' she repeated.

He nodded, without rancour.

'So let's go!' he said.

'Downhill.'

'All the way.' He took her hand. 'Be my Jill?'

'Fool.'

Chapter Thirteen

(i)

Three hours later, Gareth was about half-way to London. He pulled in at Keele for petrol, ate a sandwich standing at the service hatch and then took off again. If he kept up a steady eighty miles an hour – which you could get away with – he could make it from the vicarage gates to the flat in Mornington Crescent, London, in just over five hours.

Five hours and twenty minutes. Three minutes slower than two days before. This would be his last trip to the flat. Everything else was primed. There was just this last necessary job.

His flat was in the basement of a Victorian terraced house. It was so barely furnished it would scarcely merit that replete word in an estate agent's handout. It had been totally designed for minimal attention and the instant comfort of Gareth. Nothing else. A small neat kitchen. Bathroom, similar, with shower. Bedroom: a large double bed, one sidelight, white cupboards and wardrobe along one wall, one chair. Living-room: a settee, a lot of cushions, some bookshelves and a stereo. He had removed the books the last time. This time he took out the stereo and transferred it to the boot of his car. Blankets were already there to keep it safe and firm. He transferred his record collection to the back of the car. He took out the few other valuable or personal belongings. Then he looked round. There was not one other thing in this place he gave a damn about. He had worked very efficiently. It was ten to five.

Upstairs there lived a young man who had a job with the COI. He was never in before six. In the maisonette on the top two floors there was a rather rapid turnover of Indians: they had never bothered him nor he them. He could commit a murder with little chance of being heard.

He hoped it would not come to that but he drank a stiff measure to steady himself. The blackmail had gone on for more than three months now. It had to be stopped.

At five o'clock, Peter Fraser, a fashionably coiffured, edgily arrogant boy – man – looked late teens but his face mid-twenties – rang the bell and looked around nervously although there was no one to be seen or to see him at the foot of the basement steps. As he waited, he smoothed his hair, tugged at his tight, figure-hugging leather jerkin, moved uneasily in his expensive new jeans and rehearsed his lines. It always made him jumpy. However often you did it, he thought, you had to be careful. It was a nasty business. Paid very nicely though, thank you. He rang again, gaining confidence from his own impatience, punching the bell hard. His face, as he did this ordinary act, from slim became vulpine, the features so often referred to as faun-like by old men who thought they knew how to flatter, became vicious. All the affectations of sophistication were nowhere near enough to hide his greed.

Gareth opened the door, slowly.

'*You* took your time, didn't you?' Peter said fussily. Then he put forward one leg, rather daintily. 'Well? Do I get in or do I have to pay a forfeit?' Gareth stood aside to let him pass by. As he did so the stench of after-shave almost made him retch. 'So why do I have to come slagging up here?' Peter asked and turned, pouting.

Then Gareth hit him.

It was much more of an even match than Gareth anticipated. Fraser's feyness hid a lovingly exercised body. But Gareth's anger and his violent need to get his own back outweighed the defences of the other man. They fought, in that narrow corridor, without a word. The scuffling of their feet, the impact of blows, the heaving of breath, made up the sound of a frightened and caged animal in a frenzy to be released. A banister rail was kicked out and Gareth grabbed it as a weapon. In the fight he had lost himself: there was only the consuming lust to hurt this other body as much as he could. He raised the piece of wood like a club and brought it down hard on Fraser's skull. The man screamed. Gareth hit him again, twice. The man began to sob, quietly, and gave up, huddled on the floor. His face was bloodied. Gareth stood up, went to the bathroom and stood, shaking, wanting to be sick. Eventually he heard the door open and shut and he looked at himself in the mirror and wondered whom he had become.

(ii)

Gareth walked slowly across the darkening Hampstead Heath, still shaken by the violence he had given out and taken. He went over the fight again and again in his mind as he trudged up the steep short slope of Parliament Hill, and he flinched at the blows, felt the thuds of his own punches, saw the bloodied face, clenched in his hand's memory the wooden rail he had gripped to raise and hit to kill. And he faced the truth: it had exhilarated him, the violence, it had made him wholly alive.

So there he was, way down the slippery slope, he thought. For he was abnormally lucid and saw absolutely clearly what such a reaction implied. Which was that he had finally lost all contact with the constraints and habits and beliefs by which he had lived out his life so far.

Now on the crest of the Heath which halted here, like a frozen rolling wave poised over London, spread murkily before him in the autumn twilight, Gareth breathed in deeply and weighed up his isolation.

It was no new thing. Ever since he could remember he had

felt isolated and all of Elaine's tender, possessive, delicate, thoughtful affection had not penetrated the chill solitary self which would not be soothed. Only in the love and sex of the early times – especially with Marianne – had he been able to break out of this cell of himself. With Jimmie there had never been anything but hearty gestures – whatever Elaine had hoped and willed, he had felt a stranger from Jimmie, from his touch, his voice, his manner and yet, obedient to the law which says that sons must love their fathers, he had blamed and trained and distorted himself for years to be a proper son. But once he had – so culpably late, he thought – learnt that he was no natural son of the man then a lifetime of bewilderment and pain and hatred gathered into a thrust of resentful fury for emotions betrayed and deceived and, as he saw it, a way of living imposed which had never fit nor fitted him for anything. All his past became meaningless.

Now as he wandered down towards the Highgate Ponds, he saw himself having nowhere else to go but the extreme political position which at least gave him something to grasp. He remembered being on the Heath one afternoon a few months previously when he had seen an old friend from University 'exercising the family', he had said, 'two kids, two dogs and the self'. They had been out of contact for some years and chatted, caught up, gossiped, the man cheerfully envying Gareth's 'interesting job' and 'success' and Gareth feeling more and more cut off from everything the man represented – a family, a steady job, a sturdy pessimistic tolerance, a feeling, it seemed to Gareth, that the world he lived in, in London, England, now, was a sane and hopeful place.

To Gareth it was a place of neither hope nor sanity. As he walked along in the darkness on this licensed common land still capable of mimicking the real countryside in the middle of the metropolitan spread, he considered for example where he might go should he stay in London that night. To one of the literary/gallery parties around town where still, as ever, the tittle-tattle of reputations would be minced through the martinis. Or to a small smart claustrophobic restaurant with someone who might be or want to be on the show: there to eat dubiously prepared food and eavesdrop and be eavesdropped on, be fobbed off with steeply over-charged wine and presented with a bill for two which was half the take-home pay of a labourer in a factory. Or seek out the latest fashionable club – the dashing smoothness of the 'in' places in Mayfair, the aesthetic-grot of the latest spot in Covent Garden, the commercial squalor of Soho where punk rockers and public school fans would honk away in Cockney and cut-glass English until it was impossible to know which was which and who was pretending. But it was all a pretence. Gareth thought, the whole ticket he had been sold, the whole myth which came in like a lion in the mid-fifties, that Britain was now on the road to being more egalitarian with fairer opportunities for all, with the class-system on its way out and the time not only of academic merit but also of the recognition of all other talents being in, with the pop stars pointed out as 'princes' (the giveaway) and quoted as evidence of serious social changes and the cult of football – itself a fine game, but being used to promote a sickeningly matey myth of one society. All that and more was a sham. Nothing that mattered had changed a bit, he thought. England was wrapped in privilege as tightly as the feet of Chinese women were once bound in bandages. It was still cancered by class. It was a society for officers and superior clerks, all of whom he felt were most effectively championed by the liberal and to Gareth utterly nauseating hypocrisy of Jimmie, who was enough in himself to turn you into a nihilist. Indeed, now, in his mind, seething with a viciousness which was almost as out of control as his body had been in the fight, Gareth felt, blackly, that he could understand nothing. Make no sense out of life. Find no purpose in it.

His head was filled with hatred. He sensed the tell-tale cold sweat break on his brow and he bent forwards, put his hands on his knees and retched, finishing off what had begun in the bathroom of his flat. A very large dog went past him followed by a woman who called out its name, possessively, warningly, 'Tommie! Tommie! Good Boy!'

What if he tried to rape the woman? What if he did the vilest things he could imagine? What was there to stop him?

The bloodied face of Peter lurched yet again into his mind. That haughty, yobbishly-chic Dorian Gray face, that slender huddled figure he had wanted to beat to insensibility. He shuddered to recall the lies and failings which had held him to get involved with such a corrupt slug. And the sex – the drugged bitter sex with the man in an utterly vain attempt to stop the blackmail. His entire life had been wrenched off its path and himself left with nothing but mockery, saturated in shame and self-loathing.

But no – none of that now. No more shame. No more guilt. No more remorse. No more hope. Follow the call of the strongest drum, he thought, follow it, follow it even though it leads you into the middle of darkness because the only alternative is to ossify into habit, into a daily routine, into a life and times he wanted to wreck.

'Tommie! Tommie!' she called out in the fading distance, and Gareth began to walk back over the black grass, over the hump of the hill and down towards the city, down, immersed in the sense of evil which spread throughout his tense exhausted brain like a poisonous root.

(iii)

Throughout the previous night, Marianne had had hot and faintly shameful erotic dreams, with Gareth as the protagonist. She had woken up furtively and gone to the window for air. She had seen Gareth setting off up the fellside with Helen. She stood back so that they would not notice her. How long had it been since he had peacock preened and pranced himself so cockily for her? The sight of him there was the impetus she needed. The prick of jealousy enlivened her resolution.

It took a lot of courage for her to seek out Helen later that morning but she did it. Helen was on the phone in the study. She waved rather too gaily, Marianne thought, and pointed rather too despairingly at the telephone. It was Bill, who had taken a great liking for Helen which he expressed by giving her the benefits of his tactics and plans almost hour by hour. Helen's rôle was to say 'Yes, Bill' or 'I see', or to laugh. Curious, because what he really appreciated about her was her political knowledge and her grasp of facts and figures. He would commend her on this, but rarely, in his company, give her any opportunity to display it. Every few sentences he forced in a reference to the Prime Minister, casually, to show that he was not over-impressed. As usual, it was Helen who had to terminate the call with a promise that she would meet him at GHQ at four-thirty to take out a covey of young canvassers who had turned up from the local comprehensive to help Jimmie after his successful speech in their hall the other evening.

'Sorry,' Helen said. She offered a cigarette which she knew would be refused. She sat behind the desk. Marianne faced her in a hard-backed chair, like someone being interviewed for a job. By the time the awkwardness of this positioning had made itself apparent to Helen, it was too late to do anything without causing an even greater awkwardness.

'How it is going?' Marianne asked this out of politeness. She wanted Jimmie to win, of course, but her question to Helen was quite transparently no more than a way into a conversation. The very formality of it put Helen on the alert.

'Quite well.' Helen decided to pay out a good stretch of line. 'Bill's pessimistic which is worrying. Jimmie says he's always like that but I'm not so sure. The national polls are showing us catching up fast with the Tories. The Trade Figures were good, the reserves are up – whatever *that* means for the voter on the council estate God only knows, but better cheerful headlines than not. The cuts in beer and petrol taxes were a bit obvious, but so is the Chancellor. But here, inside this particular constituency, I can't say. Bill says a lot of others are finding it much more difficult than usual to read the local signs.'

'Ordinary people are interested in prices,' Marianne said. She had long ago been helpfully bullied into such discussions by Jimmie. Before then she had fled or simply stayed silent whenever a subject came up which was outside the domestic gossip which was the stuff of her mother's life and had been hers. Now she was not afraid to put forward her own opinions however trite they sounded. ('The only important thing,' Jimmie had told her, 'is to say what you think. Then you will be listened to by anyone who counts. Those who sneer or reject what you say will be stupid, snobbish or both and beneath the notice of any intelligent person.')

'Is that *all* they think about?'

'Most of the women, yes. They *have* to. They have the families to feed after all. Whenever you go shopping all you hear is how this has gone up and how that has gone up.'

Helen's shopping was done in less than an hour once a week at a large supermarket near her flat. She ate sparingly and budgeted shrewdly.

'I know,' she said. 'But surely something else must preoccupy them?'

'Whether their children will get jobs when they leave school. Whether there's anything left over for some sort of treat. But chiefly it's prices. To them, that's the heart of politics.'

'And that's it?'

'It's quite a lot.' Marianne suddenly felt compelled to defend those unnamed women she had been so carelessly describing. 'What do you think they should be thinking about?'

'Put as bluntly as that, it's not an easy one.' Helen grinned. 'The Middle East? The EEC? Devolution? I agree, all a bit meaningless.'

'*You* think about those things,' Marianne said, suddenly a tinge of envy in her voice. Helen *was* so much better educated.

'Maybe I have nothing better to do.'

Marianne had also learnt when a topic was considered to be finished. Besides, she had a purpose. Helen, plainly, was waiting for her to declare it. In the infinitesimal amount of time before she spoke, she was aware that she was being scrutinised in a way in which she had not been regarded before. She could sense as if she saw it in operation that Helen was assessing how strong and how important and how sexually binding was her link with Gareth. Helen, too, in that same brief space of time, knew that Marianne was fully aware of her previous commitment to Gareth and her present confusion over him. In both bases there was a turbulence difficult to disguise and it connected the two women closely. Yet above that, perched on these powerful feelings and questionings, there was the saving grace of self-restraint.

'Were you serious about Lancaster?' Marianne began.

'The job or the flat?'

'Both, really.'

'Yes.' Helen computed all the possibilities and still emerged with a positive answer. For whatever became of Gareth, he was not likely to end up in her flat in Lancaster. 'Whenever you like.'

'The sooner the better, I think,' Marianne said, 'I'd like to give it a go while Alan's *not* at school so that I'll know exactly where he is and what he's doing all day. If it works, then I can start properly when he goes to school.'

'Are you sure you want to be as far away as Lancaster?'

'I've thought about that a lot.' Marianne's face was intent. It made her look like a troubled schoolgirl, Helen thought, and she felt old for it also made her look so innocent. 'Otherwise it would be Carlisle or Penrith or Whitehaven, wouldn't it? But the trouble is that they're all around here. It wouldn't be any different from what it is now – do you see?'

Helen nodded. She saw someone bravely trying to take their life in their own hands and do what they wanted with it at some cost. She saw Marianne facing up to difficulties of a kind she herself thought she had surmounted years ago. But in the younger woman's earnest quest her own progress stood criticised.

'I've been taking driving lessons from Lionel in Jimmie's car,' Marianne went on. 'Just around the lanes here but I've got the hang of it. There's a bit of money put by. I'll be on the lookout for a second-hand car. It only takes about an hour and a half on the motorway, doesn't it?'

Again, Helen's contribution was simply to nod. She realised that Marianne had come not so much to make a request as to talk out her plan of campaign and, as it were, confirm her resolution by hearing it spoken aloud and approved. Helen was used to this rôle and did not make the mistake of sitting back. It was necessary to give an air of participating fully.

'If I could stay with you, then, for a few days, while I have a look around for a place of my own. I *could* get one just by going down and taking pot luck for a day or two but that would be a bit daft, I think; I'm not used to living on my own so I want somewhere easy and somewhere I like, otherwise I'll get depressed. I'll only be there through the week so the more I think about it the more I think I'd be better off in digs after your place and look out for a flat but only take it if I decide to stay there and bring Alan.' She paused.

'Alan's the problem, isn't he?'

'In one way.' Marianne's solemnity was flashed away by a possessive smile which came and went quickly. 'But I wouldn't be without him for a minute. I've never regretted having him, you know. And I needn't have . . . had . . . gone through with it. Gareth.' She was glad to have found a way

165

to bring him into the conversation: she noted Helen's reaction, which totally confirmed her own instincts and deductions. So that was that. 'He said that he could arrange things very easily. Nobody minds nowadays.' A stray thought surfaced and lodged hard. 'In fact most people round here would have thought a damned sight better of me if I'd had the abortion rather than the baby.'

'It was – rough, was it?' Helen asked the question almost dreamily. From the pressure behind those last sentences, she guessed, accurately, that Marianne had little if any opportunity to relieve her emotions on this matter. She could see the reassurances of Jimmie and Elaine preventing the revelation of any pain, smothering the anxiety with such complete understanding that it never had the chance to release itself.

'It was.' Marianne paused but she had to go on. In her mind's eye she saw a caravan-train of incidents. The taunts of her mother; the 'she's an easy lay' attitude of the boys she had known as they joked about her big belly or, later, offered to give Alan a ride on their shoulders if his mother would give them a ride in return. The utter loneliness of being in the middle of the town with the baby screaming its head off and the realisation that she was, as it seemed, eternally and totally responsible for every breath the infant took. 'I didn't know – "how to handle it" is what people say but it was worse than that.' She paused but only to set herself more directly on course. 'I didn't know what I was supposed to do. Was I supposed to try to make him marry me? Was I supposed to go out and look around for other fellas? Was I supposed to dump the kid with my mother and go back to the factory as if nothing much had happened – that's what my mother thought I should do. And after all, there's supposed to be no shame in it nowadays. So they say. But there is. There's a lot. Maybe I just made it up but I don't think so. I daren't look anybody in the face and when I did it was just to dare myself. For the first year or two it was shaming day and night.'

'What did Gareth do?' Helen ought to have held her peace but could not.

'Oh.' Marianne stopped abruptly as if hitting an obstacle at full gallop. Off-guard she spoke out of that part of her knowledge she had wished to conceal. 'You know Gareth,' she said.

Helen had not the heart to deceive.

'Yes.' She hesitated. 'He would seem to be giving you everything you wanted except the one thing you needed. And yet whenever you thought it over or talked it over his actions and reasons were as watertight as a perfect alibi.'

Marianne nodded. She had put it perfectly. Helen went on.

'He would talk a lot about freedom and individual responsibility and mean it, because it means a lot to him, but it would always have a way of ending up so that you were left stuck in the mud and he went on his way doing exactly what he wanted.'

'That's right.'

The women were silent. Enough was known now.

'What does he think about this Lancaster idea?' Helen asked.

'As you'd expect.'

'Go ahead with his blessing?'

'That's right.'

'Do you think you can make it work?' Helen asked.

'I don't know.' Carefully Marianne regrouped about the subject which ostensibly had brought her into the room in the first place. 'But, you see, it's that or – as far as I can see – cooped up like poor Elaine, forever busy doing nothing until it gets you down. If I don't do something for myself – by myself – nothing will change. I'm worried about Alan, of course, but if I love him and do everything I can to look after him, then what else can I do? After that, he'll just have to take his chance like everybody else. Don't you think?'

Helen nodded and kept her memories in check. She flared with envy and regret at this woman and her child. For *she*, very sensibly, had taken Gareth's advice five years before, and chosen abortion.

(iv)

The two women in the car appeared strikingly different and yet in so many ways their roots and emotions had been similar. But to look at them you would have concluded a world of difference. The older woman, elegant, casual, lovely, eager, amused; the younger woman, stiff, plainly dressed, severe-looking, tense: the cavalier and the puritan in female form – English types apparently recurring yet again.

Elaine was determined to come into the constituency with Helen and there was nothing the younger woman could do but agree, although Elaine's *allegro con brio* form of help in some way offended her. Helen tried, doggedly but unsuccessfully, to be fair. Somehow Elaine's heroic efforts at assistance mocked the pedestrian work of herself and others. Among the other helpers, of course, Elaine was regarded as gallant and rare – beyond criticism. But Helen thought she regarded the whole campaign as too much of a romp. It was partly the spill-over of the extraordinary energy Elaine seemed to have found. Helen chided herself for the glumness which led her to be such a killjoy but it was useless to deny it. Elaine, Helen thought, not only did not take the election or the canvassing in the proper spirit or seriously enough, she doubted very much whether Elaine either knew how serious it was or what 'serious' itself was. She fought hard to put down these uncharitable reflections as they drove down to the coastal plain and along the narrow road into the town.

Elaine was perfectly aware of Helen's dislike and ascribed it to guilt because of the affair she was having with Jimmie.

She was determined not to let this spoil things between them. She still told herself that she and Helen were friends.

Helen drove her 1971 Mini with care.

'Well now!' Elaine embarked upon a conversation with a great launch down the slipway of good manners, Helen thought, and wished she wouldn't. Here it came! 'What shall we talk about?'

Caught short, Helen laughed. Elaine joined in. They stopped as abruptly as they had begun and Helen gave off the powerful impression that manoeuvring the Mini along the empty afternoon road required every iota of her mental energy.

'It's not as hard work as I thought it might be,' Elaine said, 'and much more fun. I almost feel that Jimmie has been depriving me over the years.'

'I'm sure he wouldn't do that.'

Elaine noted how smartly Helen leapt to his defence. Panic again threatened her as it did so many times a day. 'He might!' she said gaily, quickly. 'He has hidden depths. Is that what I mean? Hidden something.' No, she thought, that was too obvious, too portentous to leave in the air; Helen must not suspect that she knew. She had to keep Helen's friendship, she thought, *had* to, though why she did not know.

'You're certainly working hard,' Helen said, dully and for something to say. Her mind was still on the conversation with Marianne and still hovering about her resurgence of feeling for Gareth, which would have to be denied or released but could not be ignored.

'So are you.' Elaine found a safe subject. 'Is it all helping your thesis?'

'It will, I suppose. Yes. I suppose it will.' Brilliant riposte, Helen thought, not so much in neutral as neutered.

'I like Bill, don't you?' Elaine went on, her face lit up as she talked about the campaign. 'He's rather like Lionel.

There's something about those West Cumbrian men – when they talk to you, it's like new-baked bread.'

Even Helen had to yield to the yearning in that last sentence. There was a quality in Elaine which could move her to sympathy despite her strongest wish not to be drawn. She glanced at the older woman and was, as always, touched by the fragile beauty of her look when she was in this dulcet reverie. No wonder Jimmie had married her, she thought.

'More canvassing this afternoon,' Helen offered, cheerily.

'Oh dear! Still, it has to be done, doesn't it? That's rather how I feel about the whole thing: "Oh dear! But it has to be done." Don't you?'

'Not really.' Not at all! Why, Helen wondered, could Elaine not resolve this mix? Now the working-class beauty, now the neurotic, now the lady of the house, now the evanescent, original dreamer: Helen was tired by these constantly changing facets.

'Bill's eldest boy is a doctor. Did you know that?' Elaine asked.

'He told me.' Absurdly, Helen felt jealous of her relationship with Bill: for he too, of course, had been charmed by Elaine's efforts.

'*That* must be a good way to live. Healing people.'

'Listening to a lot of hypochondriacs, fuss-pots and all the flotsam of decaying humanity wouldn't be *my* idea of bliss,' Helen said grimly.

'Gareth wanted to be a doctor once. When he was little. He was always bandaging his toys. Sometimes I thought he used to break them deliberately so that he could bandage them up again. He was such a lovable little boy.'

'Here we are again,' Helen announced, rather unnecessarily, as they drove into the town.

' "Happy as can be." That's how the song goes, isn't it? Don't help me ... Yes, I remember the lines. "All good friends and jolly good company!" '

Elaine laughed aloud and Helen, unaccountably, wanted to scream.

(v)

She hesitated outside the door in the dark for some minutes. His car had come back half an hour before. It was almost three o'clock. Coming down the backstairs she had heard every creak magnified ten times over. But as she stood and listened she could hear no movement although two others were awake in their beds as restless as she. She was almost sick with nerves.

She opened the door. It was pitch-black. She felt along the wall for the light switch and flicked it on to get her bearings. Gareth sprang up in his improvised bed and she noticed the cuts on his face, the bruised cheekbone and the wad of handkerchief around his right knuckles before he told her to turn it off. She stood once more attentive, confused by his anger at so slight a thing, puzzled by his battered appearance, jostled into mundane calculations at odds with the clear and urgent impulse which had taken her from the safety of her bed to this possible humiliation. She had to take a chance.

'Well, well, well,' he said, finally, and she went over to him.

He took off her dressing-gown. She was naked. She could feel his hands trembling as they went over her body roughly, coarsely, hurting her but always exciting her, feeling her intensely, working her to excitement. He said no more and all the time she was aware of the tremble of his hands, his whole lean, hard body, as if a deep tremor of fear or rage were fermenting inside him. She reached out to kiss him, took him in her mouth, felt him strain and lift her, hold her and then turn her face down, take her thighs, splay them open and penetrate so far she thought he would reach her throat. She buried her face in the pillow so as not to scream.

She reached out to hold the frame of the sofa as he slid down to his feet and crouched over her, his hands passing fiercely under her body, rubbing harder the hard nipples, caressing the clitoris until it ached for more forever more. He gripped her shoulders and pressed them down hard as he thrust harder and harder into her as if to exorcise some demon which had to be brought out and destroyed. His hands went tearingly down her back and she scarcely felt the scratches which would, she knew, the next morning rise up as welts. He could be so violent that she was afraid. At times, she had known, he could be so tender that his fingers were lighter than her own, so gently taking her that it was like slipping into a pool without causing the smallest splash. Or he could, as now – but never that she could remember so drivingly fiercely – attack and dominate her so that she held on and wanted it to hold on forever as he seemed able to do.

With his left hand he reached down and encircled her waist. The feeling of his arm there, where his thrust was directed, caused her, as he knew it would, to draw in a deep breath of alarm and pleasure and open yet further to him. With his right hand he leaned out and took her hair, entangling it in his fingers, not pulling it, not hurting, but holding it firmly so that she felt him at her head too. And then, his feet planted firm, he stood and slapped into her once, twice, three times, four times, again and again the sound of his flanks slapping against her tense buttocks, and she almost cried as the tension in herself grew and began to swoon, so she held on tighter and then put up one hand to grab his hand that was in her hair and sink her nails into knuckles already bloody, as he strove, harder, slower, deeper, to drive away, drive off, into that total darkness – she came like a waterfall and cried as he, too, came and she felt his life pour into hers. There he stood, still erect, though spent, still inside her, aching for a satisfaction which never came now, tired, jaded, sick in his mind at unnameable loss, shuddering, empty, silent. There was no love in it. Not for him.

Chapter Fourteen

Mrs. Burns was playing patience. Marianne sat by the fire patching a pair of Alan's jeans. Between them were the sofa and chaise-longue which served as Gareth's make-shift bed. It was just before ten-thirty p.m., the evening of the day which had seen Gareth's arrival in the early hours.

'They're late again,' Marianne said.

'Jimmie's always late.' Mrs. Burns did not take her eyes up from the table. 'Not a bit of wonder. Everybody wanting him to solve their problems. He has enough of his own. They never remember that.' She moved the cards about deftly. It was beginning to work out.

'Helen says I can share her flat until I find digs of my own – if I want to go to Lancaster.' Marianne looked up at the older woman when she talked, glad of the respite from this sewing which she did reluctantly. 'She said she would help me to find a job as well. She says everybody's short of secret-aries so it shouldn't be too hard. I've heard you can get forty or fifty pounds a week down south with my speeds. Some say sixty.'

Gareth came in. Mrs. Burns looked up and nodded quiz-zically. The explanation he had given for what she called his 'shocking condition' had not impressed her at all. Marianne looked up, offered a smile, saw that Gareth was in no mood for it and dropped her eyes to her work. He had set up his stereo equipment in the corner near the piano. He went and put on a record and then plugged in the earphones – new, white discs, large as saucers.

'Have you been helping Jimmie on your travels today?' Mrs. Burns asked, innocently enough.

'I haven't seen Jimmie all day. Not for a couple of days.' He paused, ready for any more questions. There were none. He put on his earphones and settled down.

Marianne had once admired what she thought of as his independence more than anything. She had to work so hard to do what she wanted. She felt a tremendous pressure of obligations – to her mother, who, after all, lived a miserable life, to Jimmie and Elaine, who had helped her so much, to Mrs. Burns, whom she helped a lot in quiet ways, even, crazily enough, to Gareth, who had, she still believed, taught her something worth learning. And then there was the overwhelming responsibility for Alan. She did not regret all this – she was as she was – but Gareth's ability to be on his own and somehow stand apart from everyone else, neither borrowing from them nor owing them anything – that was something she still loved in him.

Mrs. Burns was stuck again. She looked from Gareth to Marianne sadly.

'I don't care what you say, you'll find it very hard on your own, just you and Alan. You can be modern up to a point but beyond that it doesn't work.'

'Why not?'

'A child needs its mother around it, whatever they say, all the talk in the world won't alter that. It's all very well rushing off to make money – there's nothing wrong with it – except if you end up neglecting a child and you'll have to live with that and maybe regret it for life. You *can* regret things for life, you know, and it's very hard.'

'I can't stay here, though. I'm just a sort of glorified lodger. I feel I'd go mad if I stayed stuck up here much longer. It's nice – everybody's very nice – but it's so tucked-away and shut off. Even the television's usually bust: Jimmie doesn't mind, of course – then he has London. But ...'

'Elaine?' Mrs. Burns looked calmly at Marianne. 'Elaine would have been the same wherever she was and here at least she's happy.' Long ago Mrs. Burns had classified her daughter as 'weak' – which meant 'unable to look after herself properly'. Nothing, she thought, would or could alter that.

'She's certainly getting on with it at the moment!' Marianne rushed to repair what she thought of as the breach of manners in letting it be implied that she was able to criticise or condemn Elaine. 'I've never *seen* her so determined.'

'As long as she doesn't wear herself out,' Mrs. Burns nodded, in appreciation. 'You're right, though, something's got into her.'

'It's since Gareth came back.'

Both women looked at him. His eyes were closed. Whatever music it was poured into his ears alone and was unheard by them. He rocked slightly as he sat, and occasionally drew lightly on his cigarette.

'Gareth's just strung you along,' Mrs. Burns said, evenly. 'All the time.'

'No he hasn't. What I've done I've done because I wanted to! It's been my own choice. My own free choice.'

'I can't understand all that talk.' The old woman once more brooded over the rows of cards. 'He should have married you and when he didn't you should have left him.'

'He offered.'

'Did he?'

'He still does.'

'I see.'

'But it isn't as easy as you say. It just isn't.'

Mrs. Burns recognised the distress in the voice and spoke very gently. 'I know that, lass. It's never easy for us. But we must make the best of things, mustn't we?' There was the sound of a car coming up the short drive and she shook her head at the intractable cards. The good run had petered out.

She collected them up tidily and tried to ease her joints into action without alerting the arthritis which was remorsely spreading its course throughout her body. 'That'll be them.'

'I've said I'll leave him,' Marianne said, glancing at Gareth still apparently unconscious of the two women.

'Did you mean it?'

'Yes, I did.'

'Well then. There we are. You all lead your lives far too fast. There's plenty of time. Too much, I sometimes think.' She hobbled a little and then settled to her usual motion and went over to Gareth where she prised away and lifted one of the white earpieces, out of which floated the sound of a Beethoven quartet. 'Cocoa?' She bellowed this in his ear, and, not so very playfully, cuffed this strange and worrying grandson of hers.

'Let me make it,' Gareth replied.

'It's my job.' She let the earpiece go and it snapped back. He laughed and did not hear the rest of what she said, which was 'You get back to never-never land where you belong.'

Elaine came in, looking flushed and triumphant, followed by Harold.

'Harold drove me back,' Elaine announced, too full of herself to take time to greet anyone, tugging at her gloves, walking the width of the room, so agitated with life that it seemed to set off an invisible crackle of kindling about the place. 'Bill persuaded poor Jimmie to take some new leaflets or pamphlets – which are they? never mind – over to Ireby.' The gloves were dropped on the card-table; she unbuttoned her coat rapidly. 'We canvassed all afternoon – and it was so *cold*.'

She let the coat fall over the back of a chair and then, sweeping her eyes about the room with that mischievous smile which asserted her new confidence in her new wellbeing, she marched over to Gareth. Harold went to get himself a drink; no one else wanted one.

Elaine knocked smartly on the headphones. Gareth, irritated, opened his eyes angrily and then, seeing Elaine's face, entered into her spirit.

'Good evening,' she said, 'I'm sorry if I've disturbed you. Do you have a minute or so? Thank you. I'm canvassing on behalf of Mr. Johnston, as you probably' – she turned to the others – 'I'm always worried by "probably", it sounds patronising; still, Bill says it's right' – back to Gareth – 'anyway, as you probably know, he's the Member of Parliament for this constituency and we very much hope he'll continue to be able to represent you. If you would be kind enough to tell us whom you intend to support in the election, it really would be a very great help.'

'Well now, young lady.' Gareth put on his Gruff-Professional-North Countryman's voice. ' "Appen I's'll keep what I'm goanna do in that booooth to mysen. 'Appen you've no right, no *right* to know how aaa vooote.'

'No. None at all.'

'Well, 'appen I's'll keep mum. 'Appen life's a challenge, like,' he said. 'An' 'appen that's it, lass.'

'Oh dear! Now I'm supposed to say – perhaps you have some questions I could refer to Mr. Johnston, some queries he could answer?'

' "Aappen aa've a mount of questions but we never see him to pop 'em to him.'

'That's not fair! He's up here every weekend doing at least one surgery and sometimes two or three.'

'What's he doing about the amendment to the Small Traders Saturday Street Market Protection Act?'

'I'll put you down as a "Don't know".'

'I know all right, I'm not telling, that's all.'

Elaine replaced the headphones gently. 'You're the most awkward type of all.'

Gareth turned off the music and removed the headphones.

'Back to the land of the living?' Mrs. Burns asked, on her way out.

'How can you call it that?' Gareth asked, smiling at her.

'Cocoa all round?' People murmured assent. Marianne and Elaine indicated they would help. Mrs. Burns declined it and left alone. She never felt comfortable for long when so many of them were there chattering away.

'What was the other fella like?' Harold asked.

'He'll live,' Gareth said.

'He caught you a nice one around the eye there.'

'You're taking a very fatherly interest, Harold.'

'We have to look after our Gareth, haven't we? Always have.'

'How was the meeting?' Marianne's question was plainly nervous, obviously intended to switch the attention from Gareth: protective, Elaine noticed, tenderly. If only Gareth would marry her.

'The White Knight won on points,' Harold said. 'Cheers!' He raised his glass to the company. Gareth got out his flask.

'Cheers old chap!' he echoed, rather mockingly.

'It was terrible!' Elaine announced, thrilled. 'That horrible man Weston – the revolutionary – he turned up in the audience and asked the rudest and nastiest questions. Not letting Jimmie finish. Shouting and chanting with that little pack of his. Just because nobody goes to his meetings he tries to steal Jimmie's glory, doesn't he, Harold?'

'Exactly,' Harold agreed, enjoying Elaine's liveliness. 'A little political criminal in his outlaw denim. Dresses rather like our Gareth.'

'He made the most outrageous insinuations.' Elaine herself took on a look of outrage. 'Very close to libel, I'd say.'

'Slander,' Gareth corrected her. 'Spoken, it's slander.'

'Lies, whatever you call it,' she concluded.

'Jimmie fielded them all very well,' Harold said. He had settled on the arm of Marianne's chair. She was clearly happy to have him there and he had already whispered two or three confidences in her ear which had made her blush and giggle a little. 'I suppose there's something in the Parliamentary system after all – at least it seems to teach you to cope with heckling fools and disruptive guttersnipes. The press was there in rather greater force than one would have expected.' Harold put on a patently insincere air. 'I don't understand about these things but it looked a bit like a put-up job – of course, everyone at these election times becomes as paranoid as a prima donna. But fortunately Jimmie was on top form. Madame there sat beside him on the platform looking like Beauty – whatever it is, some line of a poem that used to come in handy – Beauty under a – never mind – looking wonderful. The audience was clearly against the Marxist thugs. Still, it could have been very tricky – Jimmie gave nothing away.'

'I thought politicians were supposed to give things away, especially at election times,' Gareth said.

'Lucky for us all that what Gareth thinks doesn't count for much, isn't it?' Harold took out his last cigar of the day. 'How's the hair shirt?'

'How's the silk sheets?'

'Perfect.' He held up his glass. 'I hear you've been hitting it a bit lately.'

'Your intelligence system must be working overtime.'

'We need to keep tabs on you, don't we?'

Elaine looked at the two men, ready to be alarmed. But the exchanges were taking place so politely there was nothing, apparently, to worry about, even though her unease, sensitive always and at this time raw from the number of times it had been pricked into life, told her unequivocally that Harold and Gareth were already locked in a serious argument. She took out a cigarette, sat down, waited. Marianne felt that she should hold her breath. The more relaxed Harold became in the easy pose beside her, the tenser she herself grew.

'I see,' Gareth said. 'Under observation, am I?'

'I remember when Gareth was a toddler,' Harold said, cosily, to Marianne. 'He had the same habit then of knowing what was good for people better than they knew themselves.

Always on to his mother to give up smoking because he said it was bad for her – ahead of your time there, Gareth.'

'As usual.'

'And then he used to lecture poor old Jimmie because he couldn't save money.'

'I remember that!' Elaine laughed. 'Yes. I remember that too!'

'I'll never know why it bothered you so much, Gareth.' Harold adopted an attitude of genuine enquiry. 'Peculiar, isn't it, looking back? You really were *upset* that the old man couldn't keep hold of the shekels. You used to say to me, "You know, Uncle Harold, Daddy'll die in the workhouse." '

'Mother would have put that word in his head,' Elaine said to Marianne, who barely nodded, oppressed now by the proximity of Harold, and the obscure feeling that he was making use of her. But for what?

'What else did Gareth say?' Elaine asked, 'That *you* remember?'

'Oh, it's difficult to know where to start,' Harold said.

'How flattering.' Gareth grinned and Marianne winced as the cut at the side of his mouth opened up. The dark blood formed a small blob and then began to dribble down towards his chin. She wanted to wipe it off him. 'I'd no idea I'd made such an impression on you, Harold,' Gareth said.

'Oh yes. You were quite a turn in those days. I always said you would end up as a politician, and – well, here you are.' He finished off his glass. 'Must be on my way.' He stood up. 'A word in your ear, Marianne.'

'I'll set you to the door,' Marianne said. She got up and Harold gave her a friendly hug around the shoulders.

' "Set," ' Gareth observed. 'Pure dialect. Meaning "accompany".'

'What would we do without you, Gareth?' Harold came across and kissed Elaine affectionately on the cheek. 'Now don't you overdo things, my girl. Don't force anything.'

'I won't. Thank you for bringing me back.'

'It's always a pleasure to be in your company. It always was.' To Gareth he said, 'Night, squire!'

'See you.'

'You'll miss the cocoa,' Elaine exclaimed, loudly, and then laughed aloud at herself.

'I'll make my apologies on the way out. Good night.'

They went out. Elaine looked after him, lovingly. 'He's always been so kind to us all. I don't know how we would have managed without him over the years.'

Gareth was still looking at the door which Marianne had gone through, without looking back.

'A bloody sight better.' Gareth spoke vehemently. 'Jimmie would never have come back into Parliament to peddle those wishy-washy populist policies of his. He would have found an honest job. I would have gone to the local school instead of being crated off to a decaying stately home for unequally privileged young jerks. You wouldn't have been in and out of that expensive sanatorium where if they know what they're doing they keep it to themselves. This house would most likely have been sold and grandmother wouldn't have to sweat away like a navvy to keep it clean. And perhaps we'd have enjoyed feeling independent. Harold's made parasites of us all.' He sucked at his flask. It was empty. He got up and went to the drinks cabinet.

Elaine, who was shocked by what he had said, thought that he looked so ill she was afraid to comment on it. He drank a lot and yet forced himself to behave as if he were totally unaffected by it. She couldn't reach him.

'Harold supplies the whisky!' she said, as he filled up his flask.

'I'll drink to that.' He did so. 'Your health.'

'*So* much better,' she said, grasping the chance. '*So* much better without the pills. My head feels so *clear*. So clear sometimes that I can hardly bear it. At the meeting, sitting on that silly platform, I was scarcely nervous at all – even though we were asked not to smoke! That was *hell*! But inside my head, I wasn't – screaming – you know – no, how could you? – but inside there for so long it was as if I could hear myself, silly, crying – I suppose I'm saying all this because I'm so happy. I don't usually talk about myself, not – not how I *really* feel – it's marvellous.'

'As the gentleman said, don't overdo it.' He waited, ready to help.

She wanted to tell him that Jimmie was helping her, and although Jimmie – she could tell – did not fully believe in her recovery, he was so steady. Effectively, she had ceased to rely on Gareth. Which was wise. For his erratic attendance at the house and the obscure volatility of his moods was no help whatsoever. But she dared not tell him that, knowing that he was proud to consider himself her prop and mainstay. She knew that to tell him about Jimmie would make him think she had betrayed him and so she said nothing.

'I'll have a happy ending,' she said, after a pause. 'You'll see.'

'Yes.'

The door opened and once more a supply-train arrived in the living-room. Helen came in first and held open the door for Mrs. Burns, who pushed the trolley before her. Marianne followed with a neat stack of bedding which she deposited at Gareth's feet.

Jimmie followed, looking quite exhausted. The face which still fluttered a few feminine hearts when it appeared in public was now literally grey with fatigue. His suit was grubby and looked as if he had slept in a chair in it. He was carrying a heavy briefcase as wearily as if it were loaded with lead.

Elaine clapped her hands. 'The Triumphal Procession! The Conqueror come in from the Wars!'

Helen went to get Jimmie a Scotch.

'There's cocoa,' Mrs. Burns said, pointing to the large jug as if to curtail discussion and head off all dispute, 'fancy cakes, an apple cake, crackers with rum butter, crackers without, brown bread and butter, some scones for those who like them. Cheese and ham underneath. So there we are. Good night one and all.'

Elaine went across to kiss her mother, who left despite requests that she should stay for some refreshment of her own. Helen handed Jimmie the Scotch.

'Unless there's anything urgent, I think I'll go up too,' Helen said, 'I've a bad headache.'

'There's some aspirin in the bathroom,' Elaine said, eagerly. 'And I've some Codeine, or Anadin, or Veganin—'

'A cup of cocoa will do fine, thank you,' Helen said. Marianne handed one to her. 'I'll take it upstairs.'

'You work so hard,' Elaine said.

'Those notes were passed on, were they?' Jimmie asked anxiously.

'Yes. And we have to be at that school by eight-thirty tomorrow morning.'

'Leave here just before eight.'

'Goodnight,' she said. He went and opened the door for her.

As he came back across the room, he registered surprise at Gareth's appearance. 'Bit of a mess, old chap.'

'Bit of a scrap.'

'Hope you won.'

'So do I.'

Elaine knew they wanted to be left on their own and yet she was fed up with being eternally compliant. She made the decision to sit it out for as long as she could. Jimmie flopped down in the chair vacated by Marianne. 'What a bloody meeting!' He looked rather blankly at Gareth. 'The British Far Left must be in a class of its own for bitchiness, witch-hunting and impenetrable stupidity. All, of course, in the name of the People. The People who never vote for them and take no damned notice of them unless they resort to insults. Dandified little storm-troopers of liberalism!' Marianne looked surprised at the anger in his tone.

'I hear Weston went for you.'

'Exactly. Not my politics or the Government's record. Me.'

'And Harold,' Elaine interrupted helpfully. 'Harold was mentioned as well.'

'That was irrelevant,' Jimmie said, testily, hardly giving her a look.

'*He* didn't seem to think so. I was looking at his face. I was glad Helen was sitting beside him to keep him from jumping up!'

'Harold was irrelevant! If you *do* insist on turning up, for God's sake make some effort to comprehend what's going on.' There was an unhappy silence. 'Sorry.'

'I thought I *did* comprehend,' she said.

'I thought you had, too,' Gareth added.

'But Weston spoke such a *lot* about Harold,' Elaine added, and then wished she had not, for Jimmie looked so beaten.

'Yes,' he said gently. 'I am sorry. You are right and I am wrong.'

'I'm being tantalised,' Gareth said, smiling comfortably at Elaine's success. 'What *was* the issue?'

'Those bloody reports were the issue of course.' Jimmie's gentleness was strictly for Elaine.

'*Private Eye?*'

'Yes. Malice masquerading as morality.' Jimmie paused. He hated to be unfair and after the conversation with Harold he had to hand it to the magazine; this made him intensely irritable.

He stood up. Elaine looked frightened. Marianne blushed as if she were the cause. 'You were a real help again, truly, darling. Truly. But I think you ought to take some time off tomorrow. We can't have you breaking – we can't have you wearing yourself out all at once. There's still more than two weeks to go. We'll need more as time goes on. So have a good sleep tomorrow. Have a stroll in the afternoon – they'll be thinking you're neglecting them all around here.'

'Shall I?' She turned to Gareth. 'Shall I stay here to make up your bed?'

'I'll do it myself. But thanks.'

'I think I *will* go to bed.'

She kissed both the men and left.

'You two look as if you want to be left alone,' Marianne said as she cleared up the cups and put them on the trolley.

'We do rather, don't we, Gareth?'

'Do we?'

'Open the door, Gareth.' Marianne was pushing the trolley on which the food still lay completely undisturbed. He opened the door. 'Sweet dreams,' she said, and smiled up at him.

'Well, old chap,' Jimmie said, 'I'm tired, you look like hell if you don't mind me saying so – let's not mess about.'

'Ah. Army Officer time. I wondered when you were going to arrive at that character. It's your last stop but one! Sir!'

He stood up and clicked to attention, Gestapo heel-clicking style, and gave the Black Power salute.

'Listen, Gareth, I really *am* a bit whacked. I've a long campaign ahead of me. Which I intend to win. Despite you. So cut out the crap, will you, old chap?'

'O.K.'

'Thanks.' Both men sat down. Jimmie hesitated: he was not enjoying this. 'Look – horribly embarrassing! – but it has to be cleared up and I want you to know that whatever way it works out I still – you know, my feelings for you will be unimpaired. Now then Harold suggests that these reports in *Private Eye* – one of the reasons why I've been so angry at it I suppose – that in fact *you*—'

'Not guilty.'

'No?'

'Not my style.'

'That's what I said.' Jimmie was patently and immensely relieved. 'I apologise. Well!' He raised his glass. 'Thank God for that.'

'May the Lord, mighty in war, give us the victory. You're probably right – a war would have done my lot the world of good as you used to say, remember? Pity you couldn't lay one on. Can't say you didn't try, though. Full marks for effort.'

'I don't recall ever saying that. Never.'

'Maybe not.'

'You mean it doesn't matter whether or not I did. It *sounds* right.'

'Something like that.'

'The details in those reports are so damned accurate.'

'It's surprising what you can dig up. Plenty of friends ready to put in a bad word. No. Daylight sabotage is my line. I spend the afternoon with Weston and his mob.'

'I know.' Jimmie took a breath: the revelation that Weston had Gareth on his side had shaken him badly when Bill had told him a few hours earlier.

'I came up here to help him. Came a little earlier because of Elaine but intended to come anyway.'

'Why here?' He tried to be patient. But why? Why? Why? hammered away in his head. What did I do to you except give you a home? Why do you hate me?

'Oh, we won't win. But we can get a lot of experience here. And you give us a lot of mileage because you'll feel obliged to take us on. Other reasons. It was carefully planned before I joined, I'm told. We can't afford to lose too many deposits. Our members aren't as rich as yours.' He took a drink. 'Fair enough?'

'Fair to whom? Certainly not to the electorate.'

'They'll make up their own minds, won't they? I thought that was the idea at election time.'

Jimmie kept his voice steady. 'Weston – and you, I suppose – represent no one but yourselves. You're a tiny, extreme, arrogant clique which only gets heard at all because the system we have is so accommodating. You've no idea whatsoever about the way the world works and, in my opinion, no real regard at all for the people of this country. And yes, you're right, I will take you on.' He looked at Gareth but his step-son gave him no flicker of affection, no glance of recognition at all.

'Good. Your lot, by contrast, has such a very high regard for "the people of this country" that it browbeats the working class, tolerates unemployment, leaves poverty to the poor and bursts a gut to prop up and run the rotten system you were elected to change. The Labour Party! Don't make me laugh. You're as much a conspiracy as anyone – the same old ruling class conspiracy as ever was!'

'On any objective assessment, Weston's a fantasist,' Jimmie countered. 'He wants instant socialism without tears. But his way guarantees tears. And who will pay? And who decides? Weston doesn't even have the right questions, never mind the right answers.'

'No answers that you accept.'

'What are you going to do?'

'Anything Weston wants.'

'Break up meetings?'

'Yes.'

'Hound the other candidates? Distribute lies to try to confuse what you can't understand? Brainwash one or two sadly simple-minded young locals into sharing your delusion that you're somehow Keir Hardie with *Das Kapital* under your belts? All you have under your belts are envious little hearts, misguided lusts and contemptibly mean spirits.'

'That's rubbish.'

'Very well. There's something you can tell Weston. You know as well as I do that his smear campaign could do me a lot of harm. He won't get any votes – but he doesn't actually want *votes*, does he? Nothing as ordinary or as positive as that. Anyway, tell him that he need make no more insinuations about whether or not I was more involved in that schools contract than the official enquiry suggested. I was. Tell him that. And there are letters already in the post to

Transport House and the Secretary of the Official Enquiry. Bill Atkinson got one this evening. So did my committee. To you I can admit I was not involved in any way which – never mind the excuses. Legally, I was involved and morally I am in some definite way responsible. Now the record's rather straighter.'

'It had nothing to do with you,' Gareth said. 'It was all Harold. The Old Master Builder himself. Don't let him lay it on you. It had nothing to do with you.'

'How the hell do you know?'

'We've had it checked out. Weston has.' Gareth paused and looked amused. 'Does Harold know about these letters?'

'Not yet. I meant to tell him this evening but it was all too rushed.'

'He'll love it! He'll think you've outflanked him, Ho-hum!'

'What are you up to, Gareth?'

'My party,' Gareth said, quite viciously, 'is opposed to you. The more opposed, the better the party.'

'I see.' Jimmie drank. He was shaken. There was absolutely no mistaking the violence and hatred. 'I see,' he repeated, quietly and sadly. 'So that's it.'

'That's it.'

Jimmie leaned back and an infusion of memories, conversations, decisions, scenes, upsets, hurt, pleasures, all the complex cluster which had made up the joint life of Gareth and himself came somehow sickeningly to mind. To his dismay he found he wanted affection from this younger man he had brought up and there was no way in which he could gain it. He wanted to talk it out; he would have given an enormous amount to have had a few hours to talk it over with Helen, just to talk to someone who would listen and understand. But she had withdrawn since Gareth's arrival.

'I'll clear out,' Gareth said. 'In fact, I'll clear out tonight. There's a bed at a friend of Weston's.'

'That might be better, yes.' Jimmie kept all reproach out

of his voice. Despite his shock at the unambiguous sight of Gareth's attitude towards him, he still felt anxiety for Gareth. There was a desperation about him which went so deep, leading into a pit of his own digging, Jimmie thought, gaining insight from his own hurt.

'There'll be a bed,' Gareth went on, 'at what your worthy Cumbrian voter calls "the commune" and flees past as if it had the mark of the plague on the door. Quite a decent set-up really.'

'I'm glad.'

'Are you?'

Jimmie picked up his briefcase and swung it heavily on to his knees. He was angry now.

'In this, Gareth, are a few policy documents on Education, Health, Housing, Agriculture, Transport, Shipping, the Mines, Oil – etcetera, etcetera – most of which I have read and studied. They've been worked out over months and months – not by a grasping bunch of fashionable conspirators determined to stay in the saddle at all costs but, on the whole, by remarkably honest and honourable men and women who see a complicated society and understand the benefits of a complicated society and appreciate that patient work has got to go into its upkeep and development. You and your friends don't even begin to address yourselves to all this! Things don't fall apart over a long period of time, Gareth. They collapse suddenly if they're not attended to. Things like major industries, big institutions, they can collapse in a few months. They need the work of a lot of patient and honest people. Behind all your modish swagger you're a Luddite, you're a worshipper – if you revere anything at all, and I suspect that you don't – of the noble savage and you have some fuddled idea that each of us carries his own destiny entirely in his own hand. Romantic anarchism at its worst. That never was and never will be! Read a little history or a little poetry! Your analysis is wrong, your approach is wrong, your contempt is wrong and you're wasting yourself.'

'End of sermon?'

'Yes.'

'See you, then.' Gareth got to his feet and went to the door.

Jimmie half-hoped he would come back or say just something, just a word, however small a token to their life together. But he did not and eventually Jimmie took refuge in the documents which he had hoisted on to his knees.

Oh God, he prayed, help him, help me, help us all, worthless sinners.

III. THE MEETING

Chapter Fifteen

Over the next ten days the electorate ruminated over its choice of government.

As at all elections, there was a sudden breeze of self-confidence about the country. Politicians came out and declared what they could and would do rather than what they could not and would not do. Now and then someone forgot he was in the late seventies and risked a vision of the society he wanted to see in the future. On the whole it was pedestrian stuff – yet, even so, it was a change after the defensive dirges, empty boasts and ponderous offensives of the past few years. It even seemed possible that there might be some way to find the correct answer to the apparently insoluble problem – industrial decay plus political democracy multiplied by inflation and divided by unemployment equals what? Some said they knew and some believed them.

There were those political commentators who sensed that this might be the last of the old heavyweight championship elections. They noted the entrenched power of two or three of the minor parties. Were that to be consolidated and Parliament yet again balanced almost equally on top of two big rumps neither of which could alone either do its business or get off the pot, then it would, they thought, only be a matter of time before a new host of alignments grew up. Certain sage persons declared that the whole confusion arose from the fact that this ought to be a 'natural Labour-governing era'. However, such had been the corrosive effect of the Wilson years on the heart of those who thought about and worked actively for the Labour Party, that this could no longer be counted on. Others thought that the Tories, deep in a natural hibernation, profoundly uncertain of their rôle in contemporary society, were being called out too early. Yet they had to respond despite having nothing to say. In this impasse there could, said sages concluded, be the chance for the new pattern to emerge.

The Trade Figures were good – no surprise. Prices of cigarettes, beer and whisky had been marked down. Not unexpectedly the price of petrol was reduced and the house market was on the bounce thanks to the easier mortgages. Our reserves went up and the Foreign Secretary paid a sudden, urgent visit, on international affairs of great concern, to the President of the United States, who received him fulsomely. Much publicity came from that.

Instant publicity came into its inheritance. Polls every day. National, local, straw, youth, black, old, regional, metropolitan, non-stop. Press conferences were artfully staged to upstage, television interviewers had well-researched questions undermined by well-worked-out strategies. Rows were fabricated before your very eyes. Agreements were entered into, broken, tested, asserted, revealed. The *Sun* told its readers 'Maggie's Tops'. The *Mirror* and the *People* declared for Labour; the *Mail* and the *News of the World* for the Tories; *The Times* for the minorities, with a side bet on the Tories; the *Guardian* and the *Observer* came out for Labour; the *Telegraphs* and the *Expresses* for the Tories; the *Sunday Times* equivocated, curiously. As did the *Financial Times* and Jimmie's local paper, which was Tory-owned. A prominent Labour Peer declared for the Tories. A prominent Liberal Peer declared for Labour. In Scotland, the sound of the bagpipes was heard throughout the land and in Wales the language of antique hill-poets urged members of an advanced capitalist society to take power unto themselves. There were bomb scares from the IRA. One ancient Labour candidate had a heart attack and died. The Prince of Wales was called on to explain a remark which might have indicated that he favoured the Scottish Nationalists. There was remarkably little corruption.

Jimmie worked very hard. He appeared on local radio programmes every other day, on local television whenever possible, in halls, canteens, clubs, Homes, schools, the Polytechnic, shopping precincts, churches, auctions, sale-rooms playgroups: he visited hospitals, institutions for many different sorts of disadvantaged person, factories, offices and local societies. He kept up his usual surgeries. He got stuck into the many issues brought up as challenges every day by the energetic young Tory candidate who did not mind sailing close to the wind if it gave him some mileage. He tried to beat off the entangling and benevolent alignments offered by the ever-willing Liberal. He was dogged by Weston and Gareth.

Gareth's defection had created a day's small and local headline. No more. Gareth had said 'no comment'. Jimmie had declared that it proved there was no brainwashing in *his* house and left it at that. Bill was disappointed. He thought the boot should have gone in. But then, Bill was worried that Jimmie was 'too nice'. He wanted a certain toughness to emerge publicly. He often discussed this with Helen, who worked hour after hour with Jimmie and because of that, it was observed, grew distinctly more strained.

On Sundays Jimmie did no canvassing. He worked at home but did not go around the houses. He did it on principle. People should be left alone on Sundays, he thought. None of the other candidates followed his example. Bill, in shirt-sleeves, inky and happy, spent the Lord's Day cursing his printing machine and turning out stack on stack of tract and message – all pointing ominously to Election Day as if to the Apocalypse.

Chapter Sixteen

(i)

They walked along to the church hand in hand. Elaine was very moved by the gesture: Jimmie rarely expressed his affection so naturally. It was a fine autumn morning, so fine and dry the feeling that came from the land that it was occupation enough just to be walking, breathing and being part of that yellow-brown landscape. The sun was isolated in the cloud-free sky, perfectly golden.

'Let's go to your church now,' Elaine said, 'the one you go to on your own.'

Jimmie smiled at her eagerness. She had walked the mile and a half to the village church with him for morning communion. This was rare enough. Now she proposed to extend their return ramble by another mile or so.

'You're too tired.'

'I'm not. Look.' She stood aside from him in the narrow winding road which went uphill to their hamlet and turned around slowly in a full circle.

'What am I supposed to see?'

'Me. Normal.' She laughed – but waited on his response none the less.

'I have some work to do.'

'Just to please me.'

'I must get back,' and quite suddenly he did feel rather oppressed and impatient that he could not instantly flick himself back home. The walk ahead seemed boring.

'Can't you spare me a few minutes?'

'Why are we standing still, talking to each other as if we were arguing?'

'I don't know.' She began to walk and then she stopped. He came up to her and she kissed him warmly and sweetly; and he received it impassively at first but remembered to return the pressure on her lips. Then she took his arm. It took so little to make her so happy, he reflected. And as they strolled and he felt her thrill to the delicate effect of a single leaf on a bough, a robin in a hedge, a nest bared by fallen leaves, a snail glittering in the sun, a vista of fields as open as the ocean, he felt that what she saw and enjoyed in life was what was there to be enjoyed and, as if a magic wand had touched him as she linked his arm, the dogged cloak of responsibilities slid off him.

'We'd better cut across the fields to the church,' he said, giving in to her wishes. 'There's a gate just around that corner.'

She said nothing but hugged his arm to her and for a moment rested her head on his shoulder, not leaving it there for too long, not wanting to hinder his progress.

The latch on the gate was jammed. They climbed over – she in the light fawn coat which swung loosely and gracefully about her slim figure, her slender legs not at all made plain by the plain walking shoes, her hair lifted lightly by the light wind, her face sparkling with the seaside delight at the treat – Jimmie, more ponderous although more used to such capers, rather stiff as he clambered over the five-barred gate, far too over-formal in his pin-striped suit, collar just a little too tight, brow sweating slightly; a middle-aged couple striking across the open land to a church as abandoned as an outworn creed.

The weather held. Their mood held. He subdued or repressed his daily fret and fight over the election, his fears about the scandal, his most private unhappiness about himself – offering it all to the fine Sunday autumn morning and seeing it, for that hour or so, blow away like a spent leaf. For

Elaine, too, it was an interlude of peace, blessedly without 'serious talk' or plans or the examination of anything more than the sights about them. It was like holding your breath, she thought, and for that instant imagining you had laid a pause on the world. Even in such a brief time they felt refreshed with each other and restored in themselves.

It was cold in the church and they stayed only a few minutes. Jimmie had no great inflood of feeling: that seemed to arrive only when he was alone.

Elaine took the copper beech twigs from the vase. The leaves were crinkled. She looked, as they walked back, for somewhere to dump them but nowhere seemed appropriate. Hedges newly trimmed, narrow roads free of litter. In the end they were carried all the way back home to the rubbish heap on which the others had been laid.

(ii)

In the afternoon, Jimmie went for another walk, this time alone, unable to resist the beauty of the day.

The autumn afternoon was brilliant, the light so clear it seemed to sting your eyes, the air so crisp and clean you felt like drinking it. And the place itself was displayed majestically.

For as he went on one of his favourite walks – about eight miles along the back roads which connected three of the northern fell villages – he walked in the bowl of an arc of hills, the Caldbeck Fells, Skiddaw and Binsey, which rose up in imperial purple, cut out sharply under the deep blue of the sky, taking this golden autumn light into the heather and bracken and returning it in such a warmth of colour as took your breath away. It was indeed a fine place to live and a fine day to be out, walking, fully able to enjoy his faculties and the sights and sounds about him. As the air freshened his lungs, he felt stronger and more certain than he had done for months.

It was partly Elaine's resolution which helped. Her decision to give up those pills had thrown a great deal more weight on others and he had taken the brunt of it: and of course her path had not been easy – the first few days of withdrawal from anything were the worst, so they said. But her resolution cheered him and he found himself repaid for his care by a stirring of affection in him which took him by surprise: he thought he had lost such feelings for ever. Or rather he thought they had been relegated to the furtive hopeless gestures such as the one he had made to Helen.

It was partly also that the arrival of Gareth – so clearly hell-bent – had braced him. There was nothing like the prospect of a confrontation to concentrate the mind.

Most of all, though, Jimmie had been unexpectedly strengthened by 'the Ruthwaite Affair'. One of the reasons for his lack of substantial success as a politician was that he rarely re-examined the reasons, which he thought of as 'basic', which had taken him into politics in the first place. Although he would have been astonished at the word, he had in fact merely drifted through the crises and changes which had shuddered through the Britain of the fifties and sixties and seventies believing that his old-fashioned socialism would always serve, like a tried and true faith. Up to a point he was right. But it had led to a laziness and a complacency which Harold's case had shattered.

For although he kept it under control, Jimmie was very frightened, retrospectively, at what he could have got involved in. Harold had let him off lightly then just as he was letting him off lightly now. This generosity, alas, and as so often, did not produce gratitude on Jimmie's part. He considered that he had been used and fooled by Harold and although he blamed himself, he still did not think any the better of Harold for doing it to him. The more he thought about it all, the more he was embarrassed and angry to see how much wool had been pulled over his eyes.

The positive side of this was that he felt that he was

reassessing his political position for the first time in years. He saw that he had compromised himself through a notion of tolerance which had led to his contradicting principles he ought to have held to. He saw that his position in the mid-right of the Labour movement was under attack precisely because men like him had made compromises like his. It was bracing to know that a new start must be made, and chastening to know that there was so much to do.

But the moment could be a source of help. If Elaine had taught him a single lesson, it had been to look on nature and take pleasure in it. So often his paper-meeting-conference-travelling-busy life took him over for weeks on end and he lost all contact with the planet he lived on. Here, though, it could not be ignored: like a new world, so vast, so open and clean, and enduring. The hills would outlast the days of all men; even those leafless beeches would outlast him. There was great comfort in that.

(iii)

On the evening of that same day, Helen invented a flimsy excuse to take her out of the house. She headed for the town. The weather had changed for the worse and she was glad of the heater in the car.

Sunday evening in a small northern industrial town with the intermittent cold rain slanting in from the sea seems to beggar description and yet writers have often been drawn to it. Street life does not exist. Pub life is subdued. Working life is largely shut off. Domestic life is confined to quarters. The slight religious life is over in time for Sunday-night peak viewing. Love-life is hidden or looking for a place to hide. Only a quiet life seems at all possible in a place where little or no life can be seen, smelt or heard. From the mournful slag heaps to the bleak terraces, from the carless main streets to deserted docks, from the ghost-town estates to the humourless suburbs the only moving thing at 8.20 p.m. was the odd car scuttling home. Here the Sabbath still held its barren humourless sway.

Helen hesitated to carry out her simple and unexceptionable plan and did a little tour of the privately owned houses which just made the quorum for a suburb. This was the part of the town which tended to get left out of general descriptions and impressions. The area was neat and cosy and even glossily contemporary. The houses were comfortable, gardens interestingly stocked, the occasional autumn bonfire bringing faith like a pipe of peace. Jimmie had brought her up here soon after the election had begun. She had been surprised. As he had expected. He liked to upset her clichés. The next day he had taken her to the biggest council estate, which she had thought of as 'soulless', 'a civic wasteland', etc. He had introduced her to a number of people who had talked about their previous houses – slums, without bathrooms, without gardens, without adequate lighting or heating or privacy. That had been salutary too. And she had been touched by Jimmie's pride in what had been achieved for 'the majority' as he always carefully put it. But this small suburb, she knew, was especially restful to her. She could relax here. She hated the reasons which explained this: that here were people slightly more likely to have read the books she read, listened to the sort of music she would listen to. For it was (alas for those schoolgirl slogans which could still bring a rush of righteous blood to the head), it was, indisputably, bourgeois. She would never openly admit that she liked it. Yet nowadays she felt safest there: the university had been a one-way passage.

The commune which housed Gareth was placed with socio-politico-economic precision at the rather favoured end of one of the most deprived streets in the town – 'at the interface', the poets of jargon would say, 'of the ongoing urban deterioration situation'.

She was let in to the house rather, she imagined, as one lets an unarmed stranger into a fortress. Gareth, she was told, unsmilingly, by the very white-faced, very long-haired, elegantly be-jeaned and bloused, extremely pretty girl who had opened the door, was upstairs and would be down soon. The girl took her place quietly at a big trestle-table and continued her business which consisted in gluing messages on to placards. Another and very similar young woman was helping her, both of them working as devotedly as nuns. On the far side of the room was Weston – the dreaded extremist – sitting stock-still in front of a typewriter as if frozen in an Arctic blizzard. There was only the one room downstairs. The interconnecting wall had been recently (she guessed) and amateurishly (she could tell) knocked down. There were one or two wooden chairs; the principal furniture consisted in large brightly embroidered cushions. The walls were plastered all over with posters – Che, Mao, Buster Keaton, Angela Davis, Soledad Brothers, Shrewsbury Three, Meetings, Declarations, Demands, Threats and Promises. As Helen sat down to wait, Weston, as if he had been waiting for her to settle herself, sprang into action and attacked the old typewriter like a clockwork cartoon figure overwound. No one spoke. The placards were on the subject of squatters' rights. They themselves were squatters in that house.

The man Weston finished his manic typing, leaned back, sighed happily, pulled out the sheet and read through his prose contentedly. The women went over, one at a time, and read, slowly and silently, what he had written. The three then spoke about it quietly and seriously and Helen, not discourteously ignored, listened not so much to what they said as to how they said it. She was trying hard to locate the background of the two girls from their accents. Weston she knew about. The girls were quite tricky. There was a slight adenoidal feature which suggested scouse: there was the occasional and arbitrary snap-lift which indicated Cockney. Yet the accent was far from either. She listened hard. The discussion became a little tense as Weston found his text, hot from the machine, criticised quite pointedly by the women.

He asseverated: they demurred. That gave them away. That demurring. Rich middle-class Home Counties, Helen concluded, grimly. Daddies quite likely stockbrokers or judges or of that ilk – probably a minor version – rich and establishment but also loners in their way. The women thinking they were La Pasionaria, imitating the working class and in doing so, parodying that class insultingly. The sort Helen hated most.

She decided to leave and was just judging her moment to get up when Gareth came downstairs. He was preceded by a young, rather plump, badly dressed blonde. It was perfectly clear they they had just been to bed together. Helen could not have stood up. The weakness and jealousy which flooded her took away all the strength she had. She stared like a child.

'Nice to see you,' Gareth said, in his most friendly manner. He came over, bent down and kissed her, quickly, before she had the time to dodge away. 'You know everybody, I suppose.' She did not but he did not introduce her. 'Everybody will certainly know you.'

No one took any notice.

The blonde girl plugged in the electric kettle and shook coffee from the jar into the five mugs all lined up on the floor beside the box of sugar cubes and the carton of milk.

'Would you like a cup, love?' She was a local girl. The voice was almost plangently Cumbrian. Helen shook her head.

'It'll be no bother,' the girl said. 'It'll be no bother at all.'

'No, thank you,' Helen scarcely heard herself whisper. Her throat felt sore. 'No thanks,' she repeated, loudly.

'Suit yourself. But it would be no bother at all.'

'Have some of this.' Gareth, who had sat down beside her, held out his flask. He looked sympathetic and squeezed her arm affectionately. She took the flask and drank a mouthful of the whisky.

'Better?'

She nodded.

'We are going,' Weston announced, 'on our pub crawl. Coming, everybody?' Everybody was so nobody replied except Gareth.

'I'll join you later,' he said.

'What for?' The blonde girl, squatting beside the steaming kettle, looked up with unsophisticated suspicion. 'What are you not coming for?'

'We have things to talk about.'

'You can talk about them with us.'

'Private things.'

'I'll wait for you here.' She knocked off the kettle and poured the scalding water on the grains.

'No you won't,' Gareth said, pleasantly.

'Yes I bloody well will.'

Gareth stood up, tugged Helen to her feet, and before anybody knew what was happening, they were out of the door.

'We'll take your car,' he said. 'Get in and start it quick.'

The girl came out of the house as Helen turned on the engine. Gareth waved. Helen drove away.

'Where to?'

'Is the Park open?'

'I don't know.'

'Why don't we go and look at the sea,' Gareth said. 'That'll always do.'

They arrived at that disputed stretch of coast which Jimmie was attempting to preserve for wildlife and his council to utilise for urban development. Helen stopped the car and gazed through the windscreen on to the choppy water. The tide was full up. The headlights illuminated the black cold water on the shoreline. Spittings of rain flicked on to the pane. Helen took out a cigarette.

'I'm out,' Gareth announced and plucked one of her menthols.

After a couple of draws he stubbed it out.

'I don't know how you can smoke the things,' he said, 'they're so cool they aren't cigarettes at all.'

He paused and smiled at her but she did not respond. She knew already that she had betrayed herself into believing she could either make it work with Gareth or play him along. But she had been wrong and already the hurt was there, gathering weight.

'Well now,' he went on, cheerfully, 'shocked, disappointed, disgusted, insulted, apathetic, or shall I put you down as a "don't know"?'

'She looks about fifteen.'

'Eighteen. They mature slowly around here.' Gareth grinned, meaninglessly. 'Don't worry. She wasn't a virgin.'

'Do you have to have everybody and everything you want?'

'Seems like it.'

'And I'm just another card in the pack.'

'You know you're not. But I am rather awkwardly aware that my moral position – as you would say – at the moment is far from strong. Although why you should behave as if we've been Darby and Joan for fifty years and I've just been discovered *in flagrante delicto* I don't really know. You do try to impose that ludicrous moral code of yours on everybody and everything. But some things cannot be eaten with a knife and fork.'

'Oh shut up, Gareth.' She spoke the words so quietly that he listened.

There was nothing out at sea. No comforting ships, no lights from across the water – nothing. She would have to find a strategy for survival again. It would be best to run away now but she could not let down Jimmie: he needed help. She was stuck. Inside the small car was quiet as a cloister.

'How do you cope?' she asked, eventually, still looking before her.

'With more than one?'

'With, I imagine, many more than one and quite a few who depend principally if not entirely on you.'

'I cope very well,' Gareth said.

'You sound utterly lifeless.' Helen turned and looked at him in surprise. Her remark had surprised her but when she saw him she saw the truth of it in his face. He looked strained and ill – the energy now a mimicry of what it had been years ago. Yet once more he felt constrained to produce a grin which seemed now so truly kin to a grimace of pain – but of what? Pain? Anger? She did not know. Yet she had caught a flash of it, the skull beneath the flesh.

'Perhaps,' Gareth said, deliberately camp, mincingly, 'I give too much of myself, sweetheart.'

'You gave a lot to me,' she said, simply.

'You're very special,' he said.

'Jesus Christ, Gareth!'

'Sorry.'

'No you're not.'

'No I'm not.'

'The other night – when I came down to you – and after that, since—'

'That first time was very good,' he interrupted her. 'Very, very high-class work. *After* that as well. But that "first-time-for-years" time was ace.'

'I thought,' she attempted to go on as if he had not interrupted. But failed. Then she said abruptly. 'You wouldn't live with me, would you? Would you?' The silence was humiliating. 'Even if I begged you,' she added softly, staring straight ahead. He made no move at all.

She started up the car. 'I'll drive you to your pub.'

'Join us. Confuse the natives.'

'No thanks.'

'Disapprove.'

'Yes.' Slowly she backed out and slowly she did her turn-around before pointing for the town.

'Of me or the politics?'

'Which pub?'

'I'll get out here.' He opened the door, then he leaned over and kissed her, lightly. 'We could go back to my place. It's empty. Fancy it?'

'I'll take you to the pub.'

'I need the exercise.' Nimbly he swung himself out of the car, nimble and agile, still attractive even in that small manoeuvre, she thought. But he had been aware of her, and he had been trying hard. He shut the door, waved, and walked away. She longed, sickeningly, to call him back, to plead with him to be with her. She should not have let him go.

She waited. Her uncertainty was now compounded by fear. She wondered what on earth was going to happen to her. She really ought to run: sometimes it was right and good to run. What was Jimmie's campaign worth compared with her peace of mind? For Gareth would continue to torment her. How many days to go? Why had she been such a fool as to think she could play him along? Why, in her life, was the ancient savage morality with its swift retribution so active? Why did he not love her?

When she had calmed herself down she started the engine once again and turned on the windscreen wipers to clear the rain which had reduced the view to a few glints of weak, yellow, refracted light. She drove slowly along the empty streets and slowly up the narrow road to the vicarage.

Chapter Seventeen

(i)

'You're worse than a murderer and I'm saying no more.'

Marianne waited. Her mother's accusing whine had just begun. Each time she announced 'I'm saying no more' it was merely to pause and recharge her venom. Since Alan's birth Marianne had been less and less able to bear with these long and bitter outpourings. This time there was no advantage in reply or retreat. It had to be endured. Like a storm at sea, it simply had to be weathered. She settled herself in the cheap chair in the bare-looking maisonette – her mother had never shown or cultivated cosy femininity – and tried to school herself to patience. Calculated the length of the pauses. Looked out of the corner of her eye at the large colour photograph of Alan which was the sole object put up for view. Remembered some of the numberless rows and confrontations she had had with this woman, her mother, who had soaked her energy, saturated her existence, and threatened to drown her in a lifelong retributive vendetta. Sat tight.

Marianne had told her mother that she was going to leave the area and look for a job. This, she had said, summoning all her steadiness, would mean leaving Alan at the vicarage for some of the weekdays at the beginning of the project.

'Just like your bloody father. Up and off. Up and off. Nobody else. Nobody else.'

It was evening, dusk. Her mother was almost bent double with her splenetic load. The mousy hair had been recently

208

and cheaply permed. It lay in frozen little wavelets, a chastened thatch. Her hands were showing the first signs of Parkinson's Disease. She smoked Silk Cut to the last millimetre. Her pinny was starched spotless. The slippers at the bottom of skinny legs in deep old-fashioned brown nylons were suddenly purple with crimson pom-poms. Beside her was the television, her sole evening solace. The wireless was on the mantelpiece next to the alarm clock. Marianne dared not look at her, the thin rejected mouth, cheeks smudged with impatient make-up, brow a concertina of anxiety – and the eyes, seeking all the sympathy in the world, yearning for all the love that could be found, still wounded by the man who had left her so long ago, lapping hungrily for any trickled drop of affection and, thwarted, glittering as vengefully as those of any Fury in the small darkening room. She began again.

'It's badness. It was in him, it's in you, it'll be in little Alan if I don't take care to watch him. It's bred. You can't get it out. I tried. God knows I tried. I worked my fingers to the bone. I sweated and slaved. I put you on a pedestal. I would have died for you. It's all wasted. You're just like him. You take what you want and you run away. You run away. You leave others to pick up the pieces. We have to pick up the pieces. Leaving that little boy on his own. It's wicked. It shows you're just a selfish, greedy, vicious, nasty specimen like he was – your bloody father! He did that. You're the same. And why up there? If that little boy has to stay anywhere he has to stay with me. I'm his proper grandmother. Nobody loves that little boy more than I do. They ruin him up there. When he comes here I can see. He runs wild. They let him run wild. He needs to be loved and looked after by me. But you don't think of that. No. Not you. You wouldn't. All you think about is self. Self, self, self, that's you. See. I know you. I know all about you. I know you better than you know yourself. I know what you'll do. You won't come back. Don't deny it. You'll stay away. You'll gad about. Don't

deny it. Then what'll I do? Who'll come to see me? Your
own mother. Flesh and blood. Of course you don't care. I
work my fingers to the bone, I sweat and slave. I sacrifice
everything. You don't care. Self. Self. Self. So what'll I
have? Nothing, that's what I'll have. I'll have nothing.
That'll just suit you. That's what you want. Him up there
where they ruin him and I can't get to see him. They don't
like me there. Don't pretend. And you on the gad somewhere
in a city. On the gad like him. Just a bloody pair. If you do –
that little boy – it'll be worse than murder. You don't have to
kill somebody, you know, to be a murderer. Your father. I'll
say no more.'

Marianne gripped the arms of her chair and waited. It
was a great deal harder than she had anticipated. Her mother
began again.

(ii)

Outside the lights of London were enticing. Harold liked his
view. It was the best part of this office. He stood and looked
over the city as someone might survey a territory conquered
or possessed. The view could have just such an inflating
effect on his ego. Only when he was very tired, though, and
only when he was playing games. As now.

Miss Eliot came in as silently as an Indian body-servant. It
was almost 10 p.m. She had taken off about an hour at seven
and come back in a different outfit – bathed, refreshed, ready
to work alongside him again. The meetings with the
company's accountants and the accountants of the takeover
contender had been arduous. His great diary-cleaning sweep
had lasted no more than a few days. Then there had been the
negotiations with the lawyers. Writs had been put out to
Private Eye but possibly a little too late. She came up to him
and handed him a large tumbler – whisky and water. He
took it without saying a word and sipped slowly. His first
that day. He had been warned again not to mix the pills with

alcohol. She went back to her chair and waited – notebook, pencil, legs crossed neatly. He heard the very slight but entirely sensuous sound of silk as she crossed her legs. She was wearing those old-fashioned silk stockings, he thought. The thought was worth relishing. He let it rub around as the whisky gently slid home.

The phone. She took it. 'The young man is at the door,' she said.

'Let him wait.' Harold hesitated. 'Ten minutes – fifteen. I want a shower.'

This was transmitted. She resumed her seat.

Harold walked across the office. He was in his stockinged feet. His jacket was off. There were drying damp patches under the arms of his white shirt. His collar was open. His exhausted trudge across that small space moved Miss Eliot, who loved him, a great deal. But she said nothing.

'Do you think we'll get it through?' he asked.

'It's more possible now than it seemed this morning,' she spoke carefully. He wanted no emollient reassurances where business was concerned. 'But they are still very worried about that *Private Eye* business.'

'Why the shit should it bother them?'

'It does.'

'Bloody cowards!' Harold looked at her and smiled open-heartedly. 'They *are*, aren't they, bloody little cowards?'

'Yes.' She relaxed just a little; a very, very little. 'Compared with you.'

'But they'll beat me in the end if I'm not careful.'

'We still have a lot of options.'

'You mean we still have a lot of fight.'

'Yes.'

'Same thing.' He agreed. 'But *time, time* – that's the bastard! Time.'

'Yes.' She wanted to follow it up but could not trust herself. Over the past couple of weeks he had become so vulnerable that this effect on her had been hard to keep in check.

She hung on hard to the routines and habits of a long and tough working partnership. If he wanted more, she knew, he would go for it. If only he would come to her.

'Well,' he said, after a considerable pause, 'you needn't stay on any longer tonight. No need for both of us to be tired out.'

'Are you sure?' It was not a question she asked, normally. It was not part of the routine. She noted that he hesitated. 'Is there anything else you want?' Her tone was so neutral that it scarcely even sounded like a question.

'Not yet,' he replied, unnaturally softly. 'Good night, Jean.'

'Good night.'

He watched her go to the door: she walked aware of this with no perceptible sign of her excitement. Harold sighed and then heaved himself through the business of taking a shower, changing, lighting a cigar, reading part of the morning's papers which had been on the table untouched since his arrival in the office at 7 a.m.

As he expected, he felt better for the effort. He pressed the buzzer and settled back. Peter Fraser came in and took a seat as if he were an applicant about to be interviewed for a job.

Harold let him sit for about three minutes without saying a word. Three full minutes, in the rich quiet office with the traffic sounds of London in the streets below reaching up as a low intermittent motorised moaning. Over the young man's face, spread across it like a large white brand, was the dressing which gave protection to his broken nose. It made him look as if he were wearing a mask, Harold decided. He wondered what would happen if he leaned forward and just ripped it off? The man would scream of course. But then what would he do? He had tried, Harold observed, not to move a muscle during those three minutes.

'This needn't take long,' Harold said, finally. 'I'd be grateful for your help, that's all.'

Peter nodded. He could wait. He had time.

Chapter Eighteen

'How small, of all that human hearts endure,
That part which laws or kings can cause or cure.'

Jimmie looked at those two lines for some minutes. Small
and all, cure and endure, cause and laws, hearts and part:
kings and human were the only two words he could not find
a rhyme for inside the couplet. *That* thought could kick off
his speech. He began to write and then stopped. It would not
do to be clever-clever or literary. It would seem as if he were
attempting to upstage the Prime Minister. He had suffered
from that in the past. He crossed out the lines, crumpled up
the page and took the few steps over to the window.

From here he looked directly into the copper beech. As a
boy he had swung on it, hidden in it, dared himself to climb
higher and higher – testing himself – attempted to construct
a tree house, made a swing, watched it daily exist, just be,
there, outside his bedroom window. He could not think of
life without it now. When he looked at it, Jimmie felt that he
understood the strange religious notion of Wordsworth that
there were indeed virtues in Nature, moral laws, which the
receptive mind and heart could perceive. For although it
was embarrassing to admit, it was true that, on some occasions, simply looking at the copper beech tree made him
feel a better man and determine to act so. He relaxed in
these thoughts.

He knew what his speech must be. It clicked into place.

His job was to deliver the expected line. All attention must be focused on the Prime Minister. No claiming any personal spotlight should be admitted. No frills, no show, no rhetoric, no local pleading – a brisk run around the estate and lead the applause for the PM. He could knock that off in an hour. He waited, the cold of the linoleum creeping through the worn soles of his ancient slippers. House quiet about him although he had heard Alan and Mrs. Burns go past his door and down the stairs, creeping so as not to disturb him. During the campaign his domestic status had gradually been elevated to that of a most delicate invalid. 'Jimmie needs peace and quiet': this, at present, was the household word. Yet this respect, now, was so little deserved, he thought.

Back to his desk. Wrenched away from the view. No poetry. Some other time. Even though Dr. Johnson's words expressed the resilient complacency of Britishness? And – no: some other time. Some other time too for his self-doubts and regrets and guilt. There was an election to be fought and won!

'We are fortunate,' he wrote, 'this evening, to have with us someone whose work and career in the Labour Movement, in the Labour Party, in Westminster, in the Nation at large, and on the wider International Scene, has ...' What? Jimmie hesitated only for a moment and then ploughed on. No self-indulgence permitted!

The morning dragged its way through. It was the Monday before the Thursday election day and there was a feeling of relief and half-real, half-stimulated frenzy. Jimmie had fixed a co-ordinating meeting for lunchtime in GHQ. He arrived punctually.

Everybody was in on it. The Chief Constable was pucker-browed and clamp-lipped about the 'security aspect'. The security aspect began to worry them all, after he had, for the final time, outlined the risks. 'On paper' – a phrase he used a great deal – on paper they were extensive. The Prime Minister travelled with two aides, with one security man vaguely in another vehicle. He walked about in the streets in a manner not completely planned and stayed in hotels which could be opened up with a boy-scout knife; he travelled on twisting routes preceded, usually at a distance beyond the call of help, by a couple of police motorcyclists obsessed with keeping their uniforms clean: and unarmed. There would be no security check at the door of the Imperial Ballroom in which the meeting was to take place and as everyone knew, the Imperial Ballroom was very likely a fire-trap and so secure that any bunch of teenagers could sneak in, as they did every Saturday night to avoid paying. No one, the Chief Constable said, need be reminded of the proximity of Ireland to this western coast, or of the links between West Cumberland and Ireland, of the nasty strike which had now lasted over fourteen months – not in this constituency, but in the neighbouring parish (his word). The IRA had promised 'surprises' before election day and – one way and another . . . the Chief Constable had a high old time and when he was done the assembled worthies looked around edgily as if expecting Al Capone to burst through from the tea-room waving a submachine-gun.

'Let's be reasonable about this,' Jimmie said, sucking his chairman's pipe, amused at the pleasure the Chief Constable was getting from his attempt to scare them all. 'On the whole, taking the round view, the odds are rather against a Kennedy-in-Dallas style assassination attempt. You coped very well with the Duke of Edinburgh. I've no doubt if you employ much the same method, the PM should escape with superficial wounds.'

'The Royals have a routine,' the Chief Constable said grimly.

'Use it for commoners, then.'

'With respect, the routine depends on Them as much as Us. It can't just be put on like a pair of old socks. The Royals have a tradition.'

'Freddie,' Jimmie said – using the Chief Constable's

Christian name which he thought, wrongly, flattered him – affecting to be weary – both of them knew what would be done and trusted it would work well, 'he's only here for four hours. He arrives. He eats, he talks, talks some more and then he goes up to London on the sleeper.'

'Time is no factor,' Freddie said, as if quoting.

'I'm sure you'll manage perfectly.'

'We shall see,' Freddie concluded, darkly.

If anyone in the district really wanted to blow up the present Prime Minister, Jimmie reflected, it would be Freddie himself, to whom all politicians since Churchill were greater or lesser 'sharks' or 'wets'.

'I like this PM!' Freddie claimed, suddenly, as if he had read Jimmie's thoughts. 'You know where you are with him. That's more than can be said for most.' He smiled around the table, aware that he had contradicted expectation and quite wolfishly pleased with himself.

'What about Weston?' Bill was beginning to have nightmares about Weston, whose nagging and tailing, disruptive activities and general confounding of the issues had persisted too long. He would not let go of the Harold-schools contract issue despite the writ and the publication of Jimmie's letter admitting 'responsibility' (which, as he might have expected, had occasioned a welter of support and served only to exonerate him. Transport House, his own committee, Bill, old friends and colleagues – support had rushed in. 'The true conscience of the liberal-democratic left,' *The Times* had called him in a third leader).

'He won't have a ticket.'

'He might,' Jimmie said. 'There are half a dozen ways he could have got hold of one.'

'You don't want us in the hall,' Freddie said to Jimmie, 'and I agree with you. I don't want my men to be seen on the telly frogmarching citizens out on the streets. We'll stay outside.'

'I can fix—' Bill stopped. The Chief Constable's glare dissolved his cultivated Gilbert and Sullivan public appearance.

'Mr. Atkinson!' Bill froze to attention at the sound of his surname and title. 'You can provide stewards. However, let me make it quite clear that citizens in this country have a right to heckle and to shout questions at a public speaker. Let's not all become namby-pamby about this matter. Public disturbance is something "up with which I will not put": vigorous public meetings are part of any general election and neither you nor anyone else will employ bully-boys in my parish. Is that clear, sir?'

Bill said no more. Jimmie moved on to the tricky matter of protocol. Who would shake the PM's hand?

'It says in *The Times*,' Helen said, later, when the dignitaries and officials had departed leaving a Sargasso Sea of tea-cups, full ashtrays, half-bitten buns and doodles, 'no PM's been this far away from London this late in an election.' It was mid-afternoon: the perfect time for gossip.

'Who would want to look that up?' Jimmie asked.

'The *Times* man.'

'But what sort of man is he?' Jimmie speculated. 'What does he drink? Does he laugh at dirty jokes? Is he an apparently sane commuter?'

'He thinks we'll lose,' Helen said.

'Us? Here? I haven't read it yet.'

'Us. Here.'

'Don't trust him.' Jimmie smiled in order to cheer her up. He had got a firm grip on his feelings now and indulged no more in any display of the sentimental longings for her he still felt. He noticed, as he had done a few times over the past week, that she looked unhappy. Though he suspected the cause he had not faced up to it. He had enough to do. 'Elections are the graveyard of the political prophet – Confucius he say – quite right too,' Jimmie murmured. 'Good old Confucius.'

'He thought the Tories would get in. The *Times* man.'

'The sort of article that starts to be anxious on our behalf because soon we might not be able to raise eleven men to field a decent opposition?'

'That's exactly what he said.' She smiled and the straightforward sweetness struck him. 'You *did* read it.'

'Not guilty. Common enough cliché among the lads. "More in sorrow than anger" always brings out the gentler sports for metaphors.'

'The PM's certainly doing his whirlwind best.'

'Well.' Jimmie paused and sucked deeply at the delicate china cup of thick tea Bill had provided. No alcoholic drink until after the meeting. 'There are whirlwinds and there's the quick dash for the last bus. Mr. Carter went all over the USA in jets for two or three years every *week* – two thousand miles for breakfast, three thousand five hundred for lunch, back home, a quick shake of the beans and off fifteen hundred miles up the road to talk to some minority grouped squaws. Every week. Our PM – all credit to him – has indeed visited Bristol, Cardiff and Leeds over the last fortnight and spent yesterday in Glasgow and Edinburgh. Rough, I agree. Whirlwind? Hardly.' He reached out and put his hand firmly on her wrist. 'OK?' She nodded, miserably, cast down a little by his sympathy. 'It'll soon be over. On Saturday you'll be back in Lancaster. If you think back on it at all it will be as a rather badly organised bit of fieldwork that yielded only what you could have guessed in the greater comfort of the college library.'

'It seems so odd to think that I *will* be back there,' she said. 'It's *that* part of my life which appears unreal.' The thought of returning to her lonely, settled, time-tabled life repelled her: and yet she could not stay.

'The whole business is very odd,' Jimmie agreed. 'And the other part is even odder.'

'The other part?'

'Non-life. Commonly called death. More tea?'

'You're in a good mood,' she said. She loved this scruffy, busy room. Next-door Bill made calls on two phones simutaneously – but he did not bother Jimmie. He wanted 'his boy' to rest up while he could.

'It always puts me in a good mood, campaigning,' Jimmie said, truthfully. 'I meet a lot of people, some of whom I like and respect enormously. I talk about what I believe in, which makes it clear to me that I do believe in something. It's a battle – I like that aspect too. Sometimes! You're all right, aren't you?'

'Yes.' She looked at him anxiously. Had Jimmie seen or suspected anything about Gareth? 'Don't I look it?'

'A bit exhausted. We all are. No wonder. Done marvels really. Fullest canvass I've ever managed to do.'

'Only three more days.'

'Four,' Jimmie corrected her. 'We run though until Friday lunch because of the villages way up in the fells – remember?'

'What do you think?'

'I think I'll just lose,' Jimmie said. He pulled a face. '*Just* – but still – lose. The trouble is that when they re-organised the boundaries I lost a slab of my "natural" vote and inherited a slab of *their* natural vote. Alas. And you? What do you think?'

'It's so unfair!' She showed the affection she had concealed at some cost recently – on the rebound from Gareth? Yes, she had to admit it. She wanted affection – like a wound needing to be staunched. 'You're such a good man – simply to lose because of a national swing and an unfortunate boundary change – it's unfair!'

'But you agree. I *will*, just lose.'

'Yes. And bloody Weston.'

'It isn't him.' Jimmie was surprised. 'I haven't heard you criticising him before.'

'I detest that sort of lower-middle-class playing around with politics to pull in the vaguely upper-middle-class girls and go on a great ego-trip. That's all it is. Gareth should never have fallen for it.'

'It's Gareth then.'

Helen did not reply. Jimmie let the Angel pass over his grave and then snapped into his military manner like a marionette.

'Time we got the show on the road,' he said. 'I've changed my mind. I think I'll win. Bill! Bill! To the barricades! More pamphlets!'

Bill grinned as 'his boy' came into the room, indeed rather like a very large, handsome, shaggy mountain of a boy, open and eager for the fray.

'Bill! Will we win?'

'We've got no bloody alternative!' Bill replied, happily, allowing himself a full, guilt-free swearword to celebrate the imminent arrival of his hero the Prime Minister.

Chapter Nineteen

'Isn't he broad?' they said, or 'Isn't he fat?' or 'Isn't he tall?' or 'Isn't he tired?' or 'He isn't as serious as he is on television,' or 'He isn't as grey as he is on television,' or 'He smiles just like he does on television.'

Smiling was the order of the evening. The Prime Minister smiled as he got out of the train, the Mayor smiled, his wife smiled, *his* wife smiled, Elaine smiled, Jimmie smiled, shook hands, click, flash, click, 'Just a moment,' 'Another one,' 'Hold it there, please'; the crowd smiled, children smiled they knew not why, sceptical observers standing some way off, they smiled too, the committee smiled and shook hands and the councillors smiled, each and every one and so did *their* wives: what was behind the smiles, who knew? What was in front was the man who held most power in the land however disarmingly *he* smiled and handshook and beamingly presented himself to all about him.

'If you have a moment, Prime Minister,' 'We're BBC News, Prime Minister,' 'We're Border Television, Prime Minister,' 'We're the local radio, Prime Minister,' 'We're the *Evening Star*, Prime Minister.' Prime Minister, Prime Minister – what lovely words they were and everyone wanted to say them more than once, sometimes say them again and again as if the words with the man himself before them would rub away at the Aladdin's lamp of their lives and suddenly produce genies galore – flash! – click – 'Just another one, Prime Minister,' 'Could you shake his hand,

Prime Minister?' 'That's the Prime Minister,' children were told and the town band played 'Colonel Bogey'.

This was a town where carnivals still counted. The Rose Queen and her attendants, for example, would be expected to spend the equivalent of a month's wages on the material for their costumes which could be worn only for that day. The competition between the coast towns was tough and it had never shown a sign of dying out. For the Prime Minister, the least they could do was give him a procession, as Bill said, especially here in what had, but for a single lapse, been a stronghold of Labour faith and muscle since the thirties.

The Prime Minister was, clearly, impressed. He was not used to such treats. Britain had become electronic and sophisticated for its election spasms. Bill had laid on a cavalcade. A torchlight procession from the railway station to the Imperial Ballroom. The town which by day collected drab adjectives as industriously as a spider collects flies, now by night and *en fête* showed off its paces.

'This,' said the Prime Minister, as he climbed into the open-roofed car and looked up at the black clear starlit sky and then again to the river of lights brandished by the schoolchildren, 'this', repeated the Prime Minister, as he beckoned up Jimmie beside him and settled himself firmly and looked approvingly at the jaded gaggle of reporters from the nationals who were also entertained by the sight of real excitement and festivity – something at last on which to exercise those powers of descriptive prose so praised at school, so underemployed on the great dailies which they had served with heavy helpings of political fare throughout the campaign – 'this is something like a bloody election! Thanks, Jimmie.'

The two men, never friends, were reproduced all over the dailies next morning – the Prime Minister's left arm affectionately around Jimmie's shoulders, his right arm raised in his most optimistic wave for months. And so he motored slowly to the meeting.

The shops had kept on their lights and brought out the Jubilee bunting and the Union Jacks. The other towns had sent in their bands and the ranks of marching bandsmen, mostly ex-colliers, swelled as the procession moved up the main street. The Chief Constable was in close attendance and noticed his men so smartly turned out. He, too, had done his bit; mounted police had been called on and the obedient horses walked steadily beside the flaming torches, the overcrowded cars, the pavements.

It was a show of strength. Jimmie and Bill had worked their guts out on it. The crowd was packed with supporters from towns ten, fourteen and thirty-eight miles away. All manner of favours had been called in to make this impact. The route was short and the two streets very narrow which turned the crowd into a 'vast crowd' (*Daily Mirror*), 'cheerful mob' (*Guardian*), 'surprisingly large and enthusiastic reception' (*The Times*). Schoolteachers had been nobbled and kids promised fire to play with. Clubs of all sorts and sports had been dragooned by Bill – threats had not been overlooked, debts had. The result was like a brief but sensationally unexpected Roman Carnival which flared through that town and thence on to the television screens of the nation like a firework display.

'This should do us no harm,' the Prime Minister said as he waved his papal benediction over the crowd and grinned.

'It's my last throw,' Jimmie said, waving and grinning more modestly as the car moved forward at funeral pace.

'Bad as that?'

'No. But just bad enough. Just that bit.'

'Same everywhere,' the Prime Minister said. 'But we can still do it.' Waves, grins, hellos, how are yous. 'Tonight's important for me,' he confessed grimly, still smiling.

'I hope we get it right.' A blast from the Iron and Steel Band of Cumbria who joined the procession just before the Ballroom.

'If I'd waited any longer,' the Prime Minister said, 'we'd

have been—' In the noise the exact word was lost: but its meaning was plain.

Weston and Gareth and company were not hurling their chants outside the Ballroom and so Jimmie concluded, correctly, that they had managed to outwit Bill and get inside. He would have put money on it.

More cameras inside. 'The Prime Minister!' 'The Prime Minister!' 'Here he is!' There was a standing ovation as the party ambled comfortably down the main aisle towards the stage.

'You know,' the Prime Minister said as he got into his stride, 'this isn't a bad old country. We have our ups and downs. The trouble is we take the ups too much for granted and we take the downs too much to heart. Sometimes I don't recognise the old place. Especially when I'm abroad. I read about these reports in the press of America or Italy or wherever I happen to be. "Britain sunk in gloom," they say. "Pound sinking." Well, we put a stop to that! "Morale sinking." We put a stop to that too! "Industry sinking." Sometimes I wonder to myself if the place won't be at the bottom of the North Sea by the time I get back to it! And what's a little bit worrying is that all these reports abroad, you know, all this gloom and doom, starts here. Or rather it starts in London. I wish some of the editors of those big newspapers ever thought of anywhere north of Hampstead or south of Stockwell. They should come and see what I've seen tonight. They sell Britain short and of course other countries take them seriously. It does us great damage abroad. Of that there is no doubt. We're knocking ourselves into an early grave. Self-criticism – I'm all for it. Not taking certain things too seriously – yes, I agree with that. But the survival of this country is a serious matter and I sometimes wonder if the newspapers fully realise that. They should come here, to the roots of the country, and see the people who really do speak for the country.

'Now, I don't want to wash whiter than white. I don't

want to come here selling you the best brand of Britain. We have problems. Unemployment, racial difficulties, Dickensian poverty still – we are grimly aware of all that. I'm no mindless optimist – but I think we get the picture wrong if we don't see things in balance as they are. And there *have been* improvements. Here in this town many of you live in three-bedroomed houses with gardens and some privacy where before you your fathers and their fathers lived in hutches not houses, back-to-back terraces, outside toilets, nowhere for the kids to play safely, no bit of your own garden – I needn't spell it out. We've been through a social revolution. You can see it all around you. Money's tight, I know. Prices rise – true – too many – too often – final proof, if any were needed, that in its time of need, it's not the rich who rally round. They don't keep prices down the way the much-abused Unions helped us through with wages. But even so, even so – you'll admit, I think, that your children and their children are better dressed, better fed, in better health, better housed – well, I won't go on – but it doesn't *do* to deny what has been achieved. Just as, over the past two or three years, this government, your government, has tried in a quiet way to get things a bit better for those who need it most. We've put an awful lot of money into old-age pensions – we don't boast about it, but we have tried, at great cost, I admit, to skilled craftsmen – men who've served years of vigorous apprenticeship, the backbone of an industrial society such as ours – at great cost to middle management and to some professional people – we have tried to help most those who have needed most help. If you get behind the headlines and examine the facts you'll find that the less well-off have been catching up over the last two or three years and that, surely, is one of the things we all want. Because a great society is like a decent family. If it has to spend most on its weakest member, it does so. That's what decency and a family means. There are many things we can be proud of and many things we can congratulate ourselves on. Never forget that. Don't let them talk you down. You know, there's still a lot of old-fashioned snobbery about. The sort of person who used to go to Spain for his holidays but won't go now because of the "package tours", that sort of person. The sort of superior person who says he hates "tourists" even though he's a tourist himself! We all know him! Or her! Don't we? And it's much the same about democracy, you know. We've achieved great things, this century, we – the Labour Movement! We've pulled ourselves up so far we take for granted things which our grandfathers thought would belong forever to the privileged few. Well, they don't! We took them as of right. The right to the basic decencies of life! And They don't like it. So They sneer, They whine, They pretend that what we have gained is not worth having. What They mean is that They don't like sharing. Don't let Them fool you. Hold what you have and reach out for more of the liberties and benefits of a full and free life. That's what being independent people inside a compassionate Labour Party is all about! That's what this country should be about! And only you can do it!' His voice rose. He had staved off the rise of applause several times. People wanted to applaud him: the event demanded it. Now he encouraged it and took a sip of water as the audience enjoyed itself, appreciating him and also the fact that they were in the news.

For the cameras had begun to find focus. Everyone was aware of them. The red lights flashed and excited the audience further. The heavy television lights came on, flickered like lightning in slow motion, and then settled on, flushing out all shadowy crannies from the ballroom. The audience bristled. The national nine o'clock news was coming on to the air and the Prime Minister would be seen – they would be seen – 'live'.

He had his own system of cues most carefully worked out with the floor manager. He was told there would be forty-five seconds of headlines and then they would come over live to him. Off-camera still he went straight for applause again, crudely but effectively, working up that atmosphere towards a climax. 'What are we saying to the people of this country tonight?' There was a murmur, a massive rumble from the twelve hundred. They wished to have their answer articulated. Having set up the question, the Prime Minister, the seconds ticking off steadily inside his head, punched out for the effect he wanted the camera to catch when they switched from London. 'We are saying – look at what we have done – we have kept pensions up to date with inflation, we have made and carried through the most difficult social contract in our history, we have asked for and obtained sacrifices of all kinds from all of you. We have done the hard bit, the dirty work–' Twenty, nineteen, eighteen, seventeen: he paused. 'Now let's get on with the pleasant part – we've pulled the country out of the Slough of Despond,' seven, six, five, 'let's march on together to the Promised Land – why not? It's there! It's yours! Let's go on together!'

Applause – real, genuine, a burst of authentic emotional longing – and Jimmie clapping too although he was embarrassed a little at the manipulation as the camera lights went red and the lenses swept across the enthusiastic audience. He felt, as he always did, that in the end the Prime Minister was using the national feeling; using this overspill of emotion, manipulating, seizing the opportunity, wheeler-dealing.

But in that same moment Jimmie knew why he was applauding and felt again the emotional root commitment which was his touchstone. He glanced at Elaine, so fierce this night in her determination to be there and not to let him down. Her struggle too was part of what he must do, and he felt a warmth of love for her such as he had not felt for years: she was being courageous and that was very moving. In that brief time, so much shorter than the telling, Jimmie had a sense of affirmation which was almost as strong as the original revelation that had first led him to lay out his future on that of this rich but difficult, often sullen, often infuriating and self-defeating movement. Yes, his conscience was split over the closed-shop issue and his loyalties torn by the parochial attitudes of the big unions towards their smaller 'brothers'; by the hypocrisy of the rich Labour men who used the private schools and hospitals and by the hypocrisy of the Labour left which was so selective over what it saw in Eastern Europe. But these people here were better than that. It was sentimental, perhaps, he thought, but his sentimentality had shored up his beliefs more consistently than the widely proclaimed principles of others and it was here in this hall with these people that Jimmie saw his commitment and felt, as he so rarely did, that he was doing something worthwhile.

The Prime Minister waved down the applause and seemed to forget all about the cameras as he leaned forward, jutted out his chin, pushed aside his notes, thought of the eleven to twelve million watching this bulletin, knew in his heart of hearts that elections *could* be tilted in a day, knew there was everything to play for and reached out for votes. 'What do you ask of us?' he cried out – and the tone was harsher and more fierce than he had used hitherto. 'To be fair? To be successful? Yes, To be able to answer all the problems that arise from the price of bread to your son's job difficulties? Yes? To deal with the thugs who rove the streets in Northern Ireland? Yes? Well – *be* fair – we haven't done too badly. We inherited from the Tories a mess bigger than anything since the war and we rolled up our sleeves, got stuck in and made a start. Who else could have pulled off the Social Contract? Who else could have called on the Unions to help curb the evil of inflation? You have to think about that. The Unions come in for a lot of knocking and they aren't perfect – but we got them to help us and together we won a great victory. And you have to think about *this* – let's not flinch away from it. We in the Labour Movement believe in the Big Things in life. We believe in Justice. We believe that good health should be available to all, and good housing and safe old age – and we will hold to that belief and

228

to others come-what-may!' The applause threatened: he quelled it by going on: not yet, let it build. 'They are costly beliefs – most beliefs worth fighting for *are* costly beliefs. It would be easy to throw them overboard, to lighten the ship by junking the weakest members of the crew – and that I am afraid is what the Tories want to do. But make no mistake about it, we as a party and as individuals stand for a better society for *all* of us and however old-fashioned that sounds, I'll repeat it until I'm hoarse. I'm not a man given to wearing his conscience on his sleeve – you all know that – but I must tell you, and I must tell the whole of the British People, that a vote for the Tories is a vote for selfishness, I'm sorry, yes, and for trouble! For what do they propose? Nothing! Except to *undo* what we – and you – have painfully and patiently done. What do they want? More for him who already hath. What is *their* belief? *Less* fairness, *less* mutual help, *less* all-round justice – hiding under that – expensive – hairdo is someone who wants to wreck the caring society. She says so. You've heard her. And you must stop her. Be fair! Look at what they propose. Look at what they did last time – set off a galloping sickness of inflation and stagnation and unemployment that took us three very painful years to cure – three hard years wasted in just putting the pieces together again.' He saw the signal from the floor. Back to London in fifteen seconds. 'And that is what I am saying to you tonight in no uncertain terms. Be clear, please! Make no mistake about it! What we offer, what we believe, despite all the troubles we have encountered, despite the cynicism and difficulty of the age we live in, is a clear belief in fairness and a promise, a promise as strong as an oath of allegiance to the British People, that we will watch over *all* your best interests! I say again – Be Fair! Support us in the good times we have helped to bring about! Vote Fairly!'

The applause began, foot-stamping, cheers; the cameras lingered an extra twelve seconds, it was so geniune and so loud. Back in the newsroom the BBC political commentator decided to *ad-lib* his way into his report – the Prime Minister had come alight. What he said was, what should he say? 'banal'? – no – never get away with it – 'unsurprising'? – no – 'fairly commonplace'. 'Fairly commonplace' it was, he decided, as his own cue arrived – 'but,' he heard himself saying, 'it was not so much what the Prime Minister *said* as his way of saying it. Tonight, I think, we saw him at full stretch. Indeed, in twenty years' experience, I have never seen him so determined and so in touch with his audience. He has clearly thrown down a gauntlet' (back to the pre-typed script now, on the autocue) 'and Mrs. Thatcher will have to pick it up.'

Back in the hall the Prime Minister turned to Jimmie as the applause continued, and he winked. 'That should give us a leg up,' he said.

Chapter Twenty

The Prime Minister introduced Jimmie, who put aside his own written speech and spoke briefly about what he believed in. He spoke of his first involvement with the Labour Party in the war, he spoke of Attlee and Gaitskell, he spoke of Keir Hardie and a history which could be linked back to the Tolpuddle Martyrs, the Chartists and even reached back to the Diggers. He talked about the miners in the area, the pit-falls of the turn of the century, the desperate conditions, the fight for any sort of progress. He compared the past – golden for the rich, worse than dross for the poor – with the present, where at least there was some comfort, some base for achievement. He spoke of Nye Bevan and quoted from Orwell. He gathered up all that was generally pushed to the bottom of his mind by the pressure of daily circumstances and stood before the electorate for what he was. His earnest good looks, his conviction, the emotion previously stirred up by the presence of the Prime Minister – all combined to help him make what Bill was calculating to be the best speech of his career. It was Elaine there too who helped, Bill thought. She almost literally glowed with pride as he spoke of his ideals. Also Bill saw that the Prime Minister was not merely dutifully turning his head and nodding, he too was caught by that plain confession which had the stimulus of rhetoric. It was this speech that marked out Jimmie, rather old though he might be, as a useful potential Junior Minister in one of those jobs where platform flair was most useful – the

Arts, for example, or something in the Environment. But that was the calculating side of the Prime Minister. Even he, as he was prepared to say afterwards, was moved by this confession.

It was as Jimmie was leading into his peroration that the incidents occurred. Scattered about the hall, shrewdly seated in the middle of rows, about eight Weston supporters stood up, interrupted him, made the Nazi salute and began to chant in shrill unison 'Sieg Heil!' 'Sieg Heil!'

Jimmie stopped. The television cameras went on. Bill stood up and shuffled along the side aisle, waving on to a bunch of well-prepared – despite Freddie the Chief Constable – and friendly supporters. With a maximum of good-mannered and good-natured disturbance – caused by clumsiness and not by design – a dozen of his old colleagues from the local professional Rugby League team, especially cleaned up by their wives, all in white shirts and nearly strangled by club ties, muscles bulging through their smartly buttoned blazers, shuffled along to the hecklers, picked them up, put them over a shoulder and trudged off to the door with them. The smarter revolutionaries adopted well-discussed poses of 'total negative resistance' and the 'ultimate dead weight defence'. This made the Rugby players grunt just a little bit but no one lost a milligramme of sweat. 'Sieg Heil! Sieg Heil! Sieg Heil!' kept coming shrilly from the upside-down or puppet-jerked-up faces of the dissidents. Jimmie started to laugh: he whispered something to the Prime Minister, who ostentatiously shared in the joke and began to clap. So did the more amused part of the audience. So, soon, did everyone and the rioters were carried out to widespread applause and dumped, very gently, outside the front door.

(A nasty incident backstage was totally unseen and unreported. Weston and Gareth had hidden in one of the many offices. Gareth had fixed up a lead from the microphones on stage. Their disruption was timed for 9.20 – which was intended to coincide with when the Prime Minister would be live on television. That was foiled by the Prime Minister and the broadcasters, who were now switching these times daily. That failed. And the protesters in the hall had not dared make their demonstration before the agreed time. So the plan had begun at 9.20. Gareth and Weston were to walk on to the platform and grab the microphone or, failing that, Gareth would plug in his own and hand it over to Weston.

They did not reach the wings. Bill had thoughtfully placed two of his biggest friends – second-row forwards – at either side of the stage. They had been carried away by the feeling of being part of such an important enterprise as the Prime Minister's speech and were deeply moved by his performance. This full feeling came to the boil more easily than it should have done and when Weston and Gareth tried to rush them they were met with one or two short punches which stopped them dead. They did not get a look in.)

'The entertainment,' Jimmie said, as the hall cleared, the cameras swung away rather disappointedly – (the incident was never shown: 'too small' the editor-of-the-day decided) – and the audience turned back to the stage, 'was provided by a troupe of travelling actors who can never seem to find a hall of their own!' People laughed. They wanted to laugh. They would have laughed had he merely coughed. They were prepared to listen to Jimmie lash into the extremists, use the occasion, find rhetoric in the foolishness displayed, capitalise on it. But he let it go. Quietly he took up where he had left off. Quietly and soon he concluded what he had to say and sat down without that flourishing peroration of which he was clearly capable.

The audience stood up and cheered. The Prime Minister stood up with them. Helen found herself on her feet with Bill nudging and hugging her and muttering 'We'll do it yet. We'll nail the' – pause – 'yes.' 'The other' – pause – 'have done us a favour.'

Jimmie took Elaine by the hand and gently beckoned her to her feet. She was crying but he whispered that it did not matter. Those who noticed (he did not say this, but knew it to be so) were greatly moved by her loving pride – as was Jimmie himself.

The doors opened. The band started up. The meeting was over.

IV. THE RESULT

Chapter Twenty-One

The result was a mess. Between them, the Scottish Nationalists, the Ulster Unionists, the Liberals and the Welsh
Nationalists – in that order – held enough seats to affect the
balance. They could have a 'major effect', as *The Times* put
it, 'from a minority position'. The Labour Party was just in
front of the Tories but the late results – especially of a mar-
ginal seat such as Jimmie's – were vital. The BBC cursed its
bad luck in only covering Jimmie's count by radio and film
report. The Prime Minister – safely back – phoned Jimmie
at 4.30 a.m. to ask for his opinion on the result. Jimmie had
to say he still did not know for sure. The more sagacious
commentators spoke of the 'malaise of uncertainty deeply
informing the electorate'. The old hands predicted that if
Labour got in and held on, it would give away a few goodies,
engage in brisk doings for a few months, and then, refreshed
with power, return to the electorate with a variation on the
cry 'give us the tools and we will finish the job'. Those same
shrewd observers, who included Jimmie, believed that such
an appeal could meet with a strong negative response and at
that election, the Labour Party could well receive a beating
from the combination of Unionists, Nationalists and Tories
and find itself out of power. Taking this course of events as
probable, Jimmie felt despair, for he had little doubt that
such an outcome could indeed signal the disintegration of
the present Labour Party. Its idealism had been captured by
the Nationalist groups; its time of power would be seen

as an historical divergence. It would soon, he feared, become a stump of itself, large enough for the foreseeable future – but never again large enough or sufficiently broadly based to become a national party of government. Indeed, there would be an end of national majority parties. Worse than that, Jimmie feared, though maintaining for years to come the outward appearance of a certain strength, it would in fact have lost forever its internal reason for being ... The next defeat would not only shear it of members but lead it to lose heart.

As he watched the television late on the Thursday night and into the Friday morning Jimmie experienced something as near despair over a matter not strictly personal as he had ever felt. He could see nothing but a weary struggle facing the party he loved and although its mistakes and stupidities and failings were enormous it still, for him, was the only party which carried the weakest and most oppressed members of society close to its central concerns. There was in the Labour Party, he thought, the possibility that a more just, Christian, tolerant and decent place might be made. He saw in it the chance for that selflessness which alone appeared to him to be virtuous in public life. Of course he could be exaggerating. After all, according to the Swingometer and the Computer and the bevy of eager experts, the Labour Party would squeeze in. And perhaps it would dig in its heels and stay: or return to the country and be handsomely returned again to power. But his intuition was firmly against that.

He wanted to hold his seat. The easy and kindly way in which the Party had accepted his word over the Schools Contract had moved Jimmie greatly. And, in a private way, his sense of Elaine's courage and his sympathy for her struggle had begun to revive in him feelings for her that he had thought dead for ever. He longed to hold on to his place as the Member of Parliament and to stay here with Elaine and build up a life.

Helen, who was utterly exhausted and keeping herself going by drink and will-power, counting the hours, went to bed last: Mrs. Burns, Marianne and Elaine had dropped off in the early hours. Jimmie sat alone, watching the box.

Eventually, he went to his cold bed. He looked in on Elaine, went over to her, but she was deep asleep.

He could not sleep. Outside there was the wind in the copper beech, shaking it mournfully yet soothingly – the sound bringing back night on night of open-eyed vigil in that same room. He had to get back in. The party needed every seat, every bit of help. His fears for the future could be proved groundless only by his own efforts. He wanted to rush off this instant and dedicate himself to restoring the Labour Party. It could lose its way, he thought, and he was as much to blame as anyone. 'Oh God,' he said aloud, 'give me a chance to help to save it.'

Chapter Twenty-Two

(i)

Alan swung on the rope attached to a branch of the copper beech. He trekked a little way up the hill, the large knot at the rope's end in his hand, and then he ran and launched himself into space, giving out a little squeak which he imagined to be the yodel of the Tarzan he saw on television.

Eventually he grew tired of this.

There was no one to play with. In the house everyone was busy, especially his great-grandmother, who would want him to help: with the baking or the cleaning, 'just a little job'. He wanted no jobs at all.

He looked around carefully and then trotted over to the back gate, cautiously. He was a sturdily built little boy, dark, like Gareth, but with Marianne's lighter complexion. In a moment he was out of the gate and down the lonning which was against all the rules: he needed permission to do that.

At the neighbouring farm, they welcomed him. The two children there were just entering their teens but they were tolerant and generous as well as being curious about this truant from the big house. They let him help them around the farmyard.

Alan wanted to be a farmer more than anything. He kept it from everyone because he did not want them to say 'no'. He loved it down here in the stink of the yard, in and out of the byres and barns, warily circling the large geese, calling out the names of the sheepdogs, doing real work, as they kept telling him, and being useful.

Before they sent him back, they let him have a short ride on one of the ponies and then he trotted off home, plump with pleasure and self-sworn to secrecy about his adventure.

He would tell no one, he decided, not a soul. But he had been so fearless on that pony! They had said he was a 'good lad'. They had said he would 'make a cowboy!' A *cowboy*!

He trotted off to tell his great-grandmother all about it.

(ii)

The living-room was topsy-turvy. Pictures down, stacked here and there: furniture pushed aside, carpets rolled up. The cleaning had been done. A grand reorganisation was about to commence. The large sofa which had been the principal section of Gareth's improvised bed now sat jammed up against the french windows as if specially placed there for a view of the rain which had begun again. Oddly, for some reason she had not examined, Elaine had removed her Persian vase. As she was doing so she had said to herself that she was afraid Alan might break it: but she had never bothered about that before.

On the morning after the election, Lionel came in as usual and laid the fire. His jauntiness was most marked. Not only had the campaign given him 'a shot up the bum', as he said, but after a week of scheming and months of longing he was, he considered, very near to taking Mrs. Burns to the pictures on Sunday afternoon. *Gone With The Wind* was being shown in its new stretched version. He finished making up the fire, went to wash his hands and returned to begin to sort out the room. He rolled out the carpets, heaved the lighter pieces of furniture back into place – oblivious of Elaine's intention that there should be a redisposition of the furniture. Marianne came in and began to help. They picked up the table on which the papers and magazines were used to be laid.

Marianne's energy had to be put into action. Her restlessness was intense. She could scarcely contain herself. The thought of getting away from what she now saw as a benevolent trap was becoming an obsession. She lifted her end of the table and handed it across the room so vigorously that Lionel stumbled.

'Steady! You'll pull my arm off! Steady!' Marianne obeyed and he regained his poise. 'Now then, back up a bit, just a bit more – there – steady – to the left, just a bit to your left – there – a bit more – steady – it's good stuff this – and down.'

'Fuss-pot!'

'If a thing's worth doing, it's worth doing well. Somebody in the army said that.'

'We don't even know if she wants the table put back here.'

'No matter. It needs tidying up.'

He went back across to the unlit fire, as if to touch base, gain strength, for he simply gazed at it. Marianne lit a cigarette and then rather savagely picked up cushions from the pile and planted them on to the chairs.

'Why does Elaine suddenly decide to reorganise things today of all days?'

Lionel, who had been taken short by a sudden lunge of pain in his chest while carrying the table, dragged himself out of his brief anxiety. 'Spring cleaning in October? That's Elaine!' He smiled to cover the fear.

'You all spoil her!'

The old man was surprised at the bite in her tone but decided not to rise to it. All his life he had believed in 'letting well alone'; 'Live and let live' was his motto. 'Don't look for trouble,' 'Anything for a quiet life' – in his personal relationships this attitude – somewhere on the border between tolerance, self-preservation and a certain timidity – had, on balance, he thought, done less harm than most other courses he might have followed. But he did not like to hear Elaine abused or criticised in any way and he noted Marianne afresh and observed her edginess, felt the vibration of urgency.

Like a man in a comedy film, he pushed out his bare arm (the sleeves were rolled up to the elbow) and examined the large watch which ornamented his scraggy wrist. 'What time do they expect to know his result?'

'About twelve. We'll have to set off in about an hour if we want to be with Jimmie for the announcement. Last time Elaine lost her handbag and we all turned up when they were half-way through it. Jimmie looked so – neglected!' Again her irritation with Elaine was clear.

'Jimmie's never been neglected,' Lionel replied briskly. 'His mother idolised him. In that quiet way they have, mind. But she still idolised him.'

'She made him fetch and carry like a little boy, I've been told.'

'You should never listen to what you're told,' Lionel replied, briskly. The pain had gone. 'Now then. An important problem for you, Marianne – think hard. Ready? Right. Should I or should I not light this fire?'

'No. Keep it until we come back.'

'A woman who knows her own mind: a woman to watch.'

Marianne smiled. She felt totally at home with Lionel. She understood how he thought. Even Mrs. Burns was more remote. There was a detachment which Mrs. Burns could display, a keep into which she could retreat. Lionel, although he had firm codes of habit, was, like herself, warm and pliable, even eager to please, on the surface. Both of them were capable of enduring what they saw had to be endured and both had learnt to hide their feelings from others if necessary. But Lionel knew that it was not necessary to conceal his feelings from Marianne, who, he considered, read his mind as clearly as he understood hers.

'You old bugger,' she said, affectionately, and he smiled as at a compliment.

'Do you think he'll win?'

'They don't think so on the television.'

'They only get it right on television when it's obvious to everybody,' Lionel said grimly. He liked only those experts who confirmed his own opinions and prejudices.

'I've never seen him as worried.'

'He's the best local man we've ever had,' Lionel announced, soberly, as if presenting a testimonial. 'By a street. Always on tap. Whatever party. Didn't matter to Jimmie. Too soft with some of them many a time, I'd say. They took advantage.'

'But will they vote for him?'

'I don't know. Gratitude's out of fashion.' Lionel paused, but this particular lust of curiosity could not be repressed. 'I mean, Gareth doesn't know the meaning of the word.'

'No,' she said vaguely. Lionel allowed a pause for elaboration but she did not take it up. Her plans depended on her being able to manage without Gareth.

'You haven't seemed as keen on him lately,' Lionel persisted, absurdly clumsy in his attempt to deflect attention from the urgency of his enquiry. He actually took up a duster and began to pretend to dust the table they had just set down. Still Marianne would not be drawn, but Lionel sensed that it was worth pursuing. 'Of course with him not living here and – well, and these things change and change about.' A most heavy pause. 'As a matter of fact, I've been watching a twinkle in old Harold's eye lately.'

'Oh yes.'

'Now then, Marianne.' Lionel put down his duster and squared up to her, openly and naturally nosy. 'Are you really keen or are you trailing your coat to bring our Gareth to heel?'

'There's a lot to be said for Harold.'

'Not much that he doesn't say for himself.'

'That's not fair.'

'I see,' Lionel said, suddenly embarrassed. Her firm response had made him aware that he was interfering.

'Harold's got a lot of qualities,' Marianne said.

'I see said the blind man and he didn't see at all,' Lionel answered. 'Nothing would surprise me in this house at the moment. It's worse than the Bible.'

Lionel had used that last sentence on several occasions over the past few days and it had still not lost its relish for him. It had replaced T.T.F.N. as his parting shot.

When Helen came in he decided to stay in the room. He had been there once before with these two and the crackle between them had plumped his gossipy soul.

Helen was in her raincoat, ready for the off far in advance of the others. The election had taken its toll, Lionel thought. She looked tired and under stress. While Marianne seemed to vibrate with restlessness on the surface so that it could be seen in the over-eagerness of her gestures and the impatience of her conversation, Helen had the strength to bury the effects of strain but the effort over-taxed her. Though she showed less she was every bit as worried as Marianne, Lionel guessed.

Helen and Marianne barely acknowledged each other and yet superficially they were civil, even friendly. Yet if a diagram could have been drawn it would have shown that they were directly connected by a quiver full of lines straight as arrows which went the shortest distance between them and carried jealousy, hatred, suspicion, curiosity, sympathy, identification, hope, worry, bitterness, relief, fear – all stretching by the hour with tension.

'Harold's here,' Helen announced. 'Is everybody ready? Jimmie'll be worried enough without worrying about us. I've done everything that had to be done up here.' She had not looked directly at either of them. Now she almost glared at Lionel. 'Where *is* everybody?' Then, regretting it, she held out her packet of cigarettes. 'Want one?'

'I don't mind if I do. I'm getting used to these menthols.' He looked at the cigarette – slim, white and unblemished

245

between his large coal-scabbed fingers – and then shook his head. 'They're still like medicine, though.'

'Excuse me.'

Marianne lost her usual self-control and simply – and very abruptly – walked out. Lionel blushed for her bad manners. Helen flinched as the younger woman passed her by – eyes gazing straight before her like a sleepwalker.

'I hope to God there isn't going to be another ,bloody scene! The campaign was hard enough without all this—!' Helen checked herself; drew deeply on the cigarette. Tomorrow she would be back in Lancaster and it would all be over. Gareth was dead to her now: dead.

'Cup of coffee?' Lionel asked, kindly.

'Not another!' Lionel looked hurt. 'Sorry.' To make that simple apology meant that Helen had to dig deeply into her few remaining reserves of patience and tolerance. She had to hold on. She had already drunk a couple of large vodkas that morning – whisky showed on the breath. She needed to keep going and Lionel was a kind man. 'Let me make it,' she suggested. 'It'll give me something to do while everybody gets themselves organised.' She went to the door – but Lionel was owed more than that. 'Do *you* think he'll win?'

'Please.' Lionel held out the large hand which held the little cigarette: the cigarette made the gesture beseeching. 'Let me make it. Idle hands–' He paused. 'I'd like to make it.'

'To go to the kitchen and pester poor old Betty.'

'Pester?' His clumsily assumed innocence was comical.

'Good luck to you. Let the beast out, Lionel. Black with two spoonfuls and if there's a biscuit, please put it on the saucer. At least spare me the full Grantchester vicarage tea-trolley.'

'I go, I come back.'

He left, guiltily happy like a boy excused from class.

Chapter Twenty-Three

'Christ!' Helen stubbed out her cigarette in an onyx ashtray which she still could think was too good for cigarette butts. Then she walked across to the french windows and contemplated the view. She wanted to get out, get away from this – 'aquarium' she was beginning to call it.

Harold came in, shaking himself like a St. Bernard. She knew it was he and yet spoke as if to herself.

'Rain, stones, grass and trees. Bloody *nature*. Who needs it?'

Harold smiled to himself and ignored the bait. His manner was jolly.

'What on earth's happened to this room?' He stood holding his coat before him like a fumble-fingered matador.

'Elaine.'

'Ah. I'm the chauffeur. Are there any passengers?'

'Let me take that coat.' She noticed that he looked pale. Usually the alcoholic flush and constant bathing gave him the look of strong if superficial health. He had lost weight. Heavy dieting, she concluded, and smiled at his vanity.

She took the mohair coat, picked up a chair, draped the coat over it and put it beside the unlit fire. It occurred to her that it was far too wet for the simple dash from car to door. He must have lingered outside. Why? And with whom? And he watched her, too. All her actions were quick as if efficient but in fact, he thought, their rapidity merely betrayed tension. He relaxed.

'Now the real question is – where's the hooch?' He looked around the room like an explorer in a pantomime, very conscious of the anxiety – to some extent dependence – this almost fraught young woman was beaming towards him. She could be attractive, though, he had time to reflect, underneath that absurd intellectual posture of feminine carelessness. Indeed, Gareth's attentions had made her looks loosen a little towards that rather gauche sensuality which never failed to alert Harold to the possibilities of satisfaction. 'Ah!' He found the drink. 'Still in its usual place. Undisturbed by the surrounding chaos. A sound instinct's at work in this room, young lady, whatever you say. A little tipple?'

'Why not?'

'Well said. Vodka, isn't it, in the morning? Here we are. And, for me, the Bell's. I can claim the first one as medicinal – against the rain.' He looked at the whisky in his glass and winked across at her. 'So this doesn't count. God Bless.' He drank it off in one, grimaced quite horribly and then breathed in deeply. 'Now for the first drink of the day.' He refilled his glass and took over her vodka.

'Didn't you feel better when you used to do all that golfing?'

'For a while. Cheers! And then I got bored. Curious thing, isn't it, boredom? How's the love life?'

'In full working order, thank you. I thought you were beyond that play, Harold.'

'*Did* you?' He sat down and, in imitation, she too found a chair. 'The trouble with a rather intellectual lady like yourself – if you don't mind me saying so – is that you expect everything to be as it ought to be – everything has to fall into a pattern – hasn't it? Patterns are the only things that make sense. But life's a mix-up, Helen – shake it and see. Try it some time.' There was a pause. She looked hurt. He did not attempt to salve the bruise.

'Why are you so aggressive?' she asked.

'You want the truth, Helen?'

'Yes.' Her throat was dry. She felt that suddenly and unfairly she was on trial. Her emotions swirled about inside her directionless. 'Yes,' she repeated, to steady herself.

'You like the truth, don't you? Or you think you do.'

'Stop it, Harold.' She checked herself and then added, softly, 'Bugger you.' She held on to the cold glass of clear vodka as if to a raft in a storm.

'I'm pissed off with the contempt you've developed for Elaine,' Harold said calmly. 'You and Marianne both. But you especially. You're a guest here. Who the hell are you to despise her?'

'How nice for her to be surrounded by father-figures.'

'Father-figures! Bollocks! Jargon. She's a lovely woman. She has had her bad times but that sparkle in her – that leap at life, everyday things – there's only one Elaine. And now she's on her way through. And this time she'll make it.'

'Yes.' Helen, who felt rocked by his vehemence, increasingly impressed as she had become over the weeks by this man, brought up short by the impact of his force, was still determined to fight back. 'As long as everybody looks after her she's fine,' she said, firmly.

'Some people need looking after. Others deserve it. Not everybody can be competent. Elaine isn't very competent – but she's the one who suffers for that principally. But what she *is* – that is what is important. You can look at her and catch that glance and the world's a bit different, a bit more mysterious.'

'I'm surprised you didn't marry her,' Helen said, savagely. She realised that this might sound jealous and rushed on, 'Gareth's right. You've turned her into something between a pet and a victim.'

'Gareth knows damn-all about it!'

'She is his mother.'

'Gareth doesn't even know who *he* is.'

'What is there to know? About Elaine I mean.'

Harold shook his head. That would never be told.

'We'd better be on our way soon,' he said.

Helen stood up and walked across for another drink. She wanted to keep quiet, she wanted to disengage, she wanted the silence to continue, for it protected her.

'For the last three weeks,' she said, over-loudly, 'while Jimmie's been trying to fight a nasty election, at least a third of his energy has been drained off comforting Elaine because she was so upset that Gareth had left his futile radio programme, comforting Elaine because Gareth and Marianne weren't rushing off to the altar, comforting Elaine because life wasn't – I don't know – snow-white in a perfect palace of super-glass! And she's no iller than you or me! It's just her way of claiming attention – it's affectation!' Helen flung out her accusation in the manner of one expecting to be assaulted for her opinions. But Harold spoke gently, as if reflectively.

'You're wrong on all counts.' He paused. 'She sometimes would strike *me* as affected, in the early days, I agree. But then I began to understand . . . there are reasons . . .'

'Jimmie's nearly paralysed with tiredness and worry. That's a simple fact! Couldn't she see that?'

'He's always tired. His overwork's a form of Puritan extravagance. She's seen that for years.'

'She sees no one but herself!' Helen could scarcely understand why she felt so driven to denounce someone whom she would have helped and been to some extent happy with, she realised, in other circumstances. What harm had the poor woman done her that she should feel so violently about her? Yet the denunciation proceeded as if propelled by a force long-buried and longing to be aired. 'Elaine's so self-centred it hurts her. She sees nothing else – nothing at all! Everybody just has to dance around her. She's the light for all the moths and she mesmerises you just like all the rest.'

'You're a very desirable young woman,' Harold said, smiling, and he toasted her. 'You fell a bit in love with Jimmie, that's all. And he, I'd guess, just a bit, with you.'

'Oh, bugger off, Harold.'

'What I can't really understand is why you hang about for the leftovers of the Radio Romeo.'

'What business is it of yours?'

'None.' He finished his drink and looked at the empty glass. Something about his attitude prompted her. She hesitated – but only slightly – and then came across to him, took the glass, went and re-charged it, brought it back and sat nearer him on the arm of a chair. He nodded, slightly, gratefully. Her eyes now fully portrayed – and betrayed – the aching blocked misery which beset her. He had given her the opportunity to talk about herself – that most seductive of moves. Yet she was half-afraid to let herself go. What would he do with knowledge of her?

'Why do you switch the subject to me?' she asked clumsily.

'That's what you want to talk about, isn't it? Besides ... Elaine ...?' He stopped. Helen was not quite sure, yet again, as so often with Harold, whether these occasional abrupt conclusions, the switches of subject and even the topic of conversation, were genuine or trickery. 'Anyway,' he said, 'who else can you talk to?'

'From father-figure to father-confessor!'

'That's right. Bright girl.'

'Neither suits you,' she said, but there was no accusation in her voice now.

'You know that Gareth's still holding on to Marianne by every dirty trick in the book. You know about his set-up in the town. You know he has to fill his belly with Scotch to numb his guts to the pap he spews out. You know he's a scalp-hunter.'

'As a matter of fact I did know all of that. If Elaine gets your loyalty – or whatever – Gareth certainly gets the other side. Is there anything else?'

'Quite a lot.'

'So?' Despite the attempt at badinage, Helen was beginning to yield. Harold seemed so firmly in control. The surge of

251

panic which threatened to flood through her mind now, as was happening increasingly over the past few days, came in full force and she felt dizzy as she beat it off.

'Quite a lot,' Harold repeated in that neutral tone which alarmed her most.

'You ought to be on Gareth's side.' Her words came out with brittle chirpiness. 'He's another member of Elaine's Praetorian Guard.'

Gareth, Gareth she was afraid to be drawn into talk and thought of Gareth and yet it was irresistible.

'If his famous love for his mother contained one particle of genuine feeling, he would see how much she had come to depend on him – and he would have taken more care of all that. Thank God she has begun to slip that off.'

'Gareth can't be responsible for Elaine's dependence!'

'Every woman for herself?'

'Better that than all this dependence.'

'Perhaps so. But don't go round expecting to be thought of as a dutiful son when you say you're putting your mother in a safe harbour and in fact you're leaving her adrift in open sea. He's a twenty-two carat fraud.'

'Gareth,' Helen said, stiffly, 'once made me very happy. Very happy. Nobody before or since has been as "right" as he was. That counts.'

'You're a very desirable young woman.'

'Huh!' Helen finished her drink, conscious of the Hollywood gesture of 'slinging it back'. She went to get another – walking steadily – a long way, yet, from drunkenness. 'Good meal, good screw, good night! One bastard once told a friend of mine that. *You're* like that, aren't you, Harold? You don't want whores or Escort Agencies. You don't like to pay. What you want is the new metropolitan harlot – somebody about thirty with a smashed life behind them and a thin time ahead – unpaid, undisgraced, with that extra spice of desperation. Why *should* I do without Gareth? Whatever he is. I keep mentioning Marianne as regular as clockwork, never mind conscience, but he ignores her. Why shouldn't *I*?'

'Desperation? I'm surprised.'

'Are you hell! You're as smart as paint, Harold. You've been jollying me along for quite long enough.'

'I'm impressed.'

'I even know how you do it. "Wham, bam, thank you, ma'am!" Or the Dirty Tricks Department. You're greedy. That's all. It's pathetic. Just greedy. You're greedy for sensations to remind you of what life was once like. You've squashed your spirit and pickled your mind. I bet you used to – maybe you still do – flog your shagged-out old body through terrible exercises. And then you clamber through clumsy sexual acrobatics and stuff yourself with rich food and cigars and Scotch. You blister in the sun and sweat like a pig in the sauna. You diet and experiment – I know your sort – anything at all to sting you back into life. You're the walking proof that capitalist free enterprise – ha ha – turns to fat and turds!'

Harold liked the heightening anger, the flailing: it reminded him of a small wild bird caught in a net. Helen was much better that way, he thought; much.

'Tell me. Why do girls like you, from my own background – class, you would say – generally ... I've noticed this a few times, you're clever, you'll be able to tell me – why, after you've read a few books and been to a university and scrubbed your way through a year or two of work, why do you get so involved with laying down the law on morality? Why do you want to find bad in everything or everyone? Why do you look for enemies?'

'You're unusually thoughtful, Harold,' she said.

'I'm told that mortality can bring on a certain wisdom.' Harold paused and held her look quite steadily. Helen strove successfully to maintain a façade of indifference. Harold took pleasure in shattering it. 'You see, the odds are, I'm dying. I'll be phoning through later this afternoon for the result of the final tests.'

It was like a slow-motion crash. At first nothing happened, no reaction. Then she accepted the information, then absorbed it, and finally she looked away, embarrassed, bewildered and confused. She wanted to say 'Why didn't you tell me sooner?' and 'Perhaps that explains things,' and 'I don't really believe you – isn't that horrible of me – but I don't really trust you,' and 'How terrible. What can I do for you? Let me help, make up for the bad thoughts, the show-off words – just said to impress you anyway.' What she did say was, 'I'm sorry.'

'That's why I've been so busy selling the shop,' Harold replied, deftly. '*Private Eye* was just a spur.. They'll not be satisfied until I'm drawn and quartered of course – and Jimmie's rescue act was too feeble – no. I want to go in my own glory. In my own shit, you would say, if you didn't jib at the word. And you could be right. Why not see me out? I'm off abroad. Come with me.'

'Me?'

'You'd see something of the world. You'd have money – I know you despise it but at least you'll have had a fling. If you did tag along I'd settle a fair lump on you. You'd be a little bit independent. Gareth could go to hell. You could comfort me.'

'Is comfort all you want? Sorry. But – oh God! How hellish for you. I like it better when you talk about dying – about your own glory – whatever it was.' She took a deep breath. She believed in truth in all relationships. 'Why is it, Harold, sorry, but why is it that I can't quite believe you?'

'I could prove it.'

'My feelings are the best proof. They don't trust you.'

'Why not?'

'Why me?'

'Why not?'

'What you mean,' Helen said carefully, no longer holding on to the delusion that she was engaged in nothing more than a casual exchange, 'is that I'm available.'

'Aren't you?'

'Thanks.' She paused. 'You're not serious.' Her mouth was dry. The anxiety was threatening her.

'Oh yes.'

'What about Gareth?' she asked.

Harold sipped his drink and took his time. He was powerful, Helen thought, although she did not want to admit it. That bigness, the expensive clothes, the money, the coarse sensation of having made decisions that hurt, the indisputable sexiness of someone her younger self would have caricatured and derided as a class-enemy, a capitalist-exploiter, a male chauvinist ... her theoretical objections petered out when he fastened a deliberately mock-provocative look on her and answered her question.

'My guess – and your fear, I'd say – is that if Gareth settles for anyone it will be for Marianne. But he'll settle for no one if he can get away with it. He'll keep running. He can't stop now.'

'Marianne doesn't want him now.'

'I see.'

'I agree,' she said. 'About Gareth. He'll look after number one. But I have the choice still.'

'When did he last phone you? You could have got up to London in a few hours any time over the last – what was it – six years. You meet him here by accident. That right?' He smiled. 'And. suddenly he's a consideration? C'mon, Helen.'

'You want me – let's get it straight – to come and live with you?'

'Why not?'

'Are you—? Of course you must be. I'm sorry.' Helen gave in to the gust of longing that rushed through her and said that this would simplify things, solve problems, provide a life-line. 'It's horrible ... But just to find out ... to be – truly, I mean ...'

'Spit it out.'

'It's disgusting. But to be just a little financially independent! To have a little flat I owned. To have one or two
things. To have a place I could come back to and shut the
door and know that nobody could get in unless I wanted
them to because it was mine. To own your own place. It's a
horrible weakness I know, but I've longed for that so much.'

'And your subsidised grant doesn't stretch that far.'

'My grant, Harold, covers rather less than a bikini.'

He laughed. She smiled and wanted him to hold out his
hand so that she could touch him and feel in the flesh that
security which was still elusive.

'I'd set you up, yes. And – with me – it needn't last long.
No need to be in at the death. I'll do that alone like a dog. A
year or so maximum, I'd say. A short sentence.'

'How heartless I must seem to you. And greedy. I've never
been greedy about money. Just these last few years – alone in
that terrible dump surrounded by – never mind. I've never
talked aloud about money in my life before. I can't understand why. We were trained to think it didn't matter.'

'What did it feel like to be greedy?'

'Exciting.' Helen laughed. 'You old bastard. No – not exciting. A little disgusting but – full of energy. The sort of
undirected rage of energy one had as a child.'

'Did one?'

'*One.*' She picked up his mocking echo of the word. 'I
remember how hard it was to say "one" instead of I – do
you? It still feels like a plum-stone that has to be slid out
without anybody noticing. We must have a similar background, I suppose. Except that my father could be working
for you.'

'What does he do?'

'He's retired. He used to work on the line in a factory. It
deadened him. He was retired early. Mostly sits beside the
fire hawking his guts out and wondering how his daughter
vanished from his life.'

'I'll be leaving tonight for London,' Harold said. 'I'm

coming back here for a drink after the count and then I'm on my way.'

'I can't possibly decide in half a day.'

'There's no more time.'

'Why not?'

'Because win or lose, Jimmie's going to turn his attention to my affairs and drag me into a complicated battle. He has been cleared – thanks, in great part, to me – but Jimmie will pursue it. He'll be Mr. Clean now. All very honourable on his part. But the scrap – which would damage me, ultimately, only a little – will, for one thing, upset Elaine. I don't want that. For another, I could drop dead even before my time and in a solicitor's office. No. I'm off. Come aboard.'

Helen could no longer bear to sit. She stood up, hovered, aching to be touched and reassured by touch. Harold was slowly rubbing the glass between the palms of his short strong hands, hairy fingers, new-clipped nails. Why did she want to say yes? It was against all her principles. And for those principles she had sacrificed quite a lot. She had tried to live life seriously as an intellectual, as someone who believed in truthful relationships, as someone who practised equality and held to the right to be independent and above all sacrifice expediency for principle. She found herself talking her thoughts aloud to Harold.

'I used to think that my – breakdown – it wasn't *quite* that – depression, let's say – came about because I'd arrived at a stage in the argument between what I really was and what I'd made myself be which was unsolvable except through a sort of breakdown. I was two people, a past and a present, with no future for either one or both together. I had to find a way of joining them. But it could be simpler, couldn't it? Under the skin we do all yearn to be cosseted, don't we? We can't rise above our childhood, can we? Of course I want money and luxury and somebody to be with! Yet until now I'd never admit it, even to myself. Perhaps because I was

257

afraid. It's a relief – such a relief – just to be able to say that, you know! Of course I want the world! Does it matter? It isn't wrong, is it?'

'No wonder you were ill,' Harold said, not unkindly. He finished his drink.

'No?' She turned to look at him and for a curious instant he caught a striking likeness to Elaine in this self-absorbed, self-tormented young woman. She smiled hopelessly, and the resemblance vanished. Elaine's smile made Harold himself smile in response: Helen's smile made him pity her. 'No?' she asked.

'You're a worrier, Helen,' he said briskly. 'You always were, I bet. Worrying about your exams, worrying about your accent, worrying about your clothes – am I right? Worrying about what your life was worth, worrying about your parents, what your friends thought of you, what men thought of you, what you should think of them – worrying away until you trussed yourself up in worries like a mummy. It's a pity.' He stood up. 'Somewhere inside is – was – a bright, desirable kid, screwed by . . . over-education? Afraid of life. Something like that. You'll never go away.'

He went across to the drinks and poured out a bitter lemon which he sank to satisfy his thirst. Then he took out a cigar and his cutter and concentrated on that job.

Helen waited for a sign from him, but none came. She wanted to go to him and . . . and what? She did not know. He stood there, apparently totally preoccupied in cutting the end off a cigar. A few minutes before he had offered to turn her life upside down. An invisible portcullis slammed to the floor.

'You knew I would refuse before you even began, didn't you?' she said.

'Did I?' He glanced up, a neutral glance, and blew on the end of the cigar.

'Yes.' She waited. He struck a match and gently toasted the neat fat end of the cigar. Once more she felt her emotions surge turbulently inside her threatening to break loose. 'You knew I wouldn't accept.'

At last he lit the cigar and drew on it. The red circle glowed before her.

'Why did you want me to make a fool of myself?'

'Why do you think?'

She paused. 'To hurt Jimmie. Because I'm genuinely fond of Jimmie – you knew that. Maybe I *am* a little in love with Jimmie although I wouldn't say that to him of course. Elaine must be protected!'

'Go on.'

'And you don't like Jimmie much now, do you? If you ever did. He has something you can't buy. But you can filch it for a while. Or maybe it was Gareth – you wanted me to be disloyal to Gareth.'

'Why?'

To prove that you could take what you wanted. To prove that you were the man with the power. To humiliate them. Wave a wad of fivers and, see, she crashes to the ground. Blue stocking to silk stockings, at no great cost. Well I fell for it for a few minutes because I was sorry for you. That was all. Nothing else. I hope that's clear.'

'Oh quite.'

'Are you really ill, Harold?'

'I'll know soon enough.'

'That was cruel,' she said.

He had wandered across to the french windows and he stood looking out, his back to her, as she had been when he entered. He did not turn as she went out. Neither did he react at first when someone else entered almost immediately, although he had been expecting him and had arranged to see him.

Chapter Twenty-Four

'Want one?' he asked Gareth, indicating the cigar. "They're Cuban.'

'If you hadn't come looking for me, I'd have come for you, Harold. You've had it this time.'

'Can I get you a brandy? No?' He beamed across at Gareth, a ringmaster wreathed in smoke.

'You've probably ruined that man's life.'

Gareth leaned against the piano, He was so coiled in fury that his arms were crossed around his chest and shoulders and he hugged himself as if to restrain himself from springing at Harold's throat. Harold, feet apart, cigar like a dagger in one hand, stood ready for any clash.

'Drink?' Harold asked as Gareth reached for his flask.

'Piss off.'

'I agree. It's too early for civilised chaps like us.'

'You're a shit. Weston had made a new start in this area. Whatever you thought of him you needn't have done that.'

'I?'

'You.' Gareth sprang upright and went rapidly across to the drinks to fill his flask. 'Christ! I didn't realise how much I really do hate you all until this campaign. The whole lot's got to go.' His hand was steady as he poured the spirits into the metal container.

'Bring down the politicians, flush out the mandarins of Whitehall, lock up the police—' Harold laughed.

'Exactly! I mean it, Harold. Nothing else works. Reform

means that a few deluded workers find themselves elevated and think it's progress but they're conned and conned again by the status quo. You all have to be blown sky-high.' He took a drink.

'Cheers,' Harold said.

'It was a filthy trick to dig up all that dirt about Weston's private life! You nearly drove the poor guy to suicide. I spent the day before yesterday ferrying him all over the bloody county, sometimes in the boot of the car! Reporters like hounds that hadn't been fed! The poor man having to pull out altogether. All because you think he stirred it up a bit too much for you.'

'What proof do you have that I did it?'

'Of course you bloody well did. Who else could organise all that dirt to hit the press the day before the election? Maximum harm. Maximum benefit for Jimmie the White Knight. Who else would have the mind of a ferret and the loot to dig it out?' Weston had been accused not only of not supporting his wife and family, but of corruptly manipulating votes on committees in his previous constituency, of cheating on social security and non-payment of fines for assault charges.

Harold went across and poured himself a thin Scotch. His affability had been a pose but now the pose was dropped. When he turned to Gareth it was as if he turned on him.

'If your man Weston takes off from his wife and kids without paying them a penny and sets up with another lady or two in another part of the country, good luck to him say I. If he goes in for politics as well – God help him. Mr. Harry Truman said all there was to say on that matter.'

'I was on the phone to him just now. She tried to kill herself, you know that? His wife. When she read the filth your fearless free-press reporters printed about her. A neighbour found her. That make you happy?'

'Don't go too far, son.'

'I'll make bloody sure *you* don't. You're planning to hop it tonight, aren't you?'

'Marianne's fidelity to you is the eighth wonder of the world.'

'You've been playing her along, haven't you? Touching her up? Little whispers, little promises, all the lucre stinking and shining. Tease and titillate. She only goes along with it in a misguided attempt to provoke me.'

'Oh, that's the reason, is it? I see.'

'Or pity—'

'You don't sound too sure about Marianne.'

'I don't want to be sure about her.'

'Oh, I see. But if she were partial to me?'

'Her business.'

'Business?'

'Love's the biggest drug since Jesus Christ, Harold, and you know it. It's all part of the same plot. It's the grease that keeps the wheels of the establishment smooth in the groove. *It's all part of the fucking conspiracy to keep them down!* Love is lust dressed up to kill! It's the cheapest form of coercion yet discovered. Our Western industrial society lauds it and applauds it because it needs it. Why? To trap the poor sods for life, that's why. Make the stupid berks believe in love at first sight and love me forever, and love and marriage and holy holy holy matrimony and you can turn a boy of twenty-one just beginning to think straight into a wreck of twenty-five doing a job he doesn't like shut up in a box he can hardly afford with two kids he can't deal with and a wife he can't stand. That's love and life for Mr. British Citizen and Mr. American Citizen today. That's how it is. And love's the magic key. Sex – yes – plenty! But *love*! Kill it, crush it, rub it out.'

'Elaine believes in love.'

'Oh Harold, Harold. I suppose you think that's a nice one. Poor old Harold. All the dirty tricks including that little shot of cut-throat sentimentality *à la* Richard Nixon. I'll get you, Harold. Yes I will. And I'll love that. That I will.'

'You haven't done too badly so far.'

Gareth grinned: and so did Harold. They stood a few feet from each other, in the dusky light of the morning, rain still outside, copper beech darkening the room, two generations, could have been father and son, teeth bared, heads all but lowered like two bulls, the old and the young, about to fight for control.

'Yes,' Gareth confessed. 'Jimmie believed I didn't. I told him I didn't and he believed it. Good old Jimmie. Cheers!'

'He's always believed your lies.'

'As you'd know. You've pulled quite a lot on him in your time.'

'You won't understand this, Gareth, but you make me shiver. Just a bit. You're an evil little bastard.'

'Half-truths will get you nowhere.'

'Jimmie *is* a good man,' Harold said.

'You don't like him.'

'That's neither here not there. I respect him.'

'My arse.'

Harold laughed, disconcertingly loudly and abruptly. Then he asked, 'Next instalment delivered yet?'

'Got it here.' Gareth pulled out of his pocket two neatly typed sheets – double-spacing. 'On its way to *Private Eye* tonight.'

'They'll print it next week?'

'Of course. "All the dirt that's fit to print." '

'They will print it – despite my writ?'

'Oh yes.' Gareth was ebullient. 'They'll print it all right. You knew everything about that schools business. And more.'

'Oh really?'

'Oh really. Every bloody thing. *And* there's the little matter of that contract for the new hospital in South Cumbria. And – well, why should I spoil your fun by telling you in advance.' Gareth had assumed a more relaxed manner. He put on his Humphrey Bogart accent. 'You know, Harold, I could almost feel sorry for you. It'll be quite a fall.'

'It was quite a rise, though I say it myself.' Harold nodded and went across to the fireplace, looked up at the large dark watercolour hung above the mantelpiece. 'A blow for the forces opposed to Capitalism – I suppose that's how you see it. Thanks for the warning.'

'I just wanted to see your face,' Gareth said, quietly and viciously.

Harold now spoke as casually as if he were merely swopping irrelevant time-filling gossip. 'I had a long chat with your friend Peter Fraser the other night.'

The hit was palpable. Gareth glanced around as if Fraser had been conjured into being in the room; he started towards Harold. He stopped in his tracks. He was about to speak. Then he said nothing. Harold drew on his cigar and simply waited. He had not expected such a naked reaction even though he had taken care, as in his most crucial business dealings, to time the hit as finely as possible.

'And?' Gareth asked. Harold wanted more than that. He let the pause hold; he let Gareth roast a little. '*And?*' Gareth's urgency was unmistakable.

'Curiously enough,' Harold said, 'I've got a little piece of paper too.' He took out some neatly typed sheets from his side pocket. 'Rather more than you have, I'd guess. Still,' he held out the sheets, 'I'll be a gentleman and do a straight swap.'

The conflict between fear and fury was so evident in Gareth and so powerful that Harold saw the man almost buckle from the extra unexpected pressure suddenly forcing itself into a mind already distended with stress and deceit and this strange frenetic fanticism.

Not trusting himself to talk, Gareth shook his head.

'Pity,' Harold said, softly. 'It's a very, very nasty business. All round. And Mr. Fraser is an extremely vindictive young man. Care to read what he says?'

Again Gareth shook his head and with Harold holding out the pages like a senator bestowing a document on some truculent young tribune, the lights went on as a procession of women brought in the final cup of coffee.

Chapter Twenty-Five

Elaine it was who flung open the door and switched on the lights. Mrs. Burns, in her coat and wearing a hat, led the rest holding a tray of biscuits. Marianne, also in her coat, was pushing the trolley. Helen followed. And finally Alan came in, drawing a fire engine behind him.

'Hello, Harold, you old rascal!' Elaine went across and gave him a hug. Then she went across to Gareth, who kissed her. 'He looks better very day, doesn't he? Younger. Doesn't he, everybody?' She was a poor actress; it was all too clear that she was trying to cheer him up.

Nobody replied and it was Harold himself who took the curse off the demand.

'Thank you milady.' He clicked his heels and bowed. 'Always at your service. Shouldn't we be on our way?'

'I phoned through.' Helen spoke with emphasis. She was determined to continue as if nothing at all had happened and yet the effort needed just to make the most ordinary comments seemed to wound her. She wanted to sleep. She wanted to be with Gareth. She wanted to talk quietly and calmly with Jimmie as she had done before Gareth had come. All that was impossible now. She avoided Gareth's eye. 'They've still some way to go. Boxes just in from the last of the villages. We have time in hand.'

'Isn't it *exciting*?' Elaine went across and poured out the coffee. She felt unaccountably confident in herself: Jimmie was being so warm to her. Mrs. Burns was taking around the biscuits rather like a peddler showing samples. Marianne, having glanced from Gareth to Harold and back to Gareth, settled for Alan. They sat a few yards apart, the mother and son, and pushed the engine between them, each time making what was supposed to be a train noise, so that the 'di-di-di-di' and 'whosh' lapped away beneath the adult talk.

'Of course he'll win, won't he?' Elaine asked. She stood poised before Gareth as she put the question. Cup in one hand, sugar bowl in the other – she seemed to Harold as vulnerably lovely as he had ever seen her; to Marianne, play-acting; to Helen, faux-naïve and affected; to Mrs. Burns, unusually happy; and to Gareth, unreadable. 'Won't he?' she urged to Gareth's silence. 'What do you think, Gareth?'

'I'm not sure we want to hear Gareth on this subject,' Mrs. Burns said, coming alongside with the biscuits. Three generations clustered together for a brief moment. 'Still no sugar?' she asked. 'Still sweet enough?'

'They were getting very excited about it on television earlier this morning,' Marianne said and sent the engine rolling over to Alan, the fourth generation, strikingly like his father.

'I'm *sure* he'll win,' Elaine said.

Her tone ground against Helen's sensibilities so much that she could have shouted out – what does the damned woman *know*? What does she actually *know* about anything? To siphon off this lurch of irritation, she said, 'I thought he did particularly well in the last *Forum* on television. And after the Prime Minister's reception here I wouldn't be surprised if he was offered some sort of job – if he gets in – Shadow ... what? Environment would be too grand – but maybe a junior shadow post there. He isn't too old.'

'You're never too old to be a shadow,' Elaine said rather tartly. She had ceased to feel sympathetic towards Helen. She was not afraid of her any more.

'You're never too old for the greasy pole,' Gareth said. Like Helen he had to force himself to speak at all. He wanted to regroup the spent and scattered forces of his mind. But it would not do. The tyranny of what had to be done held them all in its grip, even though every individual wanted to be out of the place and away from all the others: except, possibly, Alan, blissfully playing trains with his mother.

'Your views are not in order,' Mrs. Burns told her grandson, curtly. 'Dear me, Gareth, I know this is supposed to be the land of the free but I still think you took a shocking liberty. Going against your own father.'

'Who is not . . . never mind. Who cares?'

'Do you think it's right turning up there in Harold's Rolls-Royce?' Marianne asked innocently, rushing in to fill the gap left by Gareth's uncouth reply to his grandmother.

'I think we ought to thrash that one out here and now,' Harold said, gravely.

'There was a time when a Rolls-Royce meant so much, didn't it?' Elaine said. 'So much. Like the Riviera and Ascot and débutantes coming out—'

'Coming out of what?' Gareth asked. 'We shall never know.'

'But anybody and everybody has a Rolls-Royce now,' Elaine concluded.

'Your insights,' Harold said, just a little dryly, 'are priceless.'

'I didn't mean *you*,' For a moment she was truly a little alarmed. 'I meant no offence.'

'You could not offend me if you made the biggest effort of your life.'

'What a lovely compliment.' Elaine was so moved that she blushed and stood awkward, storkishly, when Lionel entered in long raincoat, flat cap, a large red rosette like a bloodied cauliflower pinned to his chest, carrying a football rattle which was hung about with red streamers.

'Are we off then?'

'The end of the world,' Elaine said, 'must be at hand.'

Lionel grinned, conscious of the comical impression he made, standing splay-footed to enhance it. He whirled his rattle and Alan jumped up to clap as the old man chanted: 'Two – four – six – eight – who-de-we-app-re-ciate: L-A-B-O-U-R—!'

'What does that spell, Lionel?' Gareth interrupted, though not nastily.

'Something that would do you the bloody world of good. Excuse language, ladies.'

'I should think so,' Mrs. Burns said severely, looking at Alan. 'There's no call for language – politics or no politics.'

'I agree,' Gareth called out.

'You agree with everyone, Gareth,' Harold said.

Gareth did not reply.

'Am I the only one with a rosette?' Lionel demanded, determined to go on to the offensive. He looked around and took some satisfaction in the silence. Then Mrs. Burns spoke up.

'I have one.' She took it from her pocket. It was about a quarter the size of Lionel's. 'I kept it from last time.' She looked at the crumpled emblem. 'I never did like red as a colour. Anybody want it?' There was no response until Elaine said, 'I'll pin it on your coat, Mother.' She took the rosette and placed it on the old woman's stout black coat, taking care, as if placing a handsome bloom in a pretty vase or a medal on an Old Contemptible.

'What about the younger generation?' Lionel went on, pressing home his advantage. 'None of you? I don't know what we're coming to.'

'We'd better go now,' Helen said.

Elaine stepped back to admire her handiwork and then turned to the others as if addressing an audience. Harold saw her clench her left hand tightly around the handkerchief she was carrying – a gesture he recognised as an aid to bracing herself.

'I'm staying here. No – please, Mother, listen. It's better.

269

You all go. It's better Alan stays at home and I'll look after him – Marianne was worried about taking him anyway, he needs his sleep. And I'm rather tired. No! Mother, please. I just feel a little tired, I've overdone it perhaps. But I've enjoyed it all so much – the work – thanks to Helen's help, you see, Christian names are so easy now, aren't they? The canvassing and the telephoning – it was that big meeting with the Prime Minister, I couldn't sleep at all after that – in face I haven't slept since, which makes me a silly old thing but there we are. So I'll stay here with Alan – we like to play, don't we? – we can be company for each other – and I want to tidy up this room for Jimmie when he comes back.'

'Don't you shift any of the heavy stuff,' Lionel said instantly. 'Don't you dare.'

'I think she's right,' Mrs. Burns said, heavily, 'It's all been far too hectic for her.' Elaine ignored her mother's continued treatment of her as an invalid. As far as Mrs. Burns knew, Elaine was back taking her pills.

'Are you sure you don't mind?' Marianne asked.

Elaine shook her head. Lionel, wanting to help her out of the spot he saw that she was in, trotted over to the door, whirled his rattle and opened it with a flourish.

'Anyone for a haircut?' Gareth led the way. 'After you, Cecil.' Marianne, Mrs. Burns, Helen. 'After you, Claud.' They all left but for Elaine and Harold.

Elaine took Harold's arm: Lionel caught her glance, nodded and went outside, closing the door behind him.

'Harold. Yesterday.' She swallowed and then steadied herself. 'Jimmie and I were talking about the horrible – vicious – things they've been saying about you and he told me – about your illness. I didn't know until then. Oh, Harold! You should have told me.' He took her in his arms and she pressed her head comfortingly into his shoulder. He held her strongly. 'I know how horrible it is to be pitied and you of all people don't need that.' She stood away from him, her eyes shining with the film of restrained tears – her eyes so gentle and yet so brilliant, he thought, that he would carry their look with him wherever he turned. 'But you realise, in illness, how much you like people. I know you're going away to-night – don't ask me who told me, please – and I'll miss you so much. You've been a true and a good friend to me. And you're very brave. Thank you.'

She hesitated, wanting to kiss him but afraid. It was he who kissed her.

'Thank *you*,' he said and he spoke as gently as she, his tone that of a different man to the one who had talked to Helen or even Marianne. 'I've always loved you, Elaine. I have. I never told you or tried any move at all because it would have hurt you, wouldn't it? Jimmie's the man for you and that's all there is to it. No?'

'Yes.'

'Your husband.'

'Yes.' She smiled. 'You *are* being sentimental, Harold. Oh, Harold.' She hugged him fiercely. 'I wish you were well, I wish, I wish, I wish you were well, Harold!' He closed his eyes, held her, and for the first time for years, felt deeply shaken to unhappiness.

Helen opened the door and looked at them, astounded. Elaine kissed Harold lightly, playfully, on the cheek and turned to Helen with an innocent smile. 'He's all yours,' she said. 'Look after him. You'll come back after the result?' she asked anxiously.

'Of course,' Harold replied, robustly. 'To celebrate a glorious victory!'

'Yes!' she answered, just as stoutly. 'That's what we'll do.' To Helen she said: 'You'll tell Jimmie – why I decided not to come, won't you?'

Helen nodded and then went away. Harold followed her slowly.

Outside the door, Gareth was waiting for him. Harold recovered his poise and stopped in his tracks.

'Do we have a deal?' Harold enquired.

In reply, Gareth took out an envelope, put in the typed sheets, licked the flap – all the time looking at Harold unblinkingly – and then he turned the front towards him. Harold read: 'The Editor, *Private Eye*, Greek Street, Soho, London W1. In the top left-hand corner were the words 'URGENT COPY'. Gareth nodded.

'OK?' Gareth said. 'Understand?'

Harold nodded.

'God help you,' Harold replied.

They went together to the Silver Shadow and Harold drove away smoothly and swiftly. Elaine waved from the doorstep.

Had she made the right decision? Things had been going so well that she did not want to push her luck and that morning she had felt dizzy as she used to do in the bad old days. There was so much to be aware of. Jimmie was undoubtedly coming back to her, she could feel it, but she needed to be even stronger. This glorious episode – and to her the three weeks had been no less – had made her realise that yet more needed to be done, more sacrifices had to be made if she was fully to join the land of the living from which she now thought she had been largely self-exiled for so long. Her life was indeed in her own hands and she must be both careful and bold.

She began to clear up the coffee cups. Alan banged on the piano. The house was cold but she did not think to light the fire.

Chapter Twenty-Six

Elaine listened to the result on the wireless. Radio Cumbria was covering the count live and she propped the battered fifties portable radio on the Welsh dresser, which took up the length of one of the walls in the kitchen. Alan munched contentedly through his lunch. When she was alone with the little boy, Elaine felt unaccountably shy. In her reticence, he found relief from the busy and sometimes strained attentions of his mother. Nor did Elaine fuss over him as Mrs. Burns did, tenderly training him with a slow drip of instructions and imperatives. He behaved well with Elaine, neither wanting to play her up for the fun of it as with Marianne nor wanting to tease to establish himself as with Mrs. Burns. Apart from everything else, she always gave him what he asked for to eat. And she never insisted that he should either eat eggs or, even worse, finish what was on his plate.

The commentator's voice took on the racing tone which forewarned of the imminent arrival of the result. Elaine shook off the weariness that threatened to overwhelm her and braced herself for excitement. But she could not even now shake off her self-absorption. What, she wondered, treacherously, did she really want?

And then she knew. To be herself. To be wholly and fully herself. That longing, at once trite and profound, now stirred within her like a fire begun deep inside a great body of grass, and the past few weeks with the alarms and excursions had stoked it so that she was now poised. All her habits and the energy from the past taught her to force it back, repress it, conceal and damp it, stifle it even if that meant suffocating herself. But somehow giving up the pills, seeing Helen and Jimmie, the jarring effect of Gareth, the tragic news of Harold, all these events had disturbed her and, she thought, in a secret, excited way, she was coming alive. For what she wanted was to release this fire within her, to burn down the thatch of artifice which screened and shut in her spirit, to let free whatever it was that wanted to come out and be. That was what she wanted: and it was now within her reach.

She put both her hands on the cup of tea before her and concentrated on the result. Alan climbed down from the table, announced that he was going out, and went.

'Well, the count appears to be finally over now,' the commentator said, quietly, as if talking in church, 'His Worship the Mayor, Mr. Armstrong, a steelworker, steps forward to the microphone to give us the results. The candidates are pretty inscrutable. The hall's quite full – a great feeling of tiredness after a long count this morning. I imagine most of the tellers did not get such an early night themselves. There's a certain disturbance at the back – Mr. Armstrong.'

Elaine was suddenly alerted to the present. She held her breath.

'. . . and the results were as follows.' The steady West Cumbian speech sounded so rich, she thought; her father had spoken like that. 'A. J. Carruthers, Conservative: Twelve thousand, nine hundred and eighty-three votes.' 'This will be very close,' the BBC voice assured the world, 'very, very close.' 'P. S. Hatfield, Liberal: two thousand, four hundred and thirty-eight votes.' 'Looks as if yet another Liberal loses his deposit.' Now for it. 'R. L. J. Johnston, Labour, thirteen thousand, one hundred and seventy-four votes.' 'He's in! Johnston's in! He's held the seat. Good news for Labour. They need this seat very badly. Jimmie Johnston delighted on the platform, waves at his supporters, cheering him, a rattle going there, the Mayor holding up his hand for silence. Yes. This result ensures the Labour majority over the Tories. One more result. WRP. Here it is.' 'J. R. Weston, Workers Revolutionary Party: two hundred and seventeen votes.' 'Another disaster for the extreme left. Some rather nasty chanting from the WRP brigade and their supporters at the back of the hall. The Black Power salute being given. The clenched fist. A scuffle there with a BBC sound record-ist. Rather nasty altogether. Seems to be under control. No. One of the WRP women has rushed on to the platform and – was about to take a swing at Jimmie Johnston who merely caught her wrist and now appears to be making sure she is not bundled off too roughly. The police are in the back of the hall now. I can see – Gareth Johnston there arguing his case – he was working on behalf of the WRP candidate here – I think we'll go back to the studio, back to London. The main news is, Labour held the seat, reduced majority but a great victory for Jimmie Johnston. Back to London.'

Elaine knocked off the wireless. She was elated! But, a moment later, to her dismay, she felt trapped. She wanted to rush to be there between Gareth and Jimmie, to bring them together, to share the triumph of her husband and the despair of her son. She could not leave Alan. She could not leave the house. She would never be able to be rid of the house now, she realised. Jimmie would want it as a base, he would need it, she would never get out. She would never, never, live anywhere else!

The thought depressed her violently. But she held on. It would pass. She had to breathe deeply, take care, be fresh and ready to greet and welcome Jimmie, welcome the victor. She would telephone GHQ she decided – they would go there first. Yes. The thought of action cheered her up immediately. He had won – and she had helped. That mattered most of all.

Chapter Twenty-Seven

Jimmie had asked to see Gareth back at the house immediately and Gareth had agreed.

The others had let them go into the living-room alone.

Elaine had fallen asleep on the large sofa. It was still facing the french windows. Alan had taken his afternoon nap and she had come downstairs feeling very washed out. She had intended only to rest. The two men had come into the room and sat in two armchairs some distance away from her. They did not notice her.

Gareth sipped at his flask. Jimmie sat quietly for a few moments, composing himself for what he feared would be a nasty encounter. It had to be done, though, no matter how tired he felt.

'However hard you try, Jimmie,' Gareth said mockingly, 'I'm *not* going to be the naughty boy called into the headmaster's study. I can feel everyone else on tiptoe – "Hush. Hush, whisper who dares, old father Jimmie's giving Gareth his come-uppance." They are leaving us alone.'

'Except Elaine. I should be out looking for her.'

'You fuss too much. You've always fussed too much. Alan was having his sleep so she slipped out for a walk.'

'I'm worried that she might have heard the fracas on the radio.'

'Pity we bopped the sound man. Pompous faggot!'

'I thought you wanted maximum publicity for your tantrums.'

'For the record, I was trying to stop them – our lot. Although I agreed with every word they said.'

'Few with more than four letters,' Jimmie said curtly. 'That's part of your game, though, isn't it? Obscenity and sexual licence are linked by some miraculous underground sewer system to political revolution. Promiscuity is liberty, is that it?'

'Rubbish! Liberty as used in our system is no more than an empty gesture.'

'The comrades have certainly worked you over. But I'm not surprised. No ideologists have ever been interested in liberty.'

'Your Almighty was an ideologue, wasn't He?'

'Quite the contrary. It was the devil who had a system. God just tried to make the best of things. Gareth – do you have any clue as to what on earth you're playing at?'

' "Playing at." Typical! None of it really matters to you, does it?'

'Enough for me to devote my life to it – but let that pass. I want to talk to you before you rush off – because I fear that you're out of your depth and heading for serious trouble. You're being used. And you have no idea of the consequences which will follow this. There it is. You have good – admirable – instincts in some ways – your heart is in the right place, you have a good brain—'

'For Christ's sake!'

'But what do you see in it and why are you doing it?' Jimmie ignored Gareth's interruption just as he ignored the increasing restlessness of the younger man. He had been wanting to say this for the past two weeks and felt badly because he might have left it too late. It would have been more painful to have challenged Gareth during the election, but it would have been the better course, he now thought, for he saw the man lost and, worst of all, blinded by an impenetrable self-righteousness. It was his duty to try and save him. 'It's not even as if you're committed to it,' Jimmie went on, forcefully. 'Not really. Not fully. Not in the way those other poor fools are. At least they follow it through. They get up at dawn to try to force their desperate news-sheet on to indifferent workers outside bleak factory gates. They live out to the hilt this fantasy of being little Lenins inside a police state. They take their paranoia seriously. What do you do? You're a dabbler, Gareth. You've just ad-mitted it. Back in the Town Hall you were trying to stop their perfectly consistent wrecking tactics. So what *is* your game?'

'What's yours?'

'That's a cheap debating trick, Gareth.'

'I learnt it by example.'

'You have no credo at all, do you?'

'Yours sickened me of that. All your soft-core Chris-tianity– spineless shit, Jimmie, just a veneer of consistency. You don't actually believe it. You don't think there's an old man with a white beard up there. You don't believe in the resurrection and the ascension. You don't believe in eternal life. It's just a bloody sham.'

'I can't believe you would go through all this just to take some sort of misguided revenge on me.'

'You find it easy enough to believe in everything else.'

'You are not so pretentious as to think you believe in nothing, are you?'

'Nice one. When did *you* stop beating your wife?'

Jimmie hesitated but only for the fraction of a second. A convincing anonymous note had told him about Gareth's connection with *Private Eye*. He was sick at heart about what he had to say. To talk about Elaine for a few moments would give him time to sound out the ground and steady himself.

'Let me make a pedestrian amendment,' Jimmie answered. 'When will you stop upsetting my wife?'

'My mother.'

'One and the same.'

278

'I'd question that.'

'You mean you'd quarrel with it. Well?'

'You know exactly what I think,' Gareth said.

'We're not as close as we used to be.'

'We were never close.'

'Young men forget.'

'You've made her utterly dependent,' Gareth said, and at first he kept all trace of indignation out of his tone.

As he talked, Elaine stirred and froze. She recognised instantly that she was being discussed and shrank even further down into the sofa, afraid to move. She would wait for an appropriate moment, she thought, and listened half-fascinated, half-horrified.

'You brainwashed her into believing she needed pills and special treatment. You took away nine-tenths of her will and her capacity to lead her own life. You've cooped her up in this mausoleum where your dead mother's handiwork stares her in the face like a daily threat and everything reminds her that she first came here as the daughter of a housekeeper. As a servant's kid. In fact the only way I can see the marriage in the first place is as an act of charity on your part – big-hearted liberal prince taking the poor little kitchen Cinderella and her illegitimate brat – me – unto his bosom. Thanks a lot! And when she threatened to get stroppy, to be herself, to make demands that did not fit in with your smug notion of a middle-class MP's token bloody wife or when she threatened in the past to embarrass you with her uncouth behaviour and not classy enough conversation – out came the pills! The softening up operation began. Now she's either stoned or a kind of cabbage cut out of what you want her to be and when she sparkles you slap her wrist and – out come the pills!'

'I see you've given the matter some thought,' Jimmie said, softly.

'More than you, I'd guess.' Gareth's feeling towards Jimmie could no longer be concealed. There was a pause.

Elaine was about to reveal herself but she was mesmerised by what was being said about her.

'Would you? Let's stick to what we know, shall we?' He paused. Again he was prompted by his notion of Christian duty. 'Do good to them that despitefully use you.' If it would be helpful to Gareth to have certain things explained then he would go through with it as far as he could. 'There's a great deal in my marriage, as in many others, I imagine, which is private and difficult and painful. Above all – private. However, you *are* contingent—'

'My God! "Contingent!" Who the hell do you think you are? My sodding commanding officer? I'm not crawling on my hands and knees for a twenty-four-hour pass, you know.'

'My turn. When you turned up to work your mischief three weeks ago, you encouraged Elaine in a decision she had already made for herself. That fact is very important.'

'No more pills.'

'Exactly. No more pills. It was *her* decision. Her own. She had made it herself. Not yours. Remember that. But what happened then? You upset her by failing to tell her face to face that you had quit the radio. You upset her further (a) by working for Weston and (b) letting her find out at second hand from the local rag. You upset her yet again by your endless teasing and cynical using of Marianne – and not just Marianne. In my opinion you grew so guilty that you did not dare face up to her at all – you stopped coming here – and she was left to carry on without your encouragement. In fact you ceased, from her point of view, to be at all vitally interested in her at the precise moment she most needed you. What you did was wicked, Gareth. It was. She was a sick woman. You took her up and then you simply dropped her.'

'You're the one who's made her sick! I left her on her own. She has to learn to be alone.'

'Everybody needs a staff to lean on.'

'Biblical or military? Same thing – as usual! Please mind your head when leaving your seat. Any more clichés?'

'The sins of the fathers? Sorry. Forgive me.'

'Don't be so pompous.'

'You still haven't contradicted my explanation for your desertion,' Jimmie said: he must, he thought, he had to make contact with the bitter young man before him: he had to try to save him from himself.

'Desertion? Explanation? Meaningless.' Gareth spoke with unconcealed viciousness and Elaine shrank down in fear and alarm at the force of it.

'I haven't told you one important fact. We agreed it was better not to rely on you.' Jimmie tried not to seem to be scoring a point over Gareth but it was hard not to appear a little patronising. 'It meant that she had to lie to you – by implication – she could never carry off the lie direct—'

No, Elaine said to herself, don't tease him, Jimmie, please, don't tease him – he can't bear it, he never could bear it.

Gareth came in furiously. 'Elaine has lied to me only once in her life and that was over the issue of your spurious parental connection! And you forced her into that! So don't try to tell me about my mother. She hates lies – I know that. And so have you never considered the effect, say, of your little romp with Helen – the effect *that* has on her? Because she is completely aware of it. She told me. She saw you pawing her.'

'I've never been unfaithful to your mother.'

'Liar!'

'I like Helen – I'm extremely fond of her.' Jimmie spoke with a sense of hopelessness. Gareth was past caring, he thought, and out of reach. 'There have been two or three women, youngish women, over the years whom I've been fond of. And perhaps rather foolishly I've hugged them now and then, maybe a little pathetically to seek for the warmth I seem to have missed. But that's all. I've never deceived your mother. Ever.'

Elaine felt her heart soar: the final trapdoor sprang open: now she could be truly free.

She got up, stepped over the arm of the sofa and came towards them, smiling, brushing her hair with her hand.

'I wasn't spying,' Elaine said. The men looked at her in acute embarrassment. Almost overcome by shyness, she came to Jimmie, who stood up. She hugged him tightly. 'Really I wasn't. I fell asleep. I had Alan's Teddy Bear with me so that he would come and find me as soon as he woke up. It's on the sofa. You can look if you like.'

'Marianne's with Alan now,' Jimmie said. She clung on to him as if exhausted from some great feat. He patted her shoulder gently.

'I *did* suspect you,' she said with an effort. 'You and Helen. I'm so ashamed – but I did.' She pulled back and looked at him with that penetratingly innocent stare which still made him feel coarse and unworthy. 'Will you ever forgive me?'

'There's never been anything to forgive you for,' Jimmie said.

Gareth need not have been in the room. He could not bear it.

'I haven't taken any pills since the day before you arrived,' she said to Gareth, still standing, now smiling, even relaxed as she felt the security of Jimmie's arm about her shoulders. 'Jimmie keeps them in his pocket, though, just in case. They're always ready. It's been hard because I feel so light-headed and then tired, arms and legs tired but not so horribly depressed as before, not really.' She turned to Jimmie for confirmation and he nodded. 'All that canvassing – I had some good sleeps – didn't I? Without any pills. Jimmie and Dr. Tom organised it all.'

'Why was I kept out of it?' Gareth spoke thick-throatedly, guttural with the force of his anger and envy.

'Perhaps we should have—' she glanced at Jimmie who smiled gently. 'Perhaps *I* should have told you.' She paused. 'Yes. I should have told you. I'm sorry.'

'I expect he warned you off me.'

'Your father isn't your enemy, Gareth, please.'

'My enemy isn't my father, Elaine, thanks.'

'Oh Gareth, Gareth,' Jimmie began, now truly weary of this relentlessly self-absorbed man.

'In effect you encouraged her to lie to me!' Gareth said, totally unable to contain himself. 'Just as both of you lied for years about this father business. It's not that it was a shock – don't flatter yourself, Jimmie, there was much more relief than grief. But what was unforgivable and unfair was that you'd let me go through childhood, schools, adolescence with all *that* rubbishy search for Identity, university with all *that* rubbishy "Who am I?" dot, dot, sodding dot, and *then* a job and all the beginning to set up an adult life – *all* on false assumptions! How *could* you?' Elaine quailed and glanced without reproach but with shame at Jimmie who stood, almost phlegmatic through fatigue, waiting for the blows of the younger man to exhaust themselves. 'So where was I? Leaning on a rotten crutch. The real limb had been amputated years ago. I can't forgive either of you for that. You, Jimmie, especially. You called the shots, didn't you, Jimmie? If ever my mother wanted to talk you would soon wrap her up, wouldn't you? Under the carpet. Under the conscious. Under – bloody life! You're a wanker, Jimmie. I can't forgive you for what you did. For making me into what I was never intended to be.' Gareth paused. The anger came off him like heat. The white strained face, the crumpled clothes, the semi-drunken, untended, wilfully tired, self-damaged look which made Jimmie so impatient, filled Elaine with pity. This is my son, she thought, and he is in danger, I can feel it, I can feel his danger. 'The thing is,' Gareth said, and his voice fell, became dark with intensity, and slow, 'I hate you, Jimmie. And I hate your lack of fucking guts.'

'You mustn't say that,' Elaine whispered. Her mouth was dry. She licked her lips. She wanted to stop all this misunderstanding between them – stop it forever. Inside her there was a force, physical, aching, rising inexorably, almost nauseous, a lust for release; she wanted to let go, just to let go. Her ears sang under the strain. She whispered again 'You can't mean it, Gareth. You can't hate him,' and felt herself to be light-years withdrawn from the mask of the self others saw: she felt herself to be soaring away from it, ripped from what she seemed, torn, from the face she was seen by: she was letting go. She turned to Jimmie. 'He doesn't mean it,' she begged him to help her staunch or stop this impulsion, this inexorable thrust within her.

'Oh but he does.'

'*You*, of course,' Gareth said, 'with the approval of the Almighty, and in all the glory of your everlasting charity, forgive me for ever and ever, amen.'

'No,' Jimmie answered steadily, 'I can't do that. I'm beginning to despair of you.' The opportunity to challenge Gareth over *Private Eye* was slipping away. But Elaine could not be dismissed like a schoolgirl, as he had once been prone to dismiss her. He had stopped that.

Elaine felt drained: she held Jimmie's arm tightly: and then she let go and stood alone.

'Didn't St Paul say that despair was the most conceited act of all?'

'You would know,' Jimmie said.

'Please don't hate each other.' Elaine glanced from one to the other, her turmoil now surfacing. 'Don't! Don't say that. I know – Gareth – it's been hard – and Marianne, let's not talk about her, no, I said, didn't I? – not to talk about her – poor Marianne – Alan is so sweet – he sleeps still with his arms thrown back like you did – just like – but don't hate each other. Not you two. I am pulled – I saw a drawing – you must have seen it – of Red Indians. They tied a man to two young trees they'd bent over to the ground – two young saplings – and then they cut the ropes and the trees sprang up and he was torn in two.' She paused and then said firmly. 'You are my son. And I love Jimmie.'

Gareth regarded her so intently that she could not absorb his gaze for more than a few seconds.

'Perhaps Gareth's right, Jimmie,' she said urgently, her voice now becoming stronger, firmer, even commanding. 'He should know *everything*, once and for all.' She allowed no pause now, trusted herself to no hesitation and let herself go where the force within her directed. 'Yes. Once and for all. It *is* better to know everything, isn't it? It's better for me with no pills. Nothing gets in the way then. What I am is what is in me.'

'Look, darling,' Jimmie protested: but he was tired. He saw a wife for whom he had cared to the point of exhaustion and a step-son he found altogether detestable, although he could not rid himself of a wish to help, understand and cherish even there. 'It's time—'

'I'm sorry the room's such a mess,' Elaine said, warding him off. 'I started to tidy up the drawers over there and – guess! – I found your novel. It was so long ago.' She went across to the sofa on which she had been sleeping and picked up a ream of paper. 'I started to read it and fell asleep. But it was good. I liked *her*. I wish I could have been strong and – what was it? – self-sufficient – independent like her.'

'Elaine, this is enough. We're all over-tired, over-tense, we'll say things we'll regret in the morning. Let's have some tea.'

'Coward,' Gareth said, quietly.

'I must tell him,' Elaine said simply. 'I must.'

'There's no need,' said Jimmie. 'None at all.'

'Let her alone!' Gareth suddenly shouted aloud. 'You bloody censor! Let her be! What do you want to tell me?'

Elaine stood perfectly still as if in a trance. Gareth walked across to her and took her shoulders in a loving gesture but gripped her fiercely in his anger.

'Tell me.'

'Leave her alone.'

'*Tell me!*'

'I will!' She nodded and, totally incongruously it seemed, she smiled and leaned forward to kiss his mouth. Gareth recoiled as if he had been stung and left off his grip.

'Gareth.' Jimmie brought a great deal of control and authority into his voice. 'You mustn't push her any more. She is clearly upset. What you are doing is to upset her even more.'

'I want to know everything,' Gareth said, not turning to reply, staring at Elaine, whose momentary flash of happiness had gone. She was in pain. He felt it with her. 'You'll have to tell me,' he said.

'I know.'

They stood as close as lovers. Jimmie, apart, waited for it to be over, watching now with all his attention, ready to break any fall.

Chapter Twenty-Eight

'In the war,' Elaine said, and she moved away from Gareth, away from that stare, needing to be free to concentrate on herself entirely. 'Let me start, let me start at the beginning. You see, I loved dancing.' She turned and smiled. The word had brought a flicker of pleasure. 'I *loved* it. Before I was married, of course. Jimmie can't dance. He's got two left feet, haven't you, darling? I didn't mind. But I loved it so much. The music and all the steps we used to do in those days. It made you feel so *well*. I went to a lot of dances around here. Jimmie was away in the war – anyway, he never gave me a second look in those days. Liked to be off with his friends from school who used to come and stay. They all ignored me! I had one or two pals of my own – girl-friends – not *close*, because of living up here, so cut off and because I was away from school so much, but I *did* know people my own age. Mother used to say I didn't but I did. I went to dances with them.'

Jimmie quietly went and poured himself a drink. He appeared self-absorbed, even detached, but like Gareth, who stood quite still in the middle of the room, he was attentive to every syllable and nuance of Elaine.

'There were dances in the villages, of course, and dances in the town, but the best dances' – she hesitated, made with her left hand a clutching gesture as if she were in the sea attempting to grab a life-raft – 'were in the American base down at Anthorn beside the sea. They had those big bands and they were free. We danced in one of the hangars. You can't imagine!' Though she was remembering a time of sparkle and delight and though she used some of the words expected from such benign memories, her tone was altogether and totally at odds with what she was describing. It was harsh, unhappy, and even savage. 'The jitterbug. Everybody wanted to jitterbug. And there were these three men.'

Don't, Gareth felt himself wanting to say, don't go on, please don't go on, please don't, don't, go on, go on, go on.

'Phil, Joe and Marvin. Phil, Joe and Marvin. They were always together. "Buddies." That's where I first heard that word. Buddies. I didn't know – nobody told me – nobody would tell me, would they? – that Marvin had a reputation as a "heartbreaker" we used to call them in those days. He would – this is very crude – he would – I was only told later – he would promise girls everything they wanted – we all wanted to go to America then and meet Gary Cooper and Clark Gable and see Hollywood – he would say he wanted to marry you and take you there so that he could – sex! I didn't like Phil and Joe very much. They were so big and fat – enormous, like those all-in wrestlers, and pasty-faced, champing gum, coarse-looking, the smile only on the face not in the eyes at all. But they were Marvin's friends and he had lovely eyes. Hazel eyes.' She spoke warmly for a brief moment. 'Very few people have *real* hazel eyes.' And then the moment went out like a candle in a storm. 'I was far too innocent.' Now launched, her voice was fierce, no playing, no tremor of fragility. 'You *can* be too innocent. I danced with anyone who asked me to. You weren't allowed to refuse in those days. I'm sure I even flirted. To that extent I was responsible. But to me, then – although I was a woman – at that time, if you can imagine it, a kiss was very important and so you flirted to put off the kiss, not to bring it on. You flirted because it was the only way you had of showing that you really liked somebody. Everything else was too serious. Marvin was very charming. The stories about him that came back to me later were horrible and I suppose they were true. But he was so full of life. He had ten times more life than anybody else. He wanted to do so many things! And he talked so well and danced so beautifully and sang the song in my ear – you'll laugh, you'll all laugh because it's so vulgar, I suppose, but I liked that then, I liked him to sing the words in my ear and I would let him dance close. I thought I had fallen in love with him and that night I told him so. Phil and Joe were drunk as usual, they used to wonder why they couldn't "click" with girls but were always so drunk and then they would just hang around Marvin – they were like his bodyguards – or they would prowl round the walls like two awful creatures from another world, half-terrifying everybody. So that night we didn't keep going back and sitting down between dances. I remember they kept shouting across at Marvin but he told me to ignore them. He said that what I'd said was so important to him that he didn't want to spoil it in any way. He took me to the bar on my own "to celebrate", he said. I didn't drink but I had – I can't remember – some drink. He drank a lot, very fast. He said he wanted to marry me. He said it just like that. There was so much to talk about, he said, would I not go back in the bus that was laid on, would I stay, so that we could talk over this wonderful news. He could always slip out of the camp. I was very happy. It's silly to deny that, isn't it, Jimmie?'

'Yes.' Jimmie nodded, gently, just as she wanted him to.

'I can say it all now.'

'Yes. You can.'

'Go on,' Gareth said. 'Please.' He spared no glance, no thought, nothing for Jimmie.

'It was raining. We had these little torches even though there was supposed to be a blackout. We went down to the beach. The sea was very loud and Marvin put his coat around my shoulders even though I had my own coat on because it was raining so hard. I carried my dancing shoes – we all did then – in a little box. I'd put some sensible heavy shoes on because often you had to walk if the bus dropped you off at the gate. Phil and Joe trailed behind us – laughing. I didn't like that but I was with Marvin and every so often he would turn around and shout at them and they would either joke or be nice – they weren't nasty. He had his arm around me. He kept leaning down and giving me little kisses on my ear and whispering how much he loved me – he kept saying it and it was what I wanted to hear more than anything in the world – he loves me, he loves me, I thought, and although I was shy saying it I told him again how much I loved him. There was a dog. Just came up out of the night. Marvin patted it and it followed us. We came to a hut. Marvin opened it. He had to put his shoulder to the door. I held the torch. It stank of damp. There were sandbags in it, and – I don't know what else. He kicked the door shut behind him and then started, started to kiss me – very hard, very hard. He said he wanted me but I said "not until we're married" and he kissed me some more and asked again and I refused and felt awful because he kept saying he would marry me tomorrow if he could and he wanted to so much and so did I! Yes. So did I! But I couldn't. I loved him but I couldn't do it. He got more demanding and wanted to but I could not.' She stopped talking, looked at Jimmie as if seeking an explanation and said: 'He just became an animal. He tore my clothes – just – and hit me – hit me – and the other two came in – the other two – and – they held me while he did what he wanted and then he held me while the others, and then again, all of them, tearing at me, I screamed at first but they were so strong and when I screamed first time one of them pushed himself into my mouth – my mouth – so that I nearly choked and then they left me alone. I was bleeding and I was so ashamed. The police brought me home the next day in a grey blanket.'

Chapter Twenty-Nine

'No,' Gareth said, in a tone so neutral it was more like pure
sound than a meant word. 'No,' he repeated, as if learning to
speak the word.

'Mother sent for me,' Jimmie said. 'I was based at Cat-
terick at the time. The war was over. I was seeing out my
time. They gave me leave.'

'No.' Gareth shook his head and stared from one to the
other, helplessly, but still able to control himself enough to
staunch the tears which threatened, 'No.'

'The doctors said I could have an abortion,' Elaine said.
'So did the specialist. It was very rare then.'

'We managed to keep things fairly quiet,' Jimmie said,
'The three men were sent back to the States.'

'But I didn't want an abortion,' Elaine said. 'However it
had happened it was there and it was a person and I didn't
want it to be killed. It wasn't *its* – it wasn't *your* fault.' She
looked at Gareth. 'Mother wanted me to take advantage of
the "kind offer" as she saw it. Nobody would marry me under
those circumstances, she said. And *your* mother was the same,
Jimmie, I thought, although she never said, of course, being
religious. She wanted to keep out of it altogether, she said. I
think she felt "touch pitch and you shall be defiled". Sorry,
Jimmie. But *you*,' looking at Jimmie lovingly, even adoringly,
'you were so good to me. You made them give me time to
make up my own mind. You said I mustn't be forced to have
an abortion if I didn't want one. We went on walks over the

fells. It was just three or four days but in my mind it's the longest and best time of my life. Yes, best – because you were so good. I would have died without you. We got married soon after you were born, Gareth. In Leeds. There.' She sat down on one of the big armchairs and took out a cigarette which she lit with steady hands although all her movements were weary. 'There you are. Is it better for you now? Is it?'

'Yes,' Gareth heard himself say.

There was silence. Jimmie looked at Gareth, full of concern and sympathy. His own quarrel with the man now seemed so small. He wanted to show his feelings, to help.

Knowing that Gareth would spurn him, Jimmie nevertheless made the attempt. 'You see now? Perhaps you are right but she had to do it for herself, when she wanted to. It was her life.' Jimmie paused. 'She could not tell you until she was ready.'

'What *you'd* call game, set and bloody match, isn't it?' Gareth rejected Jimmie brutally and went across to his mother, standing before her almost formally. 'Thank you. It was difficult for you. Thank you for telling me at last.'

'Are you sure it will help?' she asked, looking up at him, wanting reassurance.

'How terrible for you,' Gareth said, in a tone which was reflective. 'How unbelievably horrible for you.' He bent down and kissed the top of her head.

Then he went out.

Jimmie came across to her and for some moments they sat in silence.

'It might be better,' he looked at his watch and in slow motion, as it seemed to Elaine, went on, 'If I went into town now and had the drinks in the office. I could be back in a couple of hours. They'll all be in there now, I expect. It's after work. And I could go on to the Labour Club for a short victory celebration. It would mean being back later than I promised Harold, but I'd rather do it that way round. I don't much relish the prospect of being convivial into the early hours of the morning.'

'There'll be telegrams of congratulation.'

'Yes.'

'I haven't kissed you yet, not really, not to say how proud I am of you. You deserve it. Everybody says that. Someone said your meeting had tipped the whole election in Labour's favour.'

Jimmie smiled. They embraced tentatively.

'I'll come with you,' she said.

'You're tired. You need a rest. They'll be in rather a hearty mood.'

'Do I look tired?' She drew back and set herself up, rather preeningly.

'Truth?'

'Yes.'

'I'm afraid you do,' he said – but without reproach.

'Do I look decent?' She was desperate not to be left behind and alone.

'Yes.' Jimmie smiled. He understood. 'OK. But you need to wash – change – that blue dress – and make up. I'll give you – five minutes.'

'Ten.'

'Seven and a half.'

She kissed him on the mouth and pulled him very close to her.

'I do love you so much,' she said. 'We'll be all right. You'll see. I'm better now, aren't I?' And indeed she felt re-born like someone in a fairy tale. She had a mad, irrational longing to find a mirror to see if she *looked* different.

'Perhaps you are. I hope so. Yes.'

'Shall I talk to Gareth again?'

'No. He needs to be alone just now. I'll wait for you outside. I need some fresh air. It's stopped raining.'

'Don't run away, Jimmie: please don't.'

'I'll never run away,' he said.

She wanted to cry but held in the tears.

'The day before the election,' she said, 'I went up the fell to – to think about us and to hope you would be re-elected – but really,' she smiled gently, 'really just to think about us. It was so lovely up there. We are so lucky to live here. I used to think I was in a prison, here, you know, well, that's beginning to go, but outside, on the fells, just being in the place I've been in all of my life, I feel well now, Jimmie. You always say you'll never leave the place. I couldn't leave it, either. I know that now.' She was full of herself, fully alive.

'It was such a lovely day. The heather was purple, the sea was sparkling, the fell was full of rabbits – they've all come back now, haven't they? And then I saw a kestrel, a single hawk, floating on the air currents, just rising and falling, rising and falling, holding out its wings, it seemed the freest being I had ever seen and once I would have longed to have been that kestrel – don't laugh, Jimmie – no, I know you won't laugh now at anything I say – once I would have imagined I *was* that hawk in some part of me – but when I thought about it, I thought – no – I want to be with you. It's not good to be alone. I want to be with you, Jimmie, and I'll give my life to that.

'There'll be no miracle. It will come and go – but over these weeks I've made a start and faced up to so much. Gareth *was* a help, you know, at the beginning, and I don't know if I'd have had the strength to face up to you in those first few days if it had not been for him. But then you saw I was serious and you came to help me. You were so kind. You are so good.'

Elaine came across to him and they kissed, warmly, without all the embarrassment, fears, anxieties, guilt and hopelessness of former times. Body pressed against body they kissed each other long and lovingly and felt they were again part of each other as they had been so many years ago.

'I wish I could have given you a child,' Jimmie said, his lips in her hair, his head pressed against hers. 'I'm sorry.'

'We have each other,' she said, and in the overwhelming truth of the cliché, they found the path to a life together.

'I'll go and get ready,' said Elaine, and she moved away from him reluctantly but firmly, taking the initiative. 'I love you very much.'

'See you in a few minutes,' he said, and went out into the garden to be alone.

V. AN ACCIDENTAL DEATH

Chapter Thirty

Marianne watched Gareth from the door. She thought that he knew he was being watched yet he did not glance over at her nor did she feel her presence had registered. There was something so stiff and out of joint and self-conscious about what he was doing that she was puzzled.

He was in one of the old stables. On the wall above the manger was a dartboard which had been there for years. He had placed a white handkerchief on the floor at the regulation distance from the board and he was pitching the three small arrows into the target.

Marianne came across to him. The room was lit only by the weak afternoon light coming through the rain and through the grimy skylight and windows. He did not acknowledge her although there could be no doubt at all now that he was aware of her. Reluctantly she decided to begin the task: reluctantly because she felt herself resenting the enclenched self-communion of the man before her who was, after all, the father of her son.

'I thought you'd be in here when you weren't in the attic. Jimmie said you'd wandered off. They've gone into town, to thank everybody.'

He nodded. The darts went through their short trajectory and embedded themselves in the cork surface with a satisfying thud.

'We used to slip off here, didn't we?' She laughed, falsely, to cheer him up or just to break through his silence. 'Straw in my bra. Spiky. Little red marks. And then the bites. You were a bit rough sometimes.'

He faced her and his stricken, beaten, devastated expression instantly restored her sense of priorities and her poise.

'Elaine's just told me – some of it. That she said to you. Most of it.' She paused. 'I knew a bit of it already.'

'Who else knew?'

'Oh. Nobody really. But people would make guesses around the place.'

'How do you know?'

'I've just heard some of them, that's all. Rumours. You know what small places are like.'

'Why didn't *I* hear them?'

'I suppose you were never really here long enough,' she said. 'You were away at school and then university and then you did all that on the newspapers and radio.'

'So I was cut off.'

'In a way. And people are nice. They wouldn't want to let it get back to you, I suppose. I'm just guessing.'

'Why did you come to look for me?'

'I wondered what you were going to do.'

'Now?'

'Not this minute, no. But – next.'

'About you?' His answer was very nearly a sneer and the tone of it wounded the open-hearted sympathy she was offering him.

'No. About you.'

'Easy.' He squared up to the dartboard and went into one of his characters and mimicked the accent of a cardboard caricature Red Indian in a cowboy film. 'Heap trouble. Me – "He-Who-Came-From-Big-Land-Across-Big-Sea" – must find White Man who take White Woman for squaw and go back – over there. Me – "He-Who-Came-From-Big-Land-Across-Big-Sea" – go *find* White Man,' he threw a dart, hard, at the board. 'Phil?' Another dart. 'Joe?' Then the last dart. 'Highest score mugs away,' he chanted in the sing-song dirge of the bingo callers. 'Marvin? Phil scores seventeen, Joe scores three – the sap – Marvin scores nineteen – yes, Marvin wins, Marvin it is by a short whatever. Find Marvin. See Marvin and die.'

'Please stop,' Marianne said. His self-destructive ferocity, the pain his face expressed, was beginning to alarm her. 'Please.' She reached out to touch him but he cringed from her.

'Poor woman,' he said simply, facing Marianne, his eyes glassy with the film of tears just held back; just. His voice was thin, light, threatening to break. 'Poor, destroyed, raped, lost, frantic, lonely, desecrated, howling woman walking rent open and bleeding along that bitter wet beach on a black night. The poor love.' He looked at Marianne in bewilderment. 'And inside her then . . . and out of that.' She held him tightly and he lifted up his head as if dying for lack of air. 'Imagine. Her disgust. Her terror – that little miner's daughter – imagine – what she must have felt – as I went in and was ripped out. Oh God.' He pushed her away strongly so that she stumbled. Then he clapped his hands to his temples and spoke in a parody of the local dialect. 'T'world goes round and round and round. T'world ties us all up in circles. Go away, Marianne.' He let his hands drop and repeated, 'Go away, Marianne.' She stood her ground.

'I count for less and less,' she said.

'You're quite a toughie now, Marianne.' His concern for her was already gone, she noticed. The sneer was settled firmly in the voice.

'It's about time.'

'Where did you get this toughness?' He laughed. 'Harold been taking you up, has he? Good old shit-bag, Harold. You know where Harold stands – up to his neck in horse manure.'

'You don't see me at all now, do you?' Marianne said. 'You don't see me, you don't really talk to me, you don't hear me. And Alan counts for nothing at all! *Nothing!* You've been up here three weeks now and you've played with him twice. Once was when I blackmailed you into it – for an hour that was – and what did you say? You were "violently bored". Your own son! "Violently bored." The other time was when you had missed a meeting – right at the beginning -- and he could see you were at a loose end and so he asked you to make a swing on a branch of the copper beech. He begged you to. You got Lionel to find the rope. You were too lazy to climb the tree to find a good branch – but you just about did it – and there it dangles yet – more like a hangman's noose than a boy's swing. Still. Full marks for trying. It doesn't matter so much – although hell! It does! You've screwed Helen – now and then – not very constant in that, either, I'd guess, from the way she's going to pieces. Another casualty. She was OK until you arrived, you know, she was together and controlled and pleasant. Now she's half-way freaked out! You hurt me every minute of every hour but you are not even aware of it. And simply don't notice Alan!'

'I can't bear kids. I – cannot – bear – them. Not even him. Fair play now, Marianne – I never could, could I? It's not just these – late events.'

'Stop fishing for pity.'

'Why don't we have a screw?'

Marianne took a deep breath, breathed it out slowly and spoke reasonably calmly. 'I'm sorry for you, Gareth. I've loved you and hated you and I've wanted you and longed for you and then longed to be released from you but until these last three weeks when I've seen you scampering about like a little football hooligan throwing bricks at Jimmie and grinning in triumph when he didn't throw them back – messing Helen around – messing me around – and more or less saying that you don't even like your son even though you of all people must surely know what a father means – and all of this is always excused by the great love for Elaine which runs out of steam the moment she takes Jimmie's part against you – it's not until now, until all this, that I've felt really and truly sorry for you. You are – well, I'll not say it – you are best left alone, I think. I'm not going to let you cause any more damage. Not to me, anyway. And not to Alan. You make me frightened, now, Gareth. Even now as I'm talking I think you could strike me dead and live to pity yourself for doing it. I'm leaving.'

She went out cautiously, almost backing the first few steps, because while she had been talking there had come on to Gareth's face an expression of such sensual contempt, as if he had let all the vicious and unbridled feelings within him loose on that part of him which met the world. He looked ugly – in every way ugly – and she wanted to be away from that small, cramped stable which was suddenly flooded with the portent of his worst intentions.

'Good bye!' he cried out as if in an Elizabethan play. 'Good bye, fair Marianne, and God Speed!'

She went out.

Gareth walked up to the dartboard and pulled out the three arrows, which were up to their shanks in the board. He stood for some time gazing before him, twisting the pointed darts into the palm of his left hand, seeming not to notice when they worked through the skin and drew blood.

Chapter Thirty-One

Outside there was a storm. It buffeted the vicarage as if the large building were a ship at sea. And indeed the wind in the trees, especially in the copper beech, was like the sea, and the wind boomed mightily through the old house.

Inside the room there was that high, tangible feeling of anxiety which is as powerful as a physical presence. The tensions between them all were as taut and tactile as thin steel tightropes, as if these tightropes indeed had been slung and stretched from one person to another carrying all the fraught messages which were too painful to put into words.

Jimmie was standing at the lectern scribbling on one post-card after another, the same message. He was doing the job quickly but with such evident nervousness that Elaine longed to ask him to stop. But she too was worried and fearful about the boy, and she knew that Jimmie needed some occupation to steady himself.

The radio played Brahms. Like Elaine, Helen was pretending to listen, glass in hand. Helen felt utterly played out and just holding on for the next day and the flight back to the dreary existence she would have to endure. Her lot. She had drunk steadily through the day and now was beginning to drink more under the delusion that she had somehow become immune to it. She maintained this delusion by occupying herself with *The Times* crossword puzzle as if competence at that particular quiz game would reassure all parties of her sobriety, intelligence and general coherence. She envied Harold who sat, legs crossed, lovely grey flannel suit apparently pressed an hour or so ago, heavy dark blue silk tie, white silk shirt, comfortable soft leather shoes, smoking a Romeo y Julieta cigar – sleek as a great bull otter in his external appearance: increasingly ravaged when you looked closely. To him, Helen thought, bitterly, the other, all the others, Elaine included, were no more than pawns in his uncomplicated and restless game of maximum self-satisfaction. She loathed his amorality and yet she was fascinated by the free creature he had made himself.

The front door banged. The four of them moved tensely, expectantly, and waited. When Marianne came in, wearing her raincoat, drenched, a living force to the tableau the quartet had become, they moved into her service, all of them; Harold went to pour a drink, Jimmie finished what he was doing and stood aside from the lectern, clearly ready to be of use although it was Elaine who reached Marianne first and helped her off with her coat and Helen who took it from Elaine, who clearly was more inclined to hover about Marianne and be a shield or comforter as desired. Marianne had been out looking for Alan.

'John Tennant said he'd seen them go up his fell earlier on,' Marianne said. There was relief in her voice.

'Alan and Gareth?' Elaine asked.

'Yes! He said that Gareth seemed to have a long stick and was whirling it about and he heard Alan shouting and laughing. He saw them across his top field.'

'That's the explanation then,' Jimmie said. 'Thank God for that! We were all getting scared to death. So – Gareth's taken him for a walk, found shelter when the storm came on, probably went a bit too far for the little boy's strength and is now, in all likelihood, having to piggy-back him home! Used to happen to me with Gareth himself!' His jollity was a help. Its platitudinous chumminess was exactly the right comforter. People relaxed.

'Drink this,' Harold said, bringing a glass of brandy to Marianne. 'Call it medicine.'

'Thank you.'

'Your coat should be dry in two ticks,' Helen announced from the fire. She had rather noisily and clumsily but in the end effectively dragged the fireguard into place and hung the coat over it. Immediately it began to steam dry. 'Lionel's fire's on form tonight,' she said to no one in particular, and then she went across to the window, pulled back one of the curtains and poked her head beside it to shut out the reflection of the room. 'It's winter now,' she proclaimed in a voice much louder than she would have thought necessary when fully sober. 'It's a bloody awful northern black stormy night.'

'I like it dark outside,' Elaine said, still staring with benevolence at Marianne, who was trying not to be disconcerted by the force of this attention. Although she was among them she was somehow isolated – set apart by the fear that hovered almost visibly about her.

'Gareth's known that fell since he was a nipper,' Jimmie said, in case Marianne might have any remaining anxiety. 'I used to carry him up to the top on my back when he was Alan's age, didn't I, Elaine? Remember how he squealed when we popped him in that old rucksack?' The jolliness was becoming so compulsive that it even reached out to embrace Harold, whose arrival Jimmie had greeted with anything but geniality. 'Army issue, that rucksack, Harold. Just forgot to hand it in.'

'In other words, "nicked it",' Harold said. 'It's the same the whole world over.'

'How do the sheep manage out on the fell?' Helen asked this serious question as she walked most steadily back into the middle of the room, each step as deliberate as each word and both betraying the imminent slither into that stage of intoxication where you are, as it were, right in the deep end, unable either to reach out for the bank or bounce your feet on fixed ground beneath. 'I mean,' she continued. 'it's *very* nasty outside. 'T's not t' rain 't's hail – *hail*, it's hail, hard little pellets from that great pea-shooter in the sky as Gareth might say – I was up on the top of that fell with Gareth. He was like a mountain sheep himself up there – he'll be all right, Gareth will survive.' Her speech trickled into a silence which for another few precious minutes jarred her back towards sobriety. 'Hail can cut your skin,' she concluded.

Marianne nodded at Helen and walked across to the fire. She hated to be the centre of so much concern and a great part of her already thought that she had been silly to have panicked so greatly when she had discovered that both Gareth and Alan had disappeared. It was simply that the blood-filled face of Gareth in the stable, almost unrecognisable as himself, as far from his ordinary looks as that twisted ecstatic eyes-closed champion she had seen riding above her at the moment of orgasm, that strange, cruel look had imprinted itself on her mind and she saw it again and again in her mind's eye and was afraid. Still, she felt that she had fussed too much and looked about for a diversion. Harold nodded. She moved towards the door, unable to stand still even before the warming fire.

'Come on! Let's have a sense of proportion,' Harold said and she smiled her thanks to him. 'Gareth'll come back with Alan on his shoulder like . . . St. Christopher, isn't it? Am I right, St. James?'

'Yes,' Jimmie said.

'I'll get us all some coffee,' Marianne said.

'Let me, let me,' Elaine begged.

'No. Please, Elaine,' Marianne insisted. 'It'll keep me – it's something to do . . . Grandma has it half-prepared in the kitchen anyway – I saw through when I came in.'

'I'll come with you,' Elaine persisted.

'Gareth was hurt *for* you,' Marianne said, apropos of nothing. But to herself the logic was clear. 'When I talked to him he was hurt for you.'

'Poor Gareth,' Elaine said. 'He's so unhappy. *So* unhappy.'

'No regrets, Elaine,' Harold said briskly. 'After all, Gareth is the man who wants the truth above everything else, isn't he? Only he hates being told it about himself.'

'Even you are not fair to him,' Elaine said. She spoke wanly now. The day had been so strenuous. The exhilaration which had come from her confession and her declaration to Jimmie was now waning, and she was tired out.

'Harold finds it a nuisance to be fair, don't you?' Jimmie spoke with unaccustomed anger.

'Aha!' Harold raised his glass in a toast. 'Welcome! I wondered when you'd come aboard the living again. The election's over so you can be brave. Good. Cheers!' He took a big drink.

'Your writs are posted and so *you* too are a brave man again, Harold. You've gagged the press with the law.'

'I have. Would that I could suffocate those little worms in that cheap little rag. But gagging will do for the moment.'

'Two of a kind?' Helen asked. 'You two? No. No – wrong again, Wilks. Soldier on, girl.' She looked at her empty glass, said 'What the hell', and went for another large gin.

Harold judged that this was going to be the best chance he would get. It was all over, as he had suspected. The final tests had confirmed that. He had spent the two hours since the knowledge had come through in arranging his immediate passage to an exclusive and expensive hospital/hotel in Switzerland. His money was well enough organised. The business was sold but for the formalities, although the *Private Eye* revelations had meant that he had to take less than he would otherwise have got.

Several provisions had been made including a bequest of some jewellery to Elaine. And, also for the sake of Elaine, he had decided not to pursue Gareth and not to make use in any way of the information he had got out of Fraser. He had destroyed all that.

Miss Eliot would be coming to Switzerland with him.

Now was the time for his final throw here.

'Ladies and gentlemen,' he announced, grandiloquently, 'you will all be delighted to learn that I have just had the results of those final tests, and although there is some sort of – something or other – it is not at all dangerous, let alone fatal. A couple of weeks inside, a bit of dieting and I'll be as fit as ever.'

It was very well done. No one suspected the lie, not even Jimmie, who had scrutinised him throughout.

Harold knew he had dropped a small bomb and savoured the moment, almost visibly rolling it about his mind as his face roved over the diverse reactions in the room. For an instant there was not a movement and then Elaine strode forward, impelled by real relief and delight, her arms outstretched as if welcoming the conquering hero. 'How marvellous! Oh Harold, Harold, wonderful!' She hugged him, tears in her eyes, and he stared at the others over her shoulder.

'Congratulations.' Jimmie spoke stiffly but not ungenerously and raised his glass. 'It must be a great relief.'

'*Isn't* it good news,' Elaine demanded, thrilled by what she saw as almost a miraculous escape.

'You old rhino!' Helen had given up. It was less painful to be drunk, she decided, less life but less pain. Yet her brain still ticked over. 'Hey,' she said, 'how are we to know you weren't stringing us all along to get a bit of capital out of our sympathy? Eh? How are we to know?'

'*What* an idea!' Elaine was astounded.

'No flies on Helen,' Harold laughed to himself, clearly and genuinely amused, and brought across the gin bottle to pour her another drink.

'Buzz, buzz, buzz.' Helen watched myopically carefully as the spirit splashed into the glass. '*You're* the fly one, Harold. Come on, it *was* all a con, wasn't it?'

'Of course.'

Helen held up her glass and turned to Jimmie, who

flinched to see her expression so tense with reckless misery. She made the sign of the cross with her glass. She regretted it immediately, but Jimmie, too, had to be washed out of her system. These men always hurt her too much, always left her less than she had been.

'To Eternal Life,' she declared and drank alone. 'What a sentence!'

'Well, Harold,' Jimmie said, abruptly brisk, launching himself out of the slough of dismay which threatened to suck him in, 'that puts us back on an equal footing again. Your news. I'm glad.'

'So am I, Jimmie. Equal before the law. Yes. So am I. I presume that's what you mean. Cheers, Helen. Drink up.'

'Because,' Jimmie went on, ignoring the mockery of the man as he had ignored Helen's mockery, 'certain things just have to be thrashed out. I was worried they might never be faced. Clearly you can face anything now.'

'Yes and no, Jimmie,' Harold replied, easily. He was far and away the most relaxed person in the room. 'Yes and no, as the lady said. After the little hospital interlude I still intend to hop off.'

'Clearing out?' Jimmie asked.

'Precisely.'

'Switzerland?' Jimmie asked.

'But of course,' Harold said, straight-faced.

'I can't believe a thing you tell me any more.' Jimmie spoke gravely, conscious that he was making a serious accusation.

Helen wandered over to the lectern and picked up the pack of postcards Jimmie had been signing.

' "Thank you," "Thank you," "Thank you very much," ' she sang out. 'Thankyous by the yard. Thankyous by the mile. Everybody gets thanked. Thank. *Thank*. Somewhere between Think and Tank and Spank. "Party to follow" – I hope so! "Party to follow!" Follow what? Ha. Who will it follow, Jimmie – you?'

He smiled, sorry for Helen now, sorry that she was so upset. He addressed both her and Elaine.

'If it clears up tomorrow, why don't we do some walking? Nothing serious. Up to Styhead and then maybe on to Sprinkling Tarn. You could manage that, Elaine.'

'Oh yes! Sprinkling Tarn. What a lovely name.'

Helen felt stung by the ease with which Jimmie closed ranks with his wife. 'A British Election,' she announced, exaggerating her genuine drunkenness, 'oscillates wildly between dead-slow and stop – don't you all think? It has all the convulsive characteristics of a yawn. Don't you agree? That is my final conclusion.' She smiled at Harold, who was watching her with evident amusement. 'Worth a Ph.D. don't you think, Harold, two or three more years in libraries at your expense but on your behalf. Worth another grant, eh, Harold – that annoys you, doesn't it? You old philistine, you hate the idea of thousands of people like me doing research into questions you think would be resolved by two pennyworth of common sense, don't you?'

'I do.' He nodded, solemnly, making a game of her attempted attack. 'I would sack the universities tomorrow – all the non-scientists, that is.'

'We are a country of wreckers,' Helen said. 'The monasteries – knocked down by Henry; the castles – knocked down by Cromwell; the cities – knocked down by councils; and Harold wants to be up and at the universities. Full of feeble little slugs, you think, don't you, Harold? School swots too scared of the world to poke their heads out into it. OK if they're starving. But give them living wages and pensions and things and you go mad.'

'You read my inmost thoughts,' Harold said. 'You know, it's quite uncanny.'

She yawned, hugely and rudely, and stretched, almost bursting out of her blouse. 'Time for bed.' She laughed. 'That remark was not meant to incite, inflame or otherwise provoke the company. Not that it would.' She finished her gin. 'Oh yes – Harold's the fly one. Look at him. Fit as a fiddle and happy as a pig. He's fooled us all – haven't you – all of us?'

Elaine had by now put Helen into the category of those not responsible for what they were doing. In this way she protected herself from feeling upset or provoked. She returned to her primary anxiety. 'It's very irresponsible of Gareth,' she said, uncharacteristically fiercely. 'Alan had a cold coming on.'

'I know.' Helen, who had been walking to the door, suddenly stopped short. 'Gareth's decided to be a proper father! That's it! May the Lord help that poor kid.' She laughed and continued to laugh and continued into an atmosphere which tightened from embarrassment to real concern.

'Helen.' Jimmie spoke firmly. 'Can I get you anything?'

She produced a white pill-box from her pocket.

'I'll smoke my own, thanks.' She swallowed two pills. 'They don't taste of anything. Have you noticed, Elaine? Pills have no taste at all nowadays. Perhaps they don't want us to know they are doing us good. *I* know! They're *Christian pills*! They move in mysterious ways. That's it! Perhaps God is a pill, Jimmie. An Almighty Pill.' She glanced at the ceiling. 'How about that?' She looked at Elaine. 'That's what Gareth does.'

'Coffee!' Elaine said, as the door opened. 'At last!'

Chapter Thirty-Two

It was Gareth and none of them ever forgot his appearance that night.

He had put on Jimmie's old army uniform, which was sodden from the rain and so splattered with mud it looked as if he had rolled over and over again in a swamp of it. In his left hand, which was crudely bandaged with a handkerchief, he held Jimmie's ceremonial sword. The handkerchief was bloodied, there was blood on his face, his eyes were exalted with a wild despair which instantly reminded Jimmie of Elaine at the time of her most perilous crisis and made Elaine herself almost faint with dread. Helen turned away and Harold gripped harder on the glass he held tightly in his hand, for Gareth came in doing a manic march, shouting himself on as he paraded across the room and back again.

'*Up* – two – three – four – *one* – two – three – four – left – right – wrong – right, right – left – left – out – right – on – on – ward – Chris – tian – soldiers. Atten – en – en – en – shun!'

He came to a stop before Jimmie and saluted.

As he stood there, Marianne came in the open door as slowly as a frail and sick old woman.

Jimmie, who had been about to take action, was mesmerised by the intensity and the deliberation of her walk. Elaine suddenly covered her face with her hands and gave a little cry, almost a squeal of pain. Helen forced herself to look on and stood petrified. Marianne touched Gareth on the arm and he swung around fiercely, ready to attack. When he saw who it was he stopped and reached out to touch her cheek, but she swayed out of his reach and his hand dropped to his side.

'Maid Marianne,' he said. The words fell as emptily as small pebbles in a deep dry well. He assumed a feeble, energyless imitation of an American accent and Elaine felt her stomach cringe for him as he faked so badly, so pathetically, like a guilty boy caught in a mess beyond his comprehension. 'Sure is a lovely name you've got there, babe. Sum'thin ah been a-meanin' to tell you for some time now, freckles . . .'

He dropped the sword and with it all pretence. The tears ran uncontrollably down his face and his sobbing was so strong it was unbearable, loud, animal-like, at odds with all that cultivated room represented. Marianne waited, white-faced, biting her lip like a girl, just waiting for him to stop. None of the others dared interfere. It was as if an invisible hoop encircled and ensnared these two who had been lovers and no one could enter or leave until the spell was broken.

'Just take your time,' Marianne said eventually and her voice was so weary and so sad that Elaine felt a keening grow in her heart but she stilled it. 'I want to know just how it happened.'

'I wanted to be a real father,' Gareth said and he looked around to the others not appealing to them but wanting them to know. 'So I borrowed this uniform and that sword – he liked me to dress up. I did it once before. He said I had. I'd forgotten. But he really enjoyed it. I did the Charge of the Light Brigade. In that field. Jimmie – where your church is, the one you walk to. We went in. It's empty, Jimmie. And you *know* that.' He waited for an answer, anything to be diverted from his main route. 'Why kid yourself?'

'I can't bear it,' Helen said. Harold moved across to her swiftly and took her wrist in a hard grasp.

'Go on,' Jimmie said.

'We went up the fell,' Gareth was looking at Jimmie now.

'You used to take me there. I thought about that sort of thing. I tried to tell stories but I couldn't get him interested. He was as bored as I would have been at his age. Must have been. I asked him if he wanted to go back but he was determined to get to the top. He said he wanted to stand on great-grandfather's special seat because you could touch the sky from there. Grandma must have told him that. The cloud was low enough. It was raining but he didn't mind. I'd put his raincoat on him and his Wellingtons. We agreed that we liked getting soaked. But it *was* cold. To get there quicker I went by the crags.'

He looked mutely at Marianne but she only shook her head and waited. Everyone dreaded to articulate in their minds the ending they feared. All of them stood tense, aching for news which was not the worst.

Now Gareth spoke only to Marianne, pleading with her, it seemed, to believe him, at least that.

'It was slippery so I carried him. He enjoyed it. He laughed — you know. It was a piggy-back to him, he always enjoyed those — didn't he? I wanted to leave the sword at the bottom but he wouldn't let me and I gave in — it was all for him, you see, I was trying. The thunderstorm came and I knew it was stupid but not dangerous — better to go up than down. They pass quickly enough. But it frightened him — the thunder and then the lightning — real flashes of it like something in a film — but you see it on the hills always, I tried to make a joke of it but with that bloody sword — my hand hurt — I needed all my concentration — the rocks were treacherous — it *was* ridiculous and he held on to my neck tighter and tighter. He was choking me. I tried to tell him but he was in a panic. How can a kid have such a grip? His knuckles were dug into my throat just here — here over the Adam's apple and I had to tug at his hands to try to loosen it, just to get my breath, but he would not let go. He was screaming again and *I* felt dizzy. I couldn't breathe. I couldn't stand it. I snatched at his hands and pulled. My fingers slipped off — his skin was wet – but he let go, he let go altogether and he just fell back: fell.'

After what seemed an age, Marianne nodded and went back to the door. Elaine, holding her side as if holding in a great pain, followed her. Jimmie moved across to Gareth.

Upstairs, in his bedroom, Mrs. Burns had just finished washing the little boy, doing what she could to clean away the evidence of the terrible damage. She had dressed him in his pyjamas and he lay in his small bed, eyes closed, black hair newly brushed, as if asleep. Marianne felt the constriction in her throat so powerfully that she dared not trust herself. Elaine held hard, hard against the sound in her throat but her face ran free with tears. The three women looked down on the lifeless boy. It was Mrs. Burns who spoke.

'He's stone cold,' she said, heavily, wearily. She paused and waited and then went on: 'He's at peace, anyway, wherever he is. Isn't he?'

And when Marianne gave in to her tears it was Elaine who held her and supported her.

MELVYN BRAGG

CRYSTAL ROOMS

Young Harry, an orphan from an impoverished council estate, becomes the link between starkly contrasting worlds: north and south, the deprived and the over-privileged, the powerful and the defenceless. With this compelling story of blackmail, media politics, corrupted innocence and redemptive love, Melvyn Bragg delivers an unforgettable portrait of contemporary life.

'A splendid Dickensian sweep of a book'
Richard Brooks in The Observer

'A decent and intelligent novel, one which can be read, and will be read, with a great deal of pleasure'
Allan Massie in The Scotsman

'As a guide to media London, the novel is essential reading'
T. J. Binyon in the Times Literary Supplement

'The very good Bragg has forced a complex contemporary plot to work magic'
David Hughes in the Mail on Sunday

'Bragg has scarcely ever written better . . . A state of England message transfused by fiction'
Tom Adair in Scotland on Sunday

'Melvyn Bragg writes with a lyrical nostalgia which is as important to the novel as his energy'
Penelope Fitzgerald in the Evening Standard

'Bragg is a romantic and like Dickens he mixes the journalistic with the sentimental . . . The success of this book is assured'
Victoria Glendinning in The Times

MELVYN BRAGG
THE NERVE

One August bank holiday, Ted Johnson wakes to a day of reckoning – with his past life in Cumberland, his present in London and his fantasies. An inflamed nerve troubles his eye as he veers between elation and despair, overwhelmed by the noise and bustle of the streets, unable to connect even with a visiting girlfriend. Written in 1971, Melvyn Bragg's sixth novel draws a remarkable portrait of a man's courageous fight to keep his mental balance and regain a sense of identity amid the stress and intoxication of modern city life.

'It is an extraordinary blend of delicacy and harsh simplicity which makes Melvyn Bragg a remarkable novelist . . . He writes superlatively well'
The Times

'An effortless writer. He never strains for effect, simply achieves it'
The Sunday Times

'Since his first novel, Melvyn Bragg's talent has grown until he has now achieved utter truthfulness'
Sunday Telegraph

'Bragg is a graceful and confident writer'
The Observer

'Uncommonly high talent'
The Guardian

'A novelist of power and imagination'
New Society

MELVYN BRAGG
A TIME TO DANCE

A lifetime of restraint and placid affection erupts when a retired bank manager falls for a young girl, as far removed from him in background and experience as in age. Set in Cumbria, this intensely moving evocation of an overwhelming passion and its destructive kernel of jealousy confirms Melvyn Bragg as a master of the contemporary novel.

'A book of splendours and treacheries, pungent as any consuming passion, a great, tragic, raunchy novel'
Thomas Keneally

'His best novel to date . . . The spirit of Hazlitt's Rousseauesque confessional, and of the Romantic Lakeland, and of the small provincial urbs, not to mention the spirit of the great love stories of the world – Bragg has imbibed them all, and makes us drink them up in turn. It's enough to make you as intoxicated with them as he clearly is . . . Magnetic . . . a major imaginative triumph'
The Observer

'It is a sexy book. It is a romantic book. Its heart is the dream of great passion . . . Quite takes the breath away'
The Sunday Times

'Vibrantly erotic . . . brave and searingly honest . . . compulsively gripping'
Sunday Express

'It lives and breathes lust and life'
The Mail on Sunday